Birds of the Indiana Dunes

Birds

OF THE

Indiana *Dunes*

by KENNETH J. BROCK

Shirley Heinze Environmental Fund

Cover design by Peter B. Grube. Cover photographs by Clyde Fields (Prothonotary Warbler and Baltimore Oriole) and Peter B. Grube (Wood Duck, Northern Saw-whet Owl, and Ring-billed Gulls).

Original line drawings by John K. Cassady.

Printing was covered by a grant from the Northern Indiana Public Service Company.

Manufactured in the United States of America

Library of Congress Cataloging-in-Publication Data

Brock, Kenneth J.
    Birds of the Indiana Dunes.

    Bibliography: p.
    Includes index.
1. Birds--Indiana--Indiana Dunes State Park.
2. Birds--Indiana--Indiana Dunes National Lakeshore.
3. Bird watching--Indiana--Indiana Dunes State Park.
4. Bird watching--Indiana--Indiana Dunes National
Lakeshore. I. Title.

Library of Congress Catalog Card Number   97-61101

ISBN 0-9659358-0-9

CONTENTS

THE INDIANA DUNES REGION

The Dunes Avifauna   2

Migration in the Dunes   4

The Birding Sites   9

SPECIES ACCOUNTS

The Records   25

Finding Codes   26

Occurrence Histograms   28

Migration Envelopes   28

Family Gaviidae: Loons   31

Family Podicipedidae: Grebes   33

Suborder Pelecani: Gannets and Pelicans   36

Family Phalacrocoracidae: Cormorants   37

Family Fregatidae: Frigatebirds   38

Family Ardeidae: Bitterns and Herons   38

Family Threskiornithidae: Ibises and Spoonbills   45

Family Anatidae: Swans, Geese, and Ducks   45

Family Cathartidae: Vultures   65

Family Accipitridae: Hawks   66

Family Falconidae: Falcons   74

Family Phasianidae: Pheasants, Grouses, and Quails   75

Family Rallidae: Rails   76

Family Gruidae: Cranes   82

Family Charadriidae: Plovers   84

Family Recurvirostridae: Stilts and Avocets   87

Family Scolopacidae: Shorebirds   87

Subfamily Stercorariinae: Jaegers   107

Subfamily Larinae: Gulls   111

Subfamily Sterninae: Terns   119

Family Alcidae: Murrelets   123

Family Columbidae: Pigeons and Doves   124

Family Cuculidae: Cuckoos   125

Order Strigiformes: Owls   126

Family Caprimulgidae: Goatsuckers   132

Order Apodiformes: Swifts and Hummingbirds   134

Family Alcedinidae: Kingfishers   135

Family Picidae: Woodpeckers   136

Family Tyrannidae: Flycatchers   140

Family Alaudidae: Larks   146

Family Hirundinidae: Swallows   147

Family Corvidae: Jays and Crows   150

Family Paridae: Chickadees and Titmice   152

Family Sittidae: Nuthatches   153

Family Certhiidae: Creepers   154

Family Troglodytidae: Wrens   155

Family Muscicapidae: Old World Warblers, Thrushes, and Allies   158

Family Mimidae: Catbirds, Mockingbirds, and Thrashers   165

Family Motacillidae: Pipits   167

Family Bombycillidae: Waxwings   167

Family Laniidae: Shrikes   168

Family Sturnidae: Starlings   170

Family Vireonidae: Vireos   170

Subfamily Parulinae: Warblers   174

Subfamily Thraupinae: Tanagers   200

Subfamily Cardinalinae: Cardinals and Buntings   201

Subfamily Emberizinae: Sparrows   204

Subfamily Icterinae: Blackbirds and Orioles   219

Family Fringillidae: Finches   224

Family Passeridae: Weaver Finches   230

Appendix A: Bar Graphs   231

Bibliography   245

Index   248

LIST OF MAPS

The Dunes Area	xii
Whiting Area	10
Miller Beach-West Beach Area	12
Michigan City Harbor	14
Indiana Dunes State Park	16
Beverly Shores Area	18

LIST OF BIRD DRAWINGS

Long-tailed Jaeger	24
Long-eared Owl	30
Least Bittern	39
Common Merganser	62
Oldsquaw	64
Rough-legged Hawk	69
Sora	78
Greater Yellowlegs	89
Stilt Sandpiper	106
Sabine's Gull	124
Red-breasted Nuthatch	157
Snowy Owl	166
Black-throated Green Warbler	188
Loggerhead Shrike	199
LeConte's Sparrow	205
Evening Grosbeak	230

Preface to Second Edition

More than a decade has passed since the first edition of *Birds of the Indiana Dunes* was published. During this interval interest in Dunes Area birding has expanded considerably. In addition to many new local enthusiasts, the area is now regularly visited by birders from Chicago and downstate Indiana. This increased coverage has resulted in the discovery of several new species and has provided vast amounts of new data. Indeed, some 103,000 records of the 352 Dunes Area species (up from 337 in the first edition) were used as a data base for this book. These data were manipulated, organized, and analyzed with the aid of a microcomputer.

The second edition contains lots of new information about Dunes Area birdlife; it increases our knowledge of nesting species, improves the resolution of migration patterns, and documents changes in the avian populations. This information is presented in narrative (finding data and status), graphical (migration histograms), and tabular formats (migration envelopes and peak counts). A set of bar graphs showing the distribution of each species throughout the year is appended.

This book is intended to aid those interested in enjoying the birds that live in and migrate through the Dunes Area. The graphs, tables, and numerical facts are included to enhance the reader's understanding and enjoyment of Dunes Area birdlife. Please keep in mind, however, it is the birds, not dates or numbers, that are important.

Many individuals assisted in bringing the second edition into print. I am especially indebted to the Shirley Heinze Environmental Fund for publishing this volume and to the Northern Indiana Public Service Company for a generous grant that covered printing costs. Special thanks go to Peter Grube for his creative cover design and John Cassady for his superb original line drawings. Clyde Fields shared two of his beautiful bird photographs for the cover. Steve Brown's recommendations significantly improved the maps. Emma B. Pitcher critically reviewed the manuscript and offered many extremely helpful ideas. Liz McClosky and Don Moher proofread the manuscript and greatly enhanced the text. And of course scores of observers contributed the data that provides the foundation of the book. Thanks to all.

Birds of the Indiana Dunes

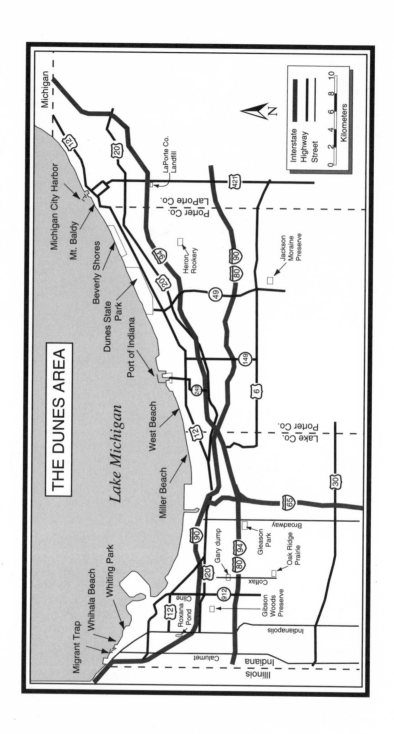

THE DUNES AREA

Lake Michigan

Michigan

Michigan City Harbor
Mt. Baldy
Beverly Shores
Dunes State Park
Port of Indiana
West Beach
Miller Beach
Whiting Park
Whihala Beach
Migrant Trap

LaPorte Co. Landfill
Heron Rookery
Jackson Moraine Preserve
Gary dump
Gleason Park
Oak Ridge Prairie
Gibson Woods Preserve
Roxana Pond
Broadway
Colfax
Cline

Porter Co.
LaPorte Co.
Lake Co.
Porter Co.

Illinois
Indiana
Calumet
Indianapolis

Interstate
Highway
Street

N

0 2 4 6 8 10
Kilometers

THE INDIANA DUNES REGION

The Indiana Dunes, named for the thin strip of sand dunes juxtaposed along Indiana's Lake Michigan shoreline, stretch across northern portions of Lake, LaPorte, and Porter Counties. Within this area precise boundaries between sand and adjacent lowlands are sufficiently vague that, in practice, "Indiana Dunes" is used in reference to the general area, rather than specifically to the sand dunes. In describing the local flora Peattie (1930), recognizing the absence of natural boundaries within this area, applied the name Indiana Dunes to the entire floor of ancient Lake Chicago (ancestral Lake Michigan), an area commonly known as the Calumet Region. Peattie's convention is adopted in this work; the term Indiana Dunes is geographically synonymous with Calumet Region. In general usage the name Calumet Region is frequently associated with the heavy industrialization and defiled environment that exists locally. In order to avoid this negative bias "Dunes Area" or simply "the Dunes" is substituted for "Calumet Region." In this volume the term High Dunes is employed when specific reference to the sand dunes is made.

Showcases within the Indiana Dunes are the State Park and National Lakeshore. The State Park consists of almost 2,200 acres of pristine dunes, wetlands, and woods that were set aside in 1923. The National Lakeshore, a mosaic of separate parcels totaling some 15,000 acres, includes a wide variety of habitats and provides access to more than 12 km of lakefront.

The Dunes Area is circumscribed by the Indiana-Illinois state line on the west; by the natural boundaries of Lake Michigan on the north; and by the Valparaiso Moraine on the south and east. For simplicity the traditional southern and eastern borders have been arbitrarily replaced by man-made features that render the boundaries more easily recognized on road maps. The southern margin follows U.S. Highway 30 across Lake County. From the Lake-Porter County line the boundary extends cross county to the intersection of U.S. Highway 6 and State Road 149. The remaining southern margin is bounded by the eastward portion of Highway 6 to the intersection with U.S. Highway 421. The eastern limit follows Highway 421 northward to Interstate 94, and continues along the latter to the Indiana-Michigan state line.

The Dunes Area is characterized by two distinct physiographic units: the High Dunes and the Lacustrine Plain. The High Dunes consist of an elongated series of locally active sand dunes, extending from the Indiana-Michigan state line to Gary. These dunes form topographic high points within the area, often towering more than 50 meters above the lake, and are generally confined to a belt within a few hundred meters of the lakeshore. Although some dunes are bare, the majority support a sparse veil of vegetation varieties that can accommodate the well-drained, sandy soil. Occurring within the High Dunes are pockets of lowlands, containing vegetation types associated with greater moisture. These wetlands include moist forests and interdunal marshes. The Lacustrine Plain constitutes the dominant landscape of the region. The plain is a rather featureless, poorly drained area consisting of marshes, shallow ponds, sluggish streams, cultivated fields, and industrial-urban development. Despite the impact of landfilling and industrialization, the Lacustrine Plain provides many excellent sites for observing birds, especially species preferring marshy or aquatic habitats.

THE DUNES AVIFAUNA

At least 352 avian species have been identified in the Dunes Area. Of these, six are either extinct or extirpated from the area. Some 113 species might be considered regular nesters, another 24 species formerly nested, or nested at least once, and unconfirmed breeding evidence exists for perhaps an additional nine species.

The most salient feature influencing Dunes Area birdlife is the presence of Lake Michigan. The lake provides suitable habitat for open water species; affects local migration patterns; and supports a wide beach that attracts numerous waders. Unique islands of habitat, undoubtedly created by Lake Michigan's geological history, plus the stabilizing effects of temperature and moisture, generate nesting sites for several passerines that are more typical of geographic regions located both north and south of the Dunes. The White-eyed Vireo, Prairie Warbler, Louisiana Waterthrush, and Hooded Warbler represent species that typically nest south of the Dunes, but breed here regularly. "Northern" species taking advantage of the Dunes' microclimate include the Veery, Chestnut-sided Warbler, and Canada Warbler. Although nests have not been found, the Alder Flycatcher is observed regularly in summer and almost certainly breeds locally.

Early Ornithological Studies in the Dunes

Before the turn of the century the Dunes Area remained a relatively unaltered wilderness. Little information exists today regarding the birds of that era; however, the presence of numerous hunting clubs in northern Lake County suggests that the avian life was unusually rich. A few tantalizing glimpses into the area's birdlife during the 1800s are available. Moore (1959), for example, gives the following quote from Drusilla Carr (ca. 1872), who in reference to the Miller Beach area stated, "The wolves stood back in the hills and cried like a woman and when we went along the beach we could see an eagle on every hill."

Several accounts of bird occurrences in the Dunes, especially near population centers, are reported in Amos W. Butler's *Birds of Indiana*, published in 1898. Butler suggested that the southern end of Lake Michigan presented an unusually fertile region for ornithological studies, and noted that, in addition to attracting maritime species, the moderating effects of the lake strongly influenced the vegetation and summer resident species. Perhaps the earliest formal account of Dunes birdlife was given by Woodruff (1907) who described the lakefront near Millers (now Miller Beach) as "An unusually rich field for the study of maritime species and occasional visitors from the far north." His list from this location included Black-bellied Plover, Semipalmated Plover, Ruddy Turnstone, Dowitcher, Red Knot, Purple Sandpiper, Baird's Sandpiper, Sanderling, Willet, Glaucous Gull, Black-legged Kittiwake, and Caspian Tern.

The first systematic observations of the area's birdlife were commenced about 1913, by two independent naturalists, Donald F. Boyd and Herbert L. Stoddard. Toward the mid-point of the century these pioneers were followed by Dr. Virginia Reuter-skiold and Raymond Grow. The following biographical sketches summarize the contributions these four individuals made to Dunes Area ornithology.

Donald F. Boyd— A well-known naturalist and meticulous note-taker, Donald Boyd was born in LaPorte, Indiana in 1882, and died in 1955. Most of his life was spent within the Dunes Area. Donald Boyd's residences included: Whiting 1906-1919; Hobart 1919-1932; Gary 1932-1944; and Portage (Boy Scout Camp) 1944-1952. Poor health forced an early retirement from the Standard Oil refinery in Whiting, allowing him to concentrate on nature studies, and ultimately to become caretaker of the Boy Scout Camp in Portage. Beginning in 1913 (while living in Whiting), Boyd developed the habit of maintaining a diary of field observations, which contained numerous wildlife observations and reams of bird data. These diaries, which were religiously recorded in yearly volumes entitled "Nature Notes," are now housed in the Calumet Region Archives at Indiana University Northwest. Boyd's detailed notes include weather summaries, information on flora (often accompanied by elaborate drawings or pressed specimens), notes on animals, nest sightings, and bird observation dates. They provide an extraordinary information source about the natural history of the region. There are also numerous short but eloquent essays on birds with intriguing titles such as, "The Rain Crow" or "The Great Northern Diver." Boyd's activities as a bander in conjunction with numerous nesting observations provide a solid picture of the Dunes Area birdlife during the first half of the twentieth century.

Herbert L. Stoddard, Sr.— Herbert Stoddard, born 24 February 1889, in Rockford, Illinois, grew up in Florida and Wisconsin. A dedicated naturalist, Stoddard taught himself taxidermy at an early age, and pursued a career in museums. He ultimately gained international recognition with the publication of *The Bobwhite Quail: Its Habits, Preservation, and Increase,* a landmark volume on wildlife management. During his tenure as a curator with the Chicago Field Museum (1913-1920), Stoddard made numerous weekend trips to the Indiana Dunes. The standard procedure was to ride the train to Millers station, and walk eastward to Mineral Springs or Tremont, where a train was boarded for the return to Chicago. According to Stoddard there were only two fisherman's shacks along this twenty mile expanse of Lake Michigan shoreline. It was on these excursions that Stoddard made a number of very significant ornithological discoveries, including early Indiana records of the Northern Goshawk, Long-tailed Jaeger, Roseate Tern, Black-backed Woodpecker, Clay-colored Sparrow, and Hoary Redpoll. Additionally, he recorded detailed accounts of all birds observed on each expedition. In 1951, Professor Russell E. Mumford, transcribed information from Stoddard's original notebook. These data, which summarize observations from some 115 trips (12 in 1914; 7 in 1915; 26 in 1916; 19 in 1917; 35 in 1919; and 16 in 1920), provide a fascinating and incredibly valuable insight into the turn of the century birdlife of the Dunes.

Virginia Reuter-skiold, M.D.— Virginia Jackola was born in Polo, Illinois, on 31 August 1903, and took her undergraduate education at Rockford College (BS 1925). In 1933 she received a Degree in Medicine, with honors in anatomy, from the University of Chicago. While attending medical school she met her future husband Dr. Knute Reuter-skiold, a member of the Medical School faculty. In the early 1940s the couple began taking weekend trips to an old farmhouse near the settlement of Baileytown (later displaced by the Bethlehem Steel plant). In 1944, Virginia began recording wildlife observations made during each weekend visit. Finally, in December 1948, both Reuter-skiolds retired and moved into the farmhouse. Almost daily for the next 15 years Dr. Virginia Reuter-skiold recorded information on birds and plants observed in the dunes near her home. The notes, recorded in small spiral-backed books, are now preserved in the Indiana University Northwest Archives.

In addition to maintaining daily check lists, which provide a wealth of invaluable data on avian migration patterns, Dr. Reuter-skiold discovered many rarities, including Ferruginous Hawk, Western Kingbird, Blue Grosbeak, Bachman's Sparrow, and Hoary Redpoll. She also recorded detailed information about the spring hawk flights. Dr. Reuter-skiold, a staunch supporter of Dunes preservation, was among the last residents to be displaced by the steel plant. In 1963 she moved to Rolling Prairie in eastern LaPorte County, where she resided until her death in 1978.

Raymond Grow— Born 22 December 1914, in Sioux Falls, South Dakota, Grow and his family moved to Gary about 1925. Although formally educated in journalism (AB Marquette University 1937) and widely viewed as a "Renaissance man" by friends and associates, Ray Grow was always a naturalist at heart. He recalled enjoying the woods as a youngster and remembered purchasing a pair of binoculars while in eighth grade. In 1951, Ray developed a deep interest in birds and joined the Chicago Ornithology Society. A few years later the acquisition of a 1954 "Chevy" provided the mobility necessary for extensive birding throughout northwestern Indiana. Ray Grow was a classic naturalist in the traditional sense, being equally conversant in ornithology, botany, and zoology. Widely regarded as a local bird authority, he made numerous contributions to Dunes ornithology. Raymond founded several Christmas Bird Counts, including the Michigan City count (now known, with a slight location adjustment, as the Indiana Dunes National Lakeshore Count); served as regional editor for the *Indiana Audubon Quarterly* Field Notes during the early 1960s; and added Indiana's first Snowy Plover, Sabine's Gull, and Boreal Chickadee to the state records. A myriad of significant observations dealing with bird movement along Indiana's lakefront were also recorded by this venerable observer. Perhaps Ray Grow's most important ornithological contribution was his study of autumn jaeger flights; his countless hours spent watching for jaegers were instrumental in documenting the regular occurrence of these Arctic wanderers along the Indiana lakefront. Raymond remained an active naturalist in the Dunes area until his death 2 April 1988.

MIGRATION IN THE DUNES

Without doubt the presence of Lake Michigan affects the movement and distribution of birdlife in the Dunes more than any other single factor. The shores of this enormous lake provide leading lines that control flight paths of migrants, and the vast open waters draw legions of transitory and wintering birds. During autumn the elongate north-south boundaries of the lake become airways along which thousands of migrants navigate toward wintering areas. Southbound birds following the shores are ultimately guided into the Dunes Area, at the toe of the lake. This avian convergence at the bottom of Lake Michigan is termed the "funnel effect." The funneling principle is invoked to explain the unusually high occurrence of shorebirds (the number of fall records is more than double the spring records for most migrants), and maritime wanderers in northwestern Indiana. In a sense, therefore, the Dunes serve as an autumn portal to the lower Midwest for southbound migrants.

Lake Michigan also provides two important avian habitats that are otherwise quite rare in the Midwest: the deep lake and the beach. Waters of the lake attract large numbers of bay and sea ducks, many of which are virtually unrecorded at inland sites in the Midwest. Additionally, the lake attracts a number of rare periodic transients, including the Purple Sandpiper, Red Phalarope, Pomarine Jaeger, Parasitic Jaeger, Great Black-backed Gull,

4

Glaucous Gull, Iceland Gull, Thayer's Gull, Sabine's Gull, Little Gull, and Black-legged Kittiwake. Extensive beaches provide resting and feeding areas for shorebirds, especially those species preferring sand rather than mudflats, e.g., Sanderling, Red Knot, and Baird's Sandpiper.

THE FUNNEL EFFECT

The deep waters of Lake Michigan also constitute a significant obstacle to migrants. During nocturnal flights many north-bound passerines overfly land's end and daybreak finds them over the lake. When landfall is visible, they often fly directly to the shore, where they immediately land for rest and feeding. This effect generates an anomalously high concentration of passerines in parks and woodlands immediately adjacent to the lake. It is equally clear that many of the small weak flyers never make landfall. A plethora of accounts describe exhausted birds seeking refuge on fishing boats or other vessels, often miles offshore. Perkins (1964), for example, presents a fascinating summary of the birds he recorded aboard a Great Lakes oreboat.   Lakefront observers also frequently note fatigued passerines struggling in off the lake. Perhaps typical is the 28 September 1958, observation by Jim Landing, who detected a small bird flying just above the water's surface, approaching Michigan City Harbor from the lake. Landing related that, "The bird approached within 100 yards, flying very feebly, then dropped onto the water.... I assumed it was going to drown, but after approximately a minute, the bird took to the air with seemingly little effort, and flew to the pier." The bird proved to be an immature Swamp

Sparrow.   Scores of other small birds are less fortunate. Tired migrants must also run a gauntlet of aggressive gulls as they approach the shore; on many occasions passerines have been observed being harassed and driven into the water by ravenous gulls.

A major spring bird-kill, described by Segal (1960), graphically demonstrates the migration hazard posed by Lake Michigan. This report tabulates results of a census of 3,636 dead birds found along 17 km of Indiana's beaches following a severe storm on the lake (see tabulation). An additional 320 birds, including the Hairy Woodpecker and Veery (not found on Segal's

THE 16 APRIL 1960 BIRD-KILL ON LAKE MICHIGAN
(from Segal, 1960)

1039	Dark-eyed Junco	21	Virginia Rail	2	Eastern Screech Owl
633	Swamp Sparrow	21	Brown-headed Cowbird	2	Eastern Bluebird
437	American Robin	18	Vesper Sparrow	2	Grasshopper Sparrow
331	American Tree Sparrow	18	Ruby-crowned Kinglet	2	Chipping Sparrow
198	Fox Sparrow	16	Eastern Towhee	2	Northern Cardinal
147	Hermit Thrush	16	Mourning Dove	1	Lincoln's Sparrow
141	Yellow-bellied Sapsucker	14	Carolina Wren	1	Sedge Wren
113	Northern Flicker	14	Yellow Rail	1	Smith's Longspur
56	Eastern Meadowlark	10	Downy Woodpecker	1	Purple Finch
50	Savannah Sparrow	10	LeConte's Sparrow	1	King Rail
47	Yellow-rumped Warbler	9	Sora	1	American Bittern
47	Brown Creeper	8	Eastern Phoebe	1	Purple Martin
47	Song Sparrow	8	Red-winged Blackbird	1	Common Snipe
37	Field Sparrow	6	Rusty Blackbird	1	House Wren
32	Henslow's Sparrow	5	Western Meadowlark	1	Lapland Longspur
32	Winter Wren	3	Whip-poor-will	1	Long-eared Owl
31	Brown Thrasher	3	European Starling	1	White-eyed Vireo
25	Golden-crowned Kinglet	2	Killdeer	1	Blue Jay
25	White-throated Sparrow	2	American Woodcock	1	Saw-whet Owl

list), were counted by John Louis (pers. comm.). The presence of several strong flyers (e.g., Mourning Dove, Killdeer, and Common Snipe) on this list attests to the storm's strength. Kills of much smaller magnitude are not rare on Lake Michigan. Cutright (1978), for example, counted 245 birds along 0.9 km of beach (near Bailly Generating Station) on 25 May 1976. Dominant species, and number of individuals, in the latter count were: Gray Catbird (24), Empidonax species (22), Common Yellowthroat (16), Magnolia Warbler (15), unidentified thrushes (12), and Chestnut-sided Warbler (10).

The Effects of Weather

That most migrants fly during fair weather when trailing winds are available is well documented in ornithology textbooks. Along the shores of southern Lake Michigan this principle is most clearly evident during the fall. Bennett (1952) discovered that the number of fall passerine migrants along the Chicago lakefront tripled on the days immediately following passage of cold fronts (compared to numbers on the day immediately prior to frontal passage). Similarly, the most exciting autumn birding in the Dunes occurs during or immediately following the passage of cold fronts. In addition to the passerine waves that follow the fronts, northerly winds stimulate a general longshore movement of water birds. On such occasions, an endless stream of loons, ducks, gulls, and terns often flow along the lakefront. Rare sightings are often associated with these blustery autumn days. Indeed, the correlation between inclement weather and good birding has been frequently noted by lakefront observers. Accordingly, the biting autumn days with strong northerly winds are often referred to as "jaeger days" by hopeful local birders.

Longshore Migrations

Scores of avian species have been observed migrating along the shores of Lake Michigan, more or less parallel to the beach. Among the water birds, movements of loons, ducks, shorebirds (Killdeer and Dunlin), gulls, and terns are common, especially on windy days, and grebe flights are occasionally noted. Most of the aforementioned species fly over the lake, or along the beach. Of special interest are the diurnal flights of land birds along the lakefront, usually tracking the crest line of the High Dunes. These flights are most frequently noted in the spring, but distinctive movements, especially of Snow Buntings, have also been noted in fall. Interestingly, birds involved in these spring flights invariably fly into the wind. Large passerine movements are often detected by observers at the hawk-watch sites; counts exceeding several hundred individuals have been tabulated within a few hours. Diurnal spring flights of the following species have been noted: Northern Flicker, Eastern Kingbird, Black-capped Chickadee, Cedar Waxwing, Tree Swallow, Barn Swallow, Bank Swallow, Northern Crow, Blue Jay, Eastern Bluebird, American Robin, European Starling, Scarlet Tanager, Rose-breasted Grosbeak, Indigo Bunting, Eastern Meadowlark, Common Grackle, Bobolink, Red-winged Blackbird, Northern Oriole, House Finch and American Goldfinch. Undoubtedly many others have yet to be recorded.

Beginning about 1990, contemporary birders discovered that fall lake-watching, especially following the passage of a cold front, provides spectacular birding. Requirements for a good lake-watch site include elevation for distant viewing, and a wind-break for shelter. At this writing the premier autumn lake-watch site is the concession stand at Marquette Park (on Miller Beach about 1 km east of the Lake Street lot). Birders from northern Indiana, Chicago, and even further afield gather at this site with each frontal passage between mid-August and December. The results have been sensational. Some of the remarkable totals accumulated over this seven-year period include: 51 Red-throated Loons, a Northern Gannet, 25 American Avocets, five Whimbrels, two Red Phalaropes, six Pomarine Jaegers, 40 Parasitic Jaegers, six Long-tailed Jaegers, 127 Franklin's Gulls, ten Little Gulls, 46 Black-legged Kittiwakes (22 of which occurred in 1995), 15 Sabine's Gulls, and a Gull-billed Tern. These results, along with hoards of the more common species, have significantly expanded our knowledge of autumn bird movements on Lake Michigan.

Observing birds on Lake Michigan requires markedly different skills and techniques than those employed on traditional bird hikes. On a lake watch the observer remains stationary, awaiting passage of the birds. Accordingly, most migrants seen along the lakefront are observed in flight. Therefore, skill in identifying flying birds and a good telescope are essential. Additionally, the birds tend to be most active on days with strong north winds, a condition that has led to evolution of a birding adage for the lake, "the more horrific the weather, the more terrific the birding."

Raptor Flights

The existence of spring hawk flights along the High Dunes was first reported in the early 1950s by Raymond Grow and Virginia Reuter-skiold, who recorded flight information near Baileytown between 1952 and 1962. The

Baileytown site consisted of a high dune that has subsequently been destroyed; however, hawks can be observed today from any location offering an unobstructed view of the lakefront and areas south of the dune crests. Currently, the most commonly used site is Johnson Beach, which consists of a stabilized dune on National Lakeshore property just outside the western margin of Dunes State Park.

Spring flights along the High Dunes must be attributed to the presence of Lake Michigan. Northbound hawks, especially buteos, enjoy a leisurely spring migration, wafting effortlessly over the Midwest on thermals and balmy southerly winds. These soaring raptors, however, display a marked aversion to flying over large bodies of water as thermals do not develop over the cool water. Consequently, upon encountering Lake Michigan the northward movement is abruptly terminated and the birds turn to a course paralleling the shoreline. Thus, the migrating hawks are concentrated in a belt immediately adjacent to the lake. In effect, therefore, the High Dunes rest directly below a narrow flight corridor that extends along the lake's southern margin.

Since 1983, considerable observer effort has been expended at the "hawk-watch sites" in an attempt to gain additional knowledge about the spring raptor flights (Brock, 1990b, Squires, 1991). This data-base has allowed some generalizations to be drawn. Most flights occur on days with winds from a southerly quadrant and the most commonly observed species are Red-taileds, Sharp-shinneds and Broad-wingeds; these species comprise more than 70% of the identified hawks. The primary flight period is between 1 March and 15 May. March and April constitute the major flight months. A good daily flight consists of 100-300 birds. Nine of the ten largest flights occurred in April (see tabulation). The average season produces about 1700 hawks; the best year was 1992, when 3774 birds were counted.

THE TEN LARGEST DAILY HAWK FLIGHTS

Day	19	26	23	25	18	14	8	22	4	20
Month	April	April	April	April	April	March	April	April	April	April
Year	1992	1984	1961	1955	1996	1990	1990	1989	1985	1992
Hours	7.5	5	5.5	6.5	5.5	6	7	5.5	5.5	5.5
Turkey Vulture	17	5	5	3	2	5	12	11	11	
Osprey	15	3	4		2			1		10
Bald Eagle			2			10	1	0		
N. Harrier	35	10	1	38	26	10	28	7	29	15
Sharp-shinned	223	140	21	128	135	52	94	63	77	92
Coopers	16	22	7	6	7	4	7	2	5	5
Goshawk				1					1	
Red-shouldered	3	1	8	2	5	75	18	2	1	3
Broad-winged	293	421	266	43	135			42		55
Red-tailed	98	28	239	274	75	142	140	173	139	128
Rough-legged	12	1	15			1	4	2	1	1
Golden Eagle			1							
Kestrel	52	17	7	1	53	12	27	16	29	4
Merlin						2				
Peregrine	1	1		2	1					1
Unidentified	4	29	60	12		61	19	22	25	1
Total	769	678	636	510	443	372	350	341	318	315

Fall raptor flights along the lakefront are far less pronounced than spring movements, and are primarily limited to the Peregrine Falcon. Peregrines are usually noted flying directly along the beaches, especially during periods of strong northerly winds. Although rare, small autumn flights of various buteos have been noted. The latter may be associated with persistent easterly winds that drift southbound birds to the east shore of Lake Michigan where they follow the shoreline southward into the Dunes. This effect is more pronounced further north, along the shoreline in Michigan, where most hawk movements are associated with easterly winds (Roy Smith, pers. comm.).

THE BIRDING SITES

The following section describes specific locations within the Dunes Area that have consistently provided reliable birding. Each site is among the better birding locations in the region. A few locations referred to in the species description are not mentioned in this section. Many of these are older sites that have subsequently been destroyed through development; others have been renamed (these sites are listed on p. 23-24).

Birding sites are divided into three categories based upon the physiographic environment in which the site is located. These categories are as follows: sites along the lakefront; sites in the High Dunes; and sites on the Lacustrine Plain. Generally each category yields a rather distinct group of habitats and birdlife. The best birding season for each site is listed with the location name.

Sites on the Lakefront

Although Indiana has some 65 km of Lake Michigan shoreline, much of the lakefront property is occupied by heavy industry, which severely limits access. In recent years land acquisition by the Indiana Dunes National Lakeshore has greatly expanded public access to the lake; however, a significant portion of the lake remains closed to birders. As a result, the relatively few points of easy access attract many observers. The observation points generally providing easy access and the best vantage points are described below.

The Migrant Trap and Whiting Park: spring and fall (Whiting Area Map) In addition to attracting species preferring open-lake habitat, Lake Michigan also strongly influences bird migration, often generating concentrated pockets of migrants during periods of heavy flight. Perhaps the best example of this effect occurs in the so-called Migrant Trap. This name was given to the site by local birders after the discovery of the astonishing number of migrants that accumulate there during spring and fall migrations. It consists of a strip of lakefront fill in extreme northwestern Indiana, less than a kilometer from the Illinois state line. The site, which occupies 600 meters of wooded lakefront, is located between the Hammond Marina and the Commonwealth Edison power plant. A large parking lot, numerous railroads, and several factories lie to the south, further isolating the Trap's vegetation, rendering it the only cover within several kilometers. Accordingly, remarkable concentrations of migrant passerines (plus occasional Soras, Virginia Rails, Woodcocks, Short-eared Owls, and Whip-poor-Wills) seek the cover afforded by these trees.

In 1996, half of the Migrant Trap was purchased by the city of Hammond and the remaining half was donated to Hammond by the Northern Indiana Public Service Company. Of the original 16 acres, 9.5 acres were set aside as a permanent migratory bird sanctuary and the remaining property was designated

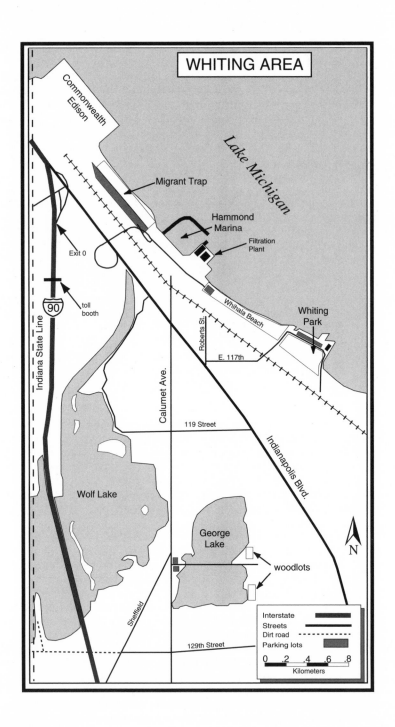

WHITING AREA

Commonwealth Edison

Lake Michigan

Migrant Trap

Hammond Marina

Filtration Plant

Exit 0

toll booth

90

Indiana State Line

Whihala Beach

Roberts St.

Whiting Park

E. 117th

Calumet Ave.

119 Street

Wolf Lake

George Lake

woodlots

Indianapolis Blvd.

N

Sheffield

129th Street

Interstate	▬▬▬
Streets	——
Dirt road	- - -
Parking lots	▬

0   .2   .4   .6   .8
Kilometers

"green space." The Indiana Department of Natural Resources holds a conservation easement on the 9.5 acre sanctuary. In addition, the site name was changed to "Hammond Lakefront Park and Sanctuary." Hammond has made a commitment to improve the sanctuary by further clean-up, enhancing the vegetation, and developing the birding trails. Northern Indiana Public Service Company has also agreed to enclose the sanctuary with a fence. A systematic ten-year plan is under development that will enhance the vegetation in one-fifth of the trap every two years. This will allow the improvements to be implemented without major habitat disruption. All work in the sanctuary will be conducted outside the migration periods.

Birding is usually best during the southbound flight (mid-August through October) when nocturnal migrants following the lakeshore are attracted to the sparse cover in the trap. Impressive spring build-ups also occur during May. The Migrant Trap is almost certainly the best single location in the region for observing migrant passerines. In recent years, fully 25% of all Dunes Area Connecticut Warbler records have come from this site. Other rare birds observed at this site include: Clay-colored Sparrow, Lark Sparrow, LeConte's Sparrow, and Harris' Sparrow.

Whiting Park, located on the lakefront approximately 2 km east of the Migrant Trap, offers similar habitat but less cover. This park attracts numerous migrants, but rarely approaches the concentrations noted in the trap; however, the mowed lawns and paved walks provide a far more pleasing habitat for the birder. Migrant passerines are often found in the trees or on the ground in the shrubbery. Rarities reported within the park include Saw-whet Owl, Kirtland's Warbler, Worm-eating Warbler, Lark Sparrow, and Henslow's Sparrow. The park breakwall also attracts an occasional Snowy Owl and has harbored Harlequin Ducks.

Miller Beach: fall (Miller Beach-West Beach Area Map) This expanse of wide sandy beach constitutes perhaps the first site in the Dunes Area to be frequented by individuals interested in observing birds. Woodruff (1907) described the beach near Millers, Indiana in the most glowing terms. At this location, which was on the edge of the High Dunes wilderness at the turn of the century, Woodruff specifically listed the following species as occurring during fall migration: Glaucous Gull, Black-legged Kittiwake, Red Knot, Purple Sandpiper, Baird's Sandpiper, and Willet.

Miller Beach is located at the foot of Lake Street in Gary. A paved parking lot on the beach provides a good view of the lake, especially on bitter autumn days when an observer is more comfortable watching from the interior of an automobile. Between Memorial Day and Labor Day a parking fee is required. The beach parking area virtually marks the southernmost extent of Lake Michigan. Thus migrating birds following both the eastern and western lakeshores southward are ultimately funneled to this site. As a result, the fall season, August through November, provides the most interesting birds. The birding is usually best on days with a brisk northerly wind, which seems to stimulate the movement of birds along the lakefront. Over the years more jaegers have been seen at Miller Beach than at any other place in Indiana (and probably the highest number at any site in the entire Midwest). Most birders prefer the Marquette Park concession stand (one km east of the lot), where they have an elevated and sheltered view of the lake.

West Beach and Long Lake: fall (Miller Beach-West Beach Area Map) These two sites comprise the West Beach unit of the Indiana Dunes National Lakeshore, and are accessible from U.S. Highway 12, at the Lake-Porter

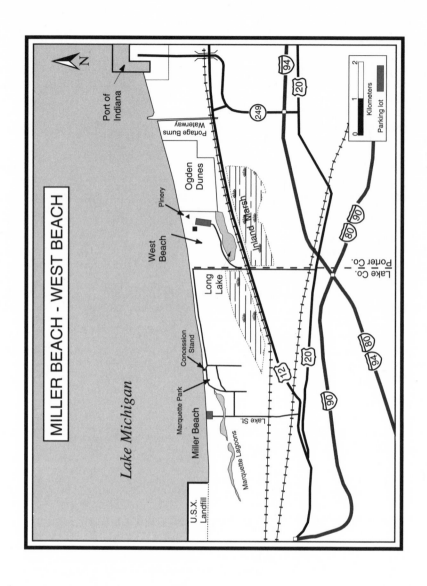

MILLER BEACH - WEST BEACH

Lake Michigan

Port of Indiana

Portage Burns Waterway

Ogden Dunes

Pinery

West Beach

Inland Marsh

Long Lake

Concession Stand

Marquette Park

Miller Beach

Lake St.

Marquette Lagoons

U.S.X. Landfill

Lake Co.
Porter Co.

Kilometers
Parking lot

N

County line. West Beach is some 4 km east of Miller Beach and offers similar open beach habitat. Parking, however, is restricted to a lot almost 200m inland from the lake. The West Beach rarities list includes Northern Gannet, Townsend's Solitaire, and Bohemian Waxwing. In winter the open dunes provide good habitat for Snowy Owls and Northern Shrikes. A small pinery, nestled between the dunes in the northeastern portion of the West Beach, occasionally yields migrant Long-eared Owls and winter finches. Long Lake, a shallow interdunal pond one km south of Lake Michigan, attracts a good selection of waterfowl during migration. Least Bitterns have been seen at Long Lake throughout the summer and probably nest there. The trees and shrubs along the northern margin of the lake attract passerines during migration. Rarities recorded at Long Lake include American White Pelican, Tundra Swan, Brant, and Eurasian Wigeon. The National Lakeshore assesses a parking fee at West Beach during summer months.

Port of Indiana: winter (Dunes Area Map) This deep-water facility is owned by the state of Indiana, and access is limited. At this writing fishermen and birders are allowed into the "Public Access Area," a site from which the harbor can be viewed. The Port of Indiana is reached by following U.S. Highway 249 northward; it leads directly to the state police gatehouse at the port entrance. From the police checkpoint proceed north, passing to the right of the Cargill grain elevators, to the public access area. Although migrant and wintering waterfowl pause to rest and feed in the port harbor, the most interesting birding occurs on windy days when a steady stream of birds track across the harbor, frequently flying almost directly over the public access area. Following a fresh snowfall Horned Larks, Lapland Longspurs, and Snow Buntings often feed on spilled grain along the access road. During winter Common Mergansers, plus assorted bay ducks, feed in the harbor when open water is available. In recent years occasional Snowy Owls have been seen perched on the breakwaters in November and December. Pacific Loon, Western Grebe, Harlequin Duck, all three scoters, Purple Sandpiper, Parasitic Jaeger, Laughing Gull, Thayer's Gull, Glaucous Gull, Great Black-backed Gull, and Black-legged Kittiwake are among the unusual species that have been recorded at this site.

Michigan City Harbor: all year (Michigan City Harbor Map) The harbor, yacht basin, beaches, and piers of Michigan City Harbor provide great opportunities for viewing Lake Michigan's birds. Over the years an impressive array of rarities, surely the highest number of any single Indiana location, has rendered Michigan City Harbor the premier birding site in the state. A list of unusual birds from the Harbor, summarized by Brock (1979), included fully 40% of all rare and accidental species on the state check list. Highlights on this list included: Northern Gannet, Magnificent Frigatebird, King Eider, Pomarine Jaeger, Lesser Black-backed Gull, Black-headed Gull, and Lark Bunting. Since 1979, the following rarities have been added to the Harbor's list: Mew Gull, California Gull, Slaty-backed Gull, Royal Tern, Arctic Tern, Marbled Murrelet, Saw-whet Owl, Western Kingbird, Kirtland's Warbler and Henslow's Sparrow. This exceptionally fine birding area is located on the northern edge of Michigan City, just north of the business district. The most convenient parking is in a lot between Washington Park beach and the yacht basin; however, an exorbitant parking fee is now assessed in spring, summer, and early fall.

Autumn is usually considered the best time to find rare birds at the Harbor, but unusual observations have been reported in every month of the year. If weather and waves permit, many birders prefer to watch from the lighthouse at the northern termination of the jetty. Unusual gulls are often observed perched

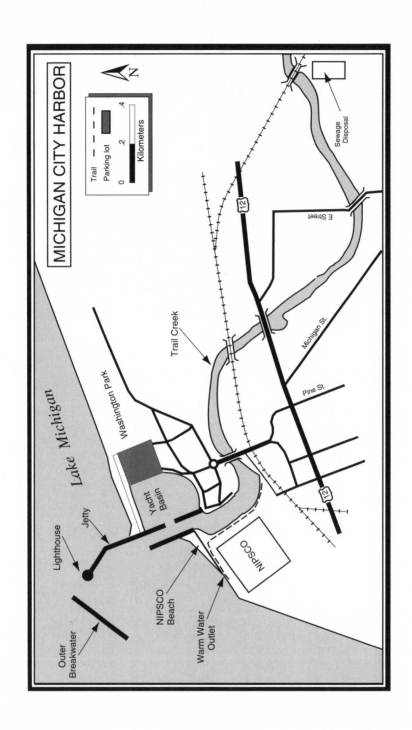

MICHIGAN CITY HARBOR

Trail
Parking lot

0   .2   .4
Kilometers

N

Lake Michigan

Outer Breakwater

Lighthouse

Jetty

Washington Park

Yacht Basin

NIPSCO Beach

Warm Water Outlet

NIPSCO

Trail Creek

Michigan St.

Pine St.

E Street

Sewage Disposal

12

12

on the outer breakwater, the Washington Park beach, and the Northern Indiana Public Service Company (NIPSCO) beach; consequently a spotting telescope is desirable. Many of the most interesting birds are seen only as they fly past the harbor. During migration the lawns and plantings of Washington Park often attract passerines. Following heavy flights, scores of wrens, vireos, warblers, and sparrows take advantage of this sparse vegetation.

Since January 1984, access to the NIPSCO area (the narrow band of lakefront adjacent to the power plant) has been open to the public. Enter near the NIPSCO guard station (south side of plant); a fenced walkway leads to the public access area. Trees and shrubs in the area attract passerine migrants and a good view of both the harbor and NIPSCO beach is provided. During hard winters the only open water available is immediately adjacent to the power plant warm-water discharge. Occasionally, unusual waterfowl are observed swimming in the discharge flume. The NIPSCO site lies directly below a passerine migration corridor along the lakefront. On spring mornings, following heavy nocturnal passerine movements, hundreds (even thousands) of migrants fly almost directly over the NIPSCO access area as they move along the lakefront. Record daily counts of many passerines have been logged at this site. The strongest movements occur on westerly winds.

Sites in the High Dunes

Sand dunes provide the most unique and aesthetically pleasing portions of the Dunes Area. Many former dunes have been removed or destroyed by industrial development, however, precious remnants are preserved at several locations, especially within the Indiana Dunes State Park and the National Lakeshore. Habitats within the High Dunes are varied, ranging from climax forests, through transition zones and interdunal marshes, to oak savannah and marram grass. In view of the close proximity of the High Dunes to Lake Michigan, the distinction between "lakefront" and "High Dunes" birding sites is somewhat arbitrary. West Beach, for example, could well be considered a High Dunes site, for it indeed rests on sand dunes (although many of the West Beach dunes were quarried in the 1920s).

Two points should be emphasized for birders visiting the High Dunes in summer. First, and most importantly, the summer woods are replete with mosquitoes. Insect repellent or protective headgear is essential. Additionally, the summer foliage is extremely dense; consequently, many more birds are heard than are seen. It is worthwhile to brush up on bird songs prior to birding woodlands of the High Dunes.

Indiana Dunes State Park: spring and summer (Indiana Dunes State Park Map) Perhaps the best known landmark in the Dunes is the State Park, which is situated at the northern termination of State Highway 49, on the shore of Lake Michigan. Occurring within the park is the greatest expanse of undamaged dunes remaining in the state. The eastern section of the park has been set aside as a wilderness area. Dunes State Park offers several habitats that render it attractive to birders: climax forest, savannah, marram grass covered dunes, blowouts, beaches and marshes. Of these, the forest, which might more accurately be described as a wooded swamp, and the marsh-woodland boundary provide the best birding. A remarkable feature of the park rests in the fact that many southern birds (e.g., White-eyed Vireo, Cerulean Warbler, Prairie Warbler, Louisiana Waterthrush, and Hooded Warbler) nest here along with typical northern species (e.g., Veery, Chestnut-sided Warbler, and Canada Warbler).

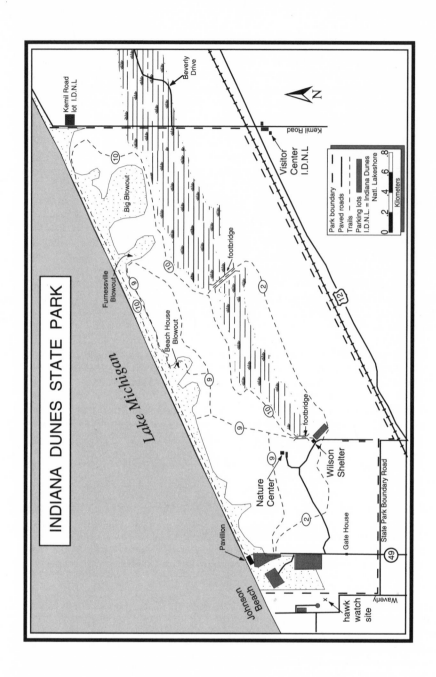

INDIANA DUNES STATE PARK

Lake Michigan

Johnson Beach

Furnessville Blowout

Big Blowout

Beach House Blowout

Kemil Road lot I.D.N.L

Beverly Drive

Kemil Road

Visitor Center I.D.N.L

N

Park boundary
Paved roads
Trails
Parking lots
I.D.N.L. = Indiana Dunes
Natl. Lakeshore

Indiana Dunes

Kilometers
0 2 4 6 8

footbridge

footbridge

Nature Center

Wilson Shelter

Pavillion

Gate House

State Park Boundary Road

Waverly

hawk watch site

12

49

2

9

10

The most popular birding areas within the park are Trails 2 and 10. Both trails can be covered by walking eastward from Wilson Shelter on Trail 2 and looping back on Trail 10. In late spring or early summer the following nesting species are almost always seen or heard along Trail 2, east of Wilson Shelter: Acadian Flycatcher, Blue-winged Warbler (toward eastern end of trail), Cerulean Warbler, Louisiana Waterthrush, and Ovenbird. Red-shouldered Hawks, Broad-winged Hawks, Barred Owls, and Hooded Warblers are occasionally detected along this section of Trail 2. The trail ultimately veers northward, crossing the interdunal marsh; shortly thereafter, it terminates at Trail 10. Trail 10 meanders between marsh, wooded swamp, and savannah habitats as it winds westward, back to Wilson Shelter. This section of Trail 10 often attracts numerous migrants, especially on cool spring days, when warblers seek insects in the lee of the tall dunes. On these occasions warblers frequently drop down into the bushes near the water where they forage on chilled insects seeking the water's warmth. Sections of Trail 10 near the footbridge and horseshoe bend are often unusually good on these cool days. Some years Prothonotary Warblers reside near the footbridge in spring and early summer.

Trail 9 follows the dune crests and requires more vigorous hiking than 2 and 10. An advantage of birding from the dune crests is that birds in nearby trees can often be observed at eye level, thereby avoiding "warbler neck" syndrome. Trail 9 also leads to the blowouts where Prairie Warblers and Field Sparrows summer. The dune crests along Trail 9 also provide a spectacular view of the surrounding woodlands and lake. During spring migration the picnic area near Wilson Shelter often attracts thrushes, warblers, sparrows, and occasional Solitary Sandpipers.

Virtually every warbler species recorded in the Dunes (including Townsend's and Black-throated Gray) has been seen in the State Park. Other rare birds reported within the park's limits are Western Grebe, Mississippi Kite, Purple Gallinule, Lark Bunting, and Clay-colored Sparrow.

Johnson Beach hawk-watch: spring (Indiana Dunes State Park Map) This site is located just outside the western boundary of the State Park (not accessible from inside the park). The site, a stabilized dune on National Lakeshore property, is reached by turning west from Highway 49, at the last possible exit prior to entering the park. This short road terminates at Waverly Road (unmarked); a right turn on the latter leads to Lake Michigan. Cross the dune crest on Waverly Road, and park in the National Lakeshore lot at the stop sign. This crossroad leads southward to the dune on which the hawk-watch site is located.

Beverly Shores Area: all year (Beverly Shores Area Map) The block of dunes between Indiana Dunes State Park and Mount Baldy, and north of U.S. Highway 12, is referred to as Beverly Shores. Centered within this area is the settlement of Beverly Shores, which, in view of its occlusion by the National Lakeshore, is often referred to as the Beverly Shores Island. Available habitats include lake, beach, wooded dunes, and interdunal marsh.

Lake and beach habitats can be examined on foot after parking in the National Lakeshore lots on Kemil Road, Lakeview, or Central Avenue. During waterfowl migration a slow drive down Lake Front Drive, keeping a watchful eye on the water, can prove quite productive; loons, waterfowl, occasional jaegers, and interesting gulls have been reported along the lakefront. The interdunal marsh, located immediately south of the primary dunes, offers excellent habitat for passerines. The length of the marsh is transected by

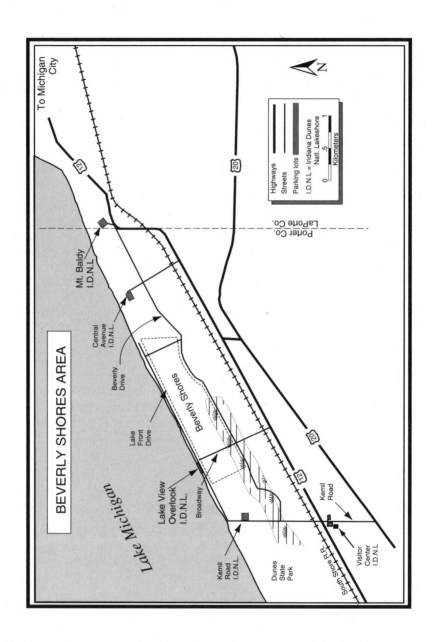

BEVERLY SHORES AREA

Lake Michigan

To Michigan City

Mt. Baldy I.D.N.L.

Central Avenue I.D.N.L.

Beverly Drive

Lake Front Drive

Lake View Overlook I.D.N.L.

Broadway

Beverly Shores

Kemil Road I.D.N.L.

Dunes State Park

Kemil Road

Visitor Center I.D.N.L.

South Shore R.R.

Porter Co.
LaPorte Co.

Highways
Streets
Parking lots
I.D.N.L. = Indiana Dunes
Natl. Lakeshore

0   .5   1
Kilometers

N

Beverly Drive, which has in the past been called (optimistically) "shrike alley" by local birders. Indeed shrikes occasionally winter in this wetland, but are not seen on most tours along Beverly Drive. The interdunal marsh, which in most areas is partially overgrown with shrubs and saplings, supports a large population of nesting species (e.g., Yellow Warbler, Common Yellowthroat, Indigo Bunting, and Swamp Sparrow). In late spring and summer scrubby second growth along the drive often echoes with calls of the Willow Flycatcher, Alder Flycatcher, White-eyed Vireo and Yellow-breasted Chat. One of the most productive areas for the latter species is near the intersection of St. Clair Street and Beverly Drive (just east of Broadway). The hot dry days of late summer often bring passerines to drink from the cool waters of the artesian well located near the west end of Beverly Drive. In May and June a slow drive along tree-shrouded Kemil Road just north of the National Lakeshore visitor center will often yield calling Acadian Flycatchers, Cerulean Warblers, and Louisiana Waterthrush.

Mount Baldy: spring (Beverly Shores Area Map) This tall active dune, located within boundaries of the National Lakeshore, is situated between Beverly Shores and Michigan City. It is accessible from U.S. Highway 12 and parking is available in a National Lakeshore lot. A stairway and walking trail lead to the dune crest. From the brow of Mt. Baldy an excellent view of the surrounding countryside is gained; Lake Michigan is clearly visible to the north and a panorama of woodlands and marshes stretches to the south.

This fine observation point is a prime location for studying the spring hawk flights in March and April. The best hawk movements occur on days with moderate to strong southerly winds; the latter invariably generate blowing sand that constitutes a distinct nuisance for birders. But on heavy flight days it is well worth the inconvenience. Hawks often pass low over the dunes allowing unusually close observation. Occasionally they fly below the dune crest, providing a rare opportunity to view flying hawks from above. In addition to the diurnal raptors, impressive flights of cranes, flickers, jays, crows, and swallows are often observed from the summit. Almost anything is possible– the American Woodcock, Barred Owl, and Short-eared Owl have all been recorded winging past Mt. Baldy.

The open sands of Mt. Baldy also attract Snow Buntings and occasional longspurs, in late fall and winter. Trees around the parking lot offer a good selection of passerines during migration and a Chuck-Will's-Widow has summered near Mt. Baldy for several years (its dawn and dusk calls can usually be heard from the parking lot).

Heron Rookery Unit: spring and summer (Dunes Area Map) This mature woodland, which is isolated by cultivated fields, is a part of the Indiana Dunes National Lakeshore. It is located in rural Porter County along the Little Calumet River between county roads 450 East and 600 East. Although the Great Blue Heron rookery is situated in eastern portions of this woodland, the best birding occurs in the western section. To bird the site, park in the small National Lakeshore lot at the intersections of county roads 450 East and 1300 North, and walk northward to the Little Calumet River channel (about 200 meters). A well maintained trail skirts the southern bank of the river. In early spring migrant warblers are often concentrated along the channel. Nesting specialties include Acadian Flycatchers, Yellow-throated Warblers, Cerulean Warblers, and Louisiana Waterthrush. Without doubt, woods along the channel support the largest American Redstart concentration in the Dunes Area.

Lacustrine Plain Sites

Perhaps more than any other physiographic unit, the Lacustrine Plain has been modified by man. Vast tracts have been drained and put into cultivation, whereas other sections have been filled to support industrial, urban, and suburban developments. Interspersed among factories, shopping centers and railroad tracks are local remnants of the former marshland, which must have provided an incredible haven for wildlife. Most of these relics consist of shallow lakes, river floodplains, or cattail marshes. Sadly, many of these vestiges are today threatened by pollution and further expansion.

Additionally, most Lacustrine Plain sites are currently influenced by man's activities. Accordingly water levels vary greatly from year to year (and often from week to week), strongly affecting the birding quality of most sites. On many occasions birders may find few, if any, birds at any given location.

Wolf Lake and George Lake: spring and fall (Whiting Area Map) Wolf Lake is located in Hammond and abuts the Indiana-Illinois state line (westernmost reaches of the lake lie in Illinois). In former years the birdlife at Wolf Lake must have been considerably richer than it is today; extensive filling has eliminated much of the marshland and drastically altered breeding habitat. Earlier this century Piping Plovers, Wilson's Phalaropes, and Black Terns nested at the lake, but these species vanished along with their habitat. Today Wolf Lake provides habitat for migrant waterfowl; in winter Common Mergansers seem to show a preference for this particular body of water. Southern portions of the lake can be reached by driving west on the western extension of 131st Street, from Calumet Avenue. This very rough dirt road is more like an obstacle course than a street. Shorebirds occasionally congregate on the southern margin of the lake; in the spring of 1980, a Curlew Sandpiper was discovered in this area. The best view of the lake is obtained from a roadside park on Calumet Avenue or from 119th Street. In April and May puddle ducks, and terns are often visible from the latter site.

George Lake (not to be confused with Lake George in Hobart) is located immediately east of Wolf Lake, across Calumet Avenue in Hammond. This shallow body of water has suffered a history similar to that of Wolf Lake. A paved road transects the lake, providing a good vantage point for viewing the lake. The lake attracts migrating waterfowl, gulls, and terns, and in dry years, shorebirds may explore narrow mudflats along the lake's margin. During the autumns of 1983 and 1984 water in the lake dropped to unprecedented low levels, providing excellent shorebird habitat. Woodcocks have nested in woodlots along the eastern margin of the lake; these tree also attract an interesting array of passerines during migration and are worth checking in spring and fall.

Roxana Pond: summer and fall (Dunes Area Map) In former years this shallow pond, which lies within a meander of the Grand Calumet River, offered the most reliable shorebird habitat in the Dunes Area. Recently, however, water levels have been too high for shorebirds. The pond is located in East Chicago just north of Roxana Street about 400m west of Indianapolis Boulevard (Roxana Street is immediately north of the Indiana Toll Road). Water levels in Roxana Pond fluctuate widely, apparently more dependent upon local industries than on precipitation. Low water levels expose extensive mudflats, which provide feeding habitat for migrant shorebirds. During low water conditions mudflats are also exposed along the banks of the Grand Calumet River, west of

Roxana Pond. The latter area can easily be birded from Roxana Street by driving west from the pond and passing under the I-90 overpass.

Most of the regular shorebirds have been seen at Roxana Pond (often in great numbers), and an impressive list of rarities has been recorded (e.g., Marbled Godwit, Hudsonian Godwit, American Avocet, Stilt Sandpiper, Long-billed Dowitcher, and Red-necked Phalarope). High water conditions, however, can entirely eliminate the mudflats; consequently, on many occasions no shorebirds will be present. Roxana Pond was also one of the last Black Tern nesting areas in the Dunes, and produced Indiana's only record of the White-winged Tern. Yellow-headed Blackbirds probably nested at the pond in 1984 and 1985. Regular nesting species include the Mallard, Blue-winged Teal, American Coot, Common Moorhen (becoming scarce), Marsh Wren, and Red-winged Blackbird.

Gleason Park: spring and fall (Dunes Area Map) This site is currently undergoing major renovation, as the U. S. Army Corps of Engineers is constructing set-back levees as part of a flood control project. It is unclear what impact these activities will have on future birding at the site. The portion of Gleason Park of interest to birders consists of an abandoned golf course and overgrown athletic field, separated by the Little Calumet River. The park is located in the southwestern quadrant of the intersection of Interstate 80-94 and Broadway, just north of Indiana University Northwest. Like most other Lacustrine Plain sites the birding at Gleason Park is strongly affected by human activities. Until about 1976, the Gary City Department of Recreation regularly pumped water from this area each spring, maintaining it as a recreation area. In subsequent years pumping was curtailed or entirely stopped allowing an extensive stand of cattails to develop. During the late 1970s and early 1980s, as the marsh ecology developed, Gleason Park proved to be one of the richest birding sites in the Dunes Area. Beginning in 1980, Yellow-headed Blackbirds nested in this youthful wetlands, providing the first Indiana nesting record in almost forty years. Additionally, a host of the more common marsh species nested in the cattail growth. In 1983, however, dredging of the Little Calumet River channel apparently lowered the local water table, greatly diminishing average moisture levels in the marsh and profoundly affecting the wetlands. By May 1985 (a spring with unusually low precipitation), the marsh was sufficiently dry that city crews cut the entire stand of cattails.

Clearly water levels in the park are highly variable, subject both to precipitation variations and man's activities. Consequently, on many occasions the habitat will be insufficient to attract waterbirds. When water levels are appropriate, however, Gleason Park can provide superb birding. On these occasions numerous migrant shorebirds pause to feed and rest in the park's shallow water; the Stilt Sandpiper, Marbled Godwit, Hudsonian Godwit, Short-billed Dowitcher, Wilson's Phalarope, and Red-necked Phalarope have all been observed. Herons, egrets, ducks, gulls, and terns also feed in the park when conditions are right.

Hammond Cinder Flats; summer and fall (Dunes Area Map) An extensive fill, just north of the intersection of 141st and Columbia Streets in Hammond, often captures runoff waters forming shallow pools. If water is present during shorebird migration this site can be quite productive. Although the cinder flats are fenced, they can be easily birded from 141st Street (a telescope is recommended). During late summer and fall Black-bellied Plovers and peeps are regular; unusual shorebirds from this location include American Avocet, Hudsonian Godwit, Western Sandpiper, and Wilson's Phalarope.

Gary (Burr Street) Dump; winter (Dunes Area Map) This site is also in a state of change; dumping was stopped in spring 1997. The Gary Sanitary Landfill is located about one km north of I-65, between Burr and Colfax Streets. Birds are often more easily observed in the J-pit, a large excavation just across Colfax Street from the Gary Dump; however, the J-pit may also become a landfill. When dumping occurs in the winter months the Gary Dump often attracts a large accumulation of gulls. It is not unusual for more than 2000 birds to be present. These large flocks invariably contain a few of the rarer species. Laughing, Franklin's, Iceland, Great Black-backed, Lesser Black-backed, Glaucous, and Thayer's Gulls have all been reported, but only the latter three can be considered regular.

Neither the dump nor the J-pit are easy to bird. Access to the dump proper is generally not possible; consequently, most observations are made from Colfax Street. The J-pit is most easily scanned from the dirt road along the pit's southern edge, but a telescope is essential. In addition to the gulls an Eared Grebe was once noted swimming in the flooded pit and Peregrines have been observed harassing local pigeons and starlings on more than one occasion. During late summer 1996, water in the J-pit attracted migrant shorebirds along with a Snowy Egret and several Little Blue Herons.

Gibson Woods Nature Preserve: spring and fall (Dunes Area Map) This 130 acre site and associated nature center, is operated by the Lake County Parks System. It is located in Hammond on Parrish Avenue. To reach the preserve from I-94 go north on Cline Avenue to 169th Street. Proceed west on 169th Street to Parrish. Turn right (north) on Parrish; the preserve entrance is about a kilometer from 169th. Gibson Woods Preserve contains one of the largest extant remnants of dune and swale in the state. This is an interesting shoreline feature developed when ancient Lake Michigan stood at a higher level. A well maintained trail system allows birders to easily cover the available habitats (oak savannah and wetlands). The area is most productive for migrant passerines, and is especially good for warblers. The grounds are open seven days a week from 9:00 a.m. until 5:00 p.m. The Nature center is also open daily from 11:00 a.m. until 4:00 p.m.

Other Sites

Several additional locations are mentioned in the species accounts. For a variety of reasons detailed discussion of these sites was deemed inappropriate for formal inclusion in the Birding Site section. In the interest of completeness, these locations are described below.

Baileytown   This small settlement was formerly located at the present site of the Bethlehem Steel Plant; it was situated between the Port of Indiana and Cowles Bog.

Bailly Generating Station   This NIPSCO power plant is located on Lake Michigan northwest of Cowles Bog.

Berry Lake   This shallow lake, now eliminated by filling, was formerly located north and slightly east of George Lake, in the Whiting-East Chicago area.

Cowles Bog   Consists of an extensive interdunal marsh, now part of the Indiana Dunes National Lakeshore. It is named after Professor H. C. Cowles (pronounced Coals) of the University of Chicago, who established many modern ecology principles during his turn-of-the-century investigations of the area. Cowles Bog lies immediately north of the intersection of U.S. Highway 12 and Mineral Springs Road; the latter transects the bog, providing access to the town of Dune Acres. Parking is available at the Chicago and South Shore Railroad lot adjacent to Mineral Springs Road and at the National Lakeshore lot east of the Dune Acres gate.

Furnessville   This area includes the woods along Furnessville Road (between U.S. Highway 20 and Kemil Road); especially the National Lakeshore property that includes the Ly-Co-Ki-We Trail.

Inland Marsh   This marsh is situated immediately south, and across Highway 12, from West Beach. This beautiful stand of cattail marshes and oak savannah, is a part of the Indiana Dunes National Lakeshore.

Moraine State Nature Preserve   This 600 acre parcel consists of wooded glacial moraine. It is located southeast of the intersection of U.S. Highway 6 and State Highway 49. The site is now managed by the Indiana Department of Natural Resources. See Dunes Area Map.

LaPorte County Landfill   This relatively new dump is located just southwest of the intersection of I-94 and U.S. Highway 421, near the eastern margin of the Dunes area. Excellent gull numbers are attracted to the site in winter. It can be birded (with difficulty) from County Road 300 North, which transects the southern edge of the landfill.

Liverpool   This name applies to a Lake County settlement that was situated along the Little Calumet River between the communities of Glen Park and New Chicago, near the present intersection of I-65 and Ridge Road.

Millers (or Miller)   This location is cited frequently in early writings about the Dunes. The name comes from a railroad station near the present site of Miller, but the citations apparently incorporate much of the surrounding area, including Miller Beach.

Mineral Springs   This name refers to a former railroad station and settlement that was located immediately south of Cowles Bog.

Oak Ridge Prairie County Park   This is a fine county park located on Colfax Street (the same street that transects the Gary Dump and J-pit) about five km south of I-94 in Griffith.

Tremont   Tremont Station was the former name of the Chicago-South Shore Railroad station located immediately south of Indiana Dunes State Park.

Whihala Beach   This Lake County park consists of a beach and thin strip of adjacent lakefront located between the Hammond Marina and Whiting Park.

SPECIES ACCOUNTS

This section describes the birds that occur, or have occurred, in the Dunes. Species names and phylogenetic arrangement follow the 6th edition of the *American Ornithologists' Union Checklist* (1983) and subsequent supplements. Where appropriate a family summary is provided as an introduction to each major avian group. Each species account normally includes Finding Data (when, where, and how likely one is to locate the bird); Status (data on migration and/or nesting); and Observations (assorted relevant information). The definition of seasons follows usage in *Audubon Field Notes*: Spring– March through May; Summer– June and July; Fall– August through November; and Winter– December through February.

The Records

The time interval over which bird information was extracted ranges from the earliest available reports (near the mid-1800s) through 31 December 1996. Important specific observations through May 1997 are also included. A record is defined as: an observation of a particular avian species made on a specified date; it may involve more than one bird. Most records are made at a single location. In some cases, however, observers visited several sites during an outing, and it was impossible to determine the exact locations at which sightings were made. In these cases the record includes birds observed at all sites visited and a general location (e.g., Indiana Dunes, Lake County, or lakefront) is employed. To avoid overweighting records of lingering birds, a single occurrence constitutes only one record even though the bird may have been seen several different days. For example, the Band-tailed Pigeon has occurred in the Dunes only once, but during its three-week visit it was recorded almost daily. This occurrence constitutes a single record. If an individual bird lingered more than one time unit on the histogram, it was counted once for each time period in which it was present.

Records, especially of rare or unusual birds, were obtained from *American Birds* , *Audubon Field Notes*, and the *Indiana Audubon Quarterly*. Except for a few controversial reports, all records from the above sources were included. Additional information was taken from the personal correspondence of Raymond Grow and James Landing and from the major references dealing with birdlife of the Dunes: Butler (1898), Woodruff (1907), Eifrig (1918), Smith (1936), Ford (1956), Keller et al. (1979), Mlodinow (1984), and Mumford and Keller (1984). Considerable data, covering the period 1912-1952, were obtained from the extensive notes and summaries of Donald H. Boyd. The single most valuable data-source for determining distribution patterns of the regularly occurring species was the daily checklists of several individuals, each of whom spent considerable time observing birds in the Dunes. These contributors, and the approximate time interval covered by each, are tabulated below.

Additionally, records and observational data were provided (unknowingly in many cases) by numerous other individuals. A partial list of contributors includes: Ellie Baker, Larry Balch, Amy Baldwin, Karl Bartel, Richard Biss, Alan Bruner, Dorthy Buck, James Bull, Bob Buskirk, William Buskirk, Ted Cable, Al and Lela Campbell, David Capp, Larry Carter, Ted Chandik, Mike Chaneske, Dave Cimprich, Charles Clark, Milt Cole, Tim Coslet, Noel Cutright,

Helen Dancey, Robert Daum, Marvin Davis, Barb Dodge, Dave Easterla, Homer Eshbaugh, Clyde Fields, Steve Getty, Brendan Grube, Peter Grube, Ralph Grundel, Nancy Gruse, James Haw, Irene Herlocker-Meyer, Lynea Hinchman, Ed Hopkins, Robert Hughes, Lois Howes, Greg Jancich, Bud Johnson, Philip Kahl, Charles Keller, Tim Keller, Jay Kendall, John Kendall, Helen Lane, David Mandel, Tim Manolis, Walter Marcisz, Carolyn Marsh, Sigrid Metzinger, Helen Michalik, Steve Mlodinow, Ted Nork, John O'Brien, Larry Peavler, Capt. J. P. Perkins, Rich Phillips, Emma B. Pitcher, Richard and Cynthia Plank, Mike Polomchak, Bud Polk, Robert Pringle, George Pyle, Scott Rea, Hank Rooney, Simon Segal, Wes Serafin, Andy Sigler, Bobbie Squires, Merrill Sweet, Robert Tweit, Joy Underborn, Francis VanHuffle, Peggy Walsh, Lawrence Walkinshaw, John White, Archie Wilson, and Belle Wilson.

Daily Check List Contributors

OBSERVER	Years
Herbert L. Stoddard*	1914 - 1920
Dr. Virginia Reuter-skiold*	1944 - 1963
Laurence C. Binford*	1951 - 1955
Henry C. West	1950 - 1966
Russell E. Mumford	1951 - 1972
John Louis	1954 - 1972
Peter B. Grube	1970 - 1984
Kenneth J. Brock	1972 - 1996
Scott F. Jackson	1979 - 1983
Fred Kase	1979 - 1983
Susan Bagby	1989 - 1996
Joy Bower	1991 - 1996
John Cassady	1994 - 1996
Jeff McCoy	1994 - 1996
* The personal notes of these individuals, plus Donald F. Boyd's, were generously provided by Professor Russell E. Mumford. The Boyd, Reuter-skiold, and Stoddard notes are now preserved in the Calumet Region Archives at Indiana University Northwest.	

The Finding Codes

Bird books and checklists have traditionally employed a set of adjectives (e.g., abundant, common, fairly common, uncommon, rare, very rare, casual, and accidental) to describe the status of avian species. Usage of these terms, however, has evolved considerably over the decades. Turn-of-the century works rarely defined these words, and the distinction between the general terms "common," "fairly common," and "uncommon" was blurry at best. Early authors also displayed a remarkable penchant for the charmingly ambiguous phrase, "not uncommon." Nor were they unduly worried about consistent interspecific use of abundance descriptors. For example, early lists often described both the Turkey Vulture and the Magnolia Warbler as "common migrants," implying that both were equally abundant. Clearly Magnolias far outnumbered vultures, but, because vultures were larger and more conspicuous, the two species were probably observed with about the same frequency.

Gradually as the amount of information expanded and the sophistication of the articles increased, explicit definitions of the status descriptors and a formal measure of encounterability were incorporated into the literature. This transition often resulted in dual definitions within a single work. The term "common," for example, might be simultaneously defined as: "Occurs in considerable numbers," and "Several can be seen in a day." Clearly the first definition reflects abundance (albeit vaguely), whereas the latter indicates encounterability. Recognizing that true species abundance is seldom known and is of only minimal value to birders, authors have in recent years tended to deemphasize the abundance aspect of the status descriptors.

Most contemporary works base status descriptors entirely upon the likelihood of encountering the species. Although this approach eliminates the dual usage problem, it is still plagued with difficulties associated with divorcing the terms from their normal English language usage. Many readers, for example, find it disconcerting to learn that a "casual" bird is more rare than a "very rare" bird. Perhaps the next logical step in this evolutionary process is to replace traditional adjectives with status descriptors having no significance outside their definitional context.

In this work numbers from one to ten, referred to as Finding Codes, have been substituted for the status descriptors. Although the Finding Code method removes the difficulties outlined above, it does require a bit of initial effort for familiarization with its application. The Finding Code reflects the effort that a competent observer should expect to spend in order to encounter a given species: a) under normal circumstances; b) in the proper habitat; c) and at the optimum time of the year. The ten Code numbers are defined below.

FINDING CODE DEFINITIONS

Code	EFFORT REQUIRED For single observer	For all observers in area
1	25 birds per hour	-
2	1 bird per hour	-
3	1 bird per half day	-
4	1 bird per day	-
5	1 bird per week	-
6	1-2 birds per season	4-20 birds per year
7	-	1-3 birds per year
8	-	1 bird every 2 years
9	-	1 bird every 20 years
10	-	1 bird per century

Although the basis of the code is mathematical (the time required to locate a species is exponentially related to the Finding Code numbers), each code has been simplified in order to render it more easily applied (i.e., code 1 is defined as 25 birds per hour, rather than one bird per 25th of an hour). Vast amounts of time, far more than a single observer could reasonably expect to spend, are required to find the rarer species; consequently, Finding Codes greater than 6 refer to the combined effort of all observers in the area.

Several aspects relating to application of the code require elaboration. First, birds with low numbers are easily found, whereas those with large numbers are more difficult; a single observer has little chance of finding birds with codes greater than 6 during a given year. Additionally, the code number assigned to a particular species is based entirely upon the ease or difficulty of finding the species, and is only indirectly related to abundance. A nesting species that constantly occupies a territory would be given a much lower code number than a migrant of similar abundance. Further, most species are somewhat seasonal in their appearance; consequently, the Finding Code indicates the time required to locate the bird during the optimum time period. This period is usually stated explicitly under "Finding data" in the individual species descriptions. Consider the Cerulean Warbler. Within the Dunes the Finding Code for this species is 3, in late May and June when territorial males are singing. This means that a competent observer (one who knows the Cerulean song in this case) could normally expect to find at least one Cerulean per half day spent in the proper habitat: the mature woods east of Wilson Shelter in Dunes State Park. The code number would increase markedly outside the late May-June time interval.

Information about the status of Dunes birds is provided by the terms transient (migrant); resident; visitant (more than ten records, but with Finding Code greater than 6); and vagrant (fewer than 10 records).

Occurrence Histograms

Accompanying the descriptions of many species are histograms plotting number of birds versus time intervals (each month is divided into three 10-day intervals; duration of the final period is adjusted to accommodate months with other than 30 days). The bar height in each case reflects the total number of individuals observed during that time interval. The Red-throated Loon example (at right) should serve to clarify the histograms. Consider the month of April; the bars indicate that ten loons were recorded in the first ten days, one in the second ten days, and two in the final ten days.

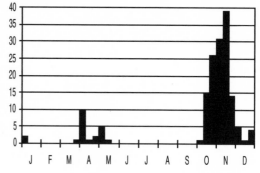

Migration Envelopes

For many species, especially those with Finding Codes above 7, only a handful of records occur each decade; consequently, migration patterns fail to emerge unless data from several decades are combined. The pattern obtained by adding all records together represents a migration envelope. The fundamental premise of the envelope is that bird migration can be represented by a statistical distribution. This concept is shown schematically as follows:

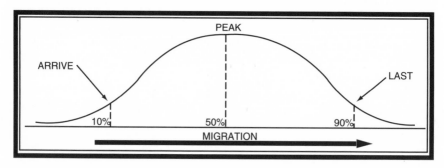

The envelope really does not reflect any single year's migration; instead, it superimposes the seasonal variations and irregularities of many years (and perhaps even long-term shifts in migration patterns) onto a single display.

For most transient species the migration envelopes are summarized in a brief table, which spells out parameters of the migration In calculating the envelope all records occurring between the migration extremes (EARLIEST and LATEST) were evaluated. A computer algorithm calculates three critical dates on the envelope: ARRIVE: 10% of the migration (actually 10% of the area under the curve), PEAK 50% of the migration, and LAST 90% of the migration. The procedure can be compared to a picket fence; each lath in the fence represents a day and lath heights reflect the total records for that date. (In order to deemphasize the effects of multiple individuals per record, 1 + ln{number of individuals} was added for each observation). The area of the fence is then calculated and the date marking the first 10% of the area, referred to as ARRIVE, is taken as the normal arrival date (i.e., 10% of all records precede this date). Midpoint on the date fence is taken as the migration PEAK, and DEPART marks the passage of 90% of the records (i.e., the average last date of observation).

Thus, about 80% of the migration occurs between the ARRIVE and DEPART dates. If fewer than 30 records exist within the migration envelope, the ARRIVE and DEPART dates were considered unreliable and not tabulated. The number of records incorporated into the calculation of each envelope is given under the right-hand column headed with N.   EARLIEST and LATEST dates are unique, consequently the observation year is included.

Consider the following sample migration envelope for the Red Knot.   The

	EARLIEST	ARRIVE	PEAK	DEPART	LATEST	N
Spring	21 May 86	- -	- -	- -	2 Jun 17	5
Fall	30 Jul 40	18 Aug	3 Sep	30 Sep	24 Oct 79	89

EARLIEST spring record was 21 May 1986 and the LATEST was 2 June 1917. Fewer than 30 spring records were available; consequently, the spring envelope is abbreviated (i.e., ARRIVE, PEAK, and DEPART dates are omitted). If between 15 and 29 records exist, the PEAK date is included. Extreme records for the fall envelope are respectively 30 July 1940 and 24 October 1979. August 18 marks the 10% point on the envelope and is taken as the average fall arrival date. Similarly, the average departure (90% of the envelope) is 30 September About 80% of the autumn Red Knots pass between the ARRIVE and DEPART dates. Midpoint on the envelope, 3 September, is taken as the migration peak. A total of 89 records (N) have occurred between the extreme fall dates.

For the few fall migrants in which adults and juvenals can be separated by plumage (e.g., shorebirds and jaegers) the Envelope is subdivided into the following categories: (all) includes all records regardless of age, (ad.) adults only, and (juv.) juvenals only. For many breeding species the true migration envelope is concealed by records of resident birds. When sufficient data exist, only records collected in the lakefront traps are used to calculate the migration envelopes. A "*" following the season indicates that only data from the lakefront sites were used to determine the envelope.

Species Deleted From First Edition

The following species were listed in the first edition of *Bird of the Indiana Dunes*, but are excluded from the present volume. Some were included in the "Hypothetical" listing and others in the "Species Accounts."

Species	Reason for Deletion
Great Cormorant	record deemed invalid
Tufted Duck	misidentified, see Brock, 1990a
Common Eider	rejected by Indiana Rare Bird Committee
Long-billed Curlew	rejected by Indiana Rare Bird Committee
Sharp-tailed Grouse	rejected by Indiana Rare Bird Committee
Whooping Crane	rejected by Indiana Rare Bird Committee
Ross' Gull	rejected by Indiana Rare Bird Committee
Kittlitz's Murrelet	rejected by Indiana Rare Bird Committee
Smooth-billed Ani	rejected by Indiana Rare Bird Committee
Northern Hawk Owl	rejected by Indiana Rare Bird Committee
Rufous Hummingbird	insufficient documentation
Swainson's Warbler	rejected by Indiana Rare Bird Committee
MacGillivray's Warbler	misidentified, see Mumford & Keller 1984
Black-headed Grosbeak	rejected by Indiana Rare Bird Committee

FAMILY GAVIIDAE: Loons

RED-THROATED LOON (*Gavia stellata*)

Finding data
Finding Code = 6, during the fall flight peak, between late October and late November. Found exclusively on Lake Michigan where the best locations are Beverly Shores (off the Lakeview picnic site), Miller Beach, and Michigan City Harbor. In recent years birders have developed the skill to identify this loon in flight, resulting in an increase in the number of annual reports. Individuals on the Lake are often far from shore; even when present their slight stature, frequent dives, and pale color, render this loon difficult to find.

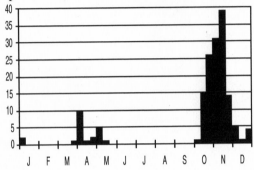

Peak counts
Spring:	5	9 Apr 1952	Lake Michigan off Gary.
Fall:	9	12 Oct 1966	Miller Beach (Mumford and Keller, 1984).

Status
The Red-throated Loon is a spring and fall transient, which occasionally lingers into winter. Migration data are as follows:

	EARLIEST	ARRIVE	PEAK	DEPART	LATEST	N
Spring	24 Mar 13	- -	9 Apr	- -	18 May 86	11
Fall	7 Oct 52	23 Oct	11 Nov	27 Nov	8 Jan 55	87

PACIFIC LOON (*Gavia pacifica*)

Finding data
Finding Code = 10; only two records. This species was reported without details (AFN 4:244) from Lake Michigan off the Indiana Dunes on 6 May 1950. Several observers identified a winter plumed bird 10 November 1984 as it fed with a flock of Red-breasted Mergansers at the Port of Indiana (IAQ 63:115).

COMMON LOON (*Gavia immer*)

Finding data
Maximum Finding Code = 2, between late October and mid-November. On
many autumn days, especially those with strong northerly winds, migrating loons are observed flying parallel to the lakefront or inland on a southerly heading. Most pass individually or in loose groups about 30 meters above the lake's surface. It is not rare to count more than 100 loons per day.

Peak counts

Spring:	743	5 Apr 1997	Beverly Shores and Dunes State Park
Fall:	952	19 Nov 1988	Beverly Shores

Status
This large loon is a spring and fall transient, being far more common in the fall.
Occasionally stragglers remain well into winter and six June records exist.
Migration data are as follows:

	EARLIEST	ARRIVE	PEAK	DEPART	LATEST	N
Spring	12 Feb 55	30 Mar	16 Apr	10 May	11 Jun 80	185
Fall	10 Sep 88	19 Oct	4 Nov	26 Nov	31 Dec 86	408

Although Eifrig (1918) suggests that this species probably nested in the Dunes area in the 19th century, and Woodruff (1907) reports a nest containing eggs near Hickory, Illinois in May 1892, there exists no recent evidence of breeding. Most June records consist of individuals in non-breeding plumage.

Observations
Impressive loon concentrations on Lake Michigan are periodically reported. On a November day in 1944, for example, Captain Perkins (1964), aboard an oreboat departing Gary at daybreak, reported: "Sailing north on the Point Betsie course, we found ourselves in the midst of Common Loons, either migrating or gathering to migrate. As far as we could see there were loons on the calm waters of Lake Michigan--not in flocks, but scattered here and there. As our ship plowed through this concentration of divers for miles, I thought surely all the loons from the North were there."

Periodic "kills" on Lake Michigan attest to the Common Loon's susceptibility to chemical and biological toxins in its feeding areas. One of the most devastating die-offs took place in November 1976 when some 1,000-3,000 dead Common Loons were found along the Indiana and Michigan shorelines (AB 31:182). The suspected killer was botulism. Other kills of smaller magnitude have also been reported.

FAMILY PODICIPEDIDAE: Grebes

Of the five grebe species occurring in the Dunes area, only the Pied-billed breeds. The Horned Grebe is a regular migrant, the Eared, Western and Red-necked Grebes are vagrants. A disproportionate fraction of the total grebe records occurred in the 1950s, when numbers of all four migrant species increased markedly. During that decade maximum daily Horned Grebe counts were frequently in the hundreds. More remarkable was the high number of records of the less common species. Between 1952 and 1965 almost half of all Eared and Red-necked Grebe records were logged.

PIED-BILLED GREBE (*Podilymbus podiceps*)

Finding data

The Finding Code = 2, during the fall migration in late September and October when large numbers often build up on Long Lake and George Lake. Smaller numbers are seen in spring. Although it breeds in the Dunes area, this species is often difficult to find in summer.

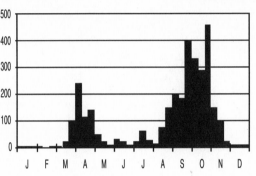

Peak counts

Spring:	33	1 Apr 1995	Multiple sites
Fall:	200	27 Oct 1951	Wolf Lake

Status

The Pied-billed Grebe is a transient and summer resident. Despite the summer resident status, this small grebe has been reported every month of the year. Long Lake provides a major nesting site within the Dunes area; however, breeding birds are widespread throughout the Lacustrine Plain. Eggs have been reported in early June and young in mid-June through August. On 6 July 1975 an adult, carrying two downy chicks piggy-back, was observed at Cowles Bog. Migration data are:

	EARLIEST	ARRIVE	PEAK	DEPART	LATEST	N
Spring	- - -	25 Mar	11 Apr	5 May	- - -	230
Fall	- - -	27 Aug	4 Oct	9 Nov	- - -	331

HORNED GREBE (*Podiceps auritus*)

Finding data

Maximum Finding Code = 3, in late October and November. Small groups often swim and feed on Lake Michigan, where they are detected by scanning the lake several hundred meters beyond the surf. Occasionally a few appear on larger inland ponds and lakes, such as Long Lake and Wolf Lake.

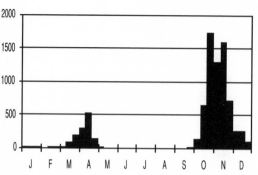

Peak counts

Spring:	200	11 Apr	1953	Beverly Shores
Fall:	500	15 Nov	1964	Wolf Lake (Mumford and Keller, 1984)

Status

The Horned Grebe, normally a spring and fall transient through the Dunes, has wintered on rare occasions. Many late March and April "hell divers" are adorned in colorful breeding plumage and a few linger into May; however, no fully acceptable breeding records exist. Woodruff's (1907) note of a downy juvenile collected 24 May 1878 at Sheffield (now part of Hammond) constitutes the only nesting evidence; however, West (1956) questions the validity of this report. Migration data are:

	EARLIEST	ARRIVE	PEAK	DEPART	LATEST	N
Spring	- - -	12 Mar	3 Apr	22 Apr	24 May 78	226
Fall	18 Sep 91	18 Oct	7 Nov	6 Dec	- - -	408

RED-NECKED GREBE (*Podiceps grisegena*)

Finding data

The current Finding Code = 8; however, this rare species was apparently more common in former years. Most reports of the Red-necked Grebe come from Lake Michigan, but it has appeared on Marquette Lagoon (near Miller Beach) on two occasions.

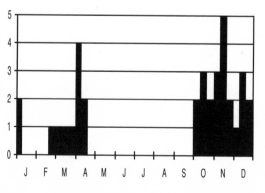

Peak counts

Spring:	2	1 Apr	1950	Michigan City Harbor
Fall:	3	17 Oct	1955	Lakefront (Raymond Grow, unpub. notes)

Status

The Red-necked Grebe is a spring, fall, and early-winter vagrant through the Dunes. Migration data are:

	EARLIEST	ARRIVE	PEAK	DEPART	LATEST	N
Spring	27 Feb 92	- -	1 Apr	- -	13 Apr 59	9
Fall	18 Sep 91	- -	16 Nov	- -	7 Jan 92	20

Observations

In view of this grebe's rarity, a 1955 oil spill on Lake Michigan, which claimed the lives of hundreds of water birds, proved especially disastrous. Nolan (AFN 10:27) states, "Of the hundreds of birds disabled and picked up in Indiana, 95 percent were Horned Grebes; a surprising total of five Red-throated Grebes were found...." Raymond Grow (unpub. notes) indicates that three of these "oiled grebes" were found during the week of 17 October and the other two discovered later.

EARED GREBE (*Podiceps nigricollis*)

Finding data

Finding Code = 8, from mid-October through November. Although many records are from Lake Michigan, the Eared Grebe demonstrates a greater affinity for ponds than the other migrant grebes. Accordingly, many have been seen at Long Lake and Roxana Pond; however, most records are from Michigan City Harbor.

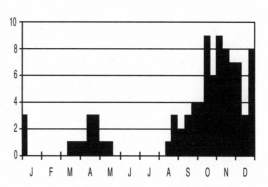

Peak counts

Spring:	1		All spring records are singletons
Fall:	4	16 Oct 1957	Michigan City Harbor
Winter:	7	31 Dec 1956	Michigan City Harbor

Status

This small grebe is primarily a fall and winter transient; only a handful of spring records exist. In 1978 a bird lingered in Roxana Pond from 19 August until 25 November.

	EARLIEST	ARRIVE	PEAK	DEPART	LATEST	N
Spring	14 Mar 93	- -	16 Apr	- -	3 May 81	9
Fall	19 Aug 78	16 Sep	1 Nov	11 Dec	5 Jan 58	45

WESTERN GREBE (*Aechmophorus occidentalis*)

Finding data
Maximum Finding Code = 8, during late fall and early winter (October through December). All records are from Lake Michigan. A majority of reports come from Michigan City Harbor and the Port of Indiana, but several birds have also been seen from Miller Beach.

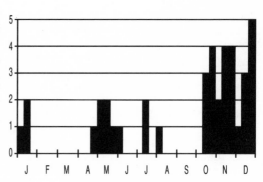

Peak counts

Spring:	1		All spring records are singletons
Fall:	3	19 Oct 1960	Miller Beach (AFN 15:44)

Status
The Western Grebe is primarily a fall vagrant; winter birds appear only in mild years when the lakefront remains ice-free. Indiana's first record of this species consisted of a 27 October 1945 sight record at Dunes State Park (Ford, 1956). The earliest fall date was 19 October 1960 at Miller Beach. All spring and summer birds were at the Port of Indiana.

SUBORDER PELECANI: Gannets and Pelicans

NORTHERN GANNET (*Sula bassanus*)

Three records; Finding Code = 9. According to Butler (1906), who studied a mounted specimen in the Michigan City store of Roman Eichstodt, an immature Gannet was killed on Lake Michigan in November 1904. A photograph of this bird, which constituted the first Indiana record of this species, was published in Butler's report. More recently, immatures were seen off West Beach and Michigan City Harbor 8 and 9 December 1991 (AB 46:270) and feeding with gulls off Miller Beach 5 November 1993 (AB 48:114).

AMERICAN WHITE PELICAN (*Pelecanus erythrorhynchos*)

Finding data
Finding Code = 8. Reports of this species in the Dunes area have increased markedly in recent years. Prior to 1986 the White Pelican was reported only four times in the Dunes area. In contrast, a total of nine birds have been reported since 1986.

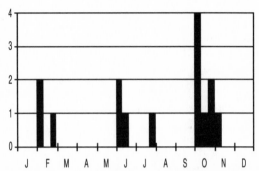

Peak counts
Spring:	0			No spring records
Summer:	2	3 Jun	1990	Beverly Shores
Fall:	2	1 Oct	1896	Miller Beach (Woodruff, 1907)
Winter:	2	7 Feb	1993	Michigan City Harbor

BROWN PELICAN (*Pelecanus occidentalis*)

Finding data
Finding Code = 10; only two records. During the summer of 1990 a bird was seen regularly along the entire lakefront between 8 June and 23 July (AB 44:1138). The following autumn (1991) a Brown Pelican was seen on three occasions between 7 and 19 October at Michigan City Harbor and Miller Beach (AB 46:95).

FAMILY PHALACROCORACIDAE: Cormorants

DOUBLE-CRESTED CORMORANT (*Phalacrocorax auritus*)

Finding data
Maximum Finding Code = 2 from late September through October. The cormorant is often seen along Lake Michigan's shores, either swimming, flying, or resting on some exposed perch. Perhaps the best location to observe this species is on a water-intake island situated in Lake Michigan about 1 km off the Migrant Trap. Birds are almost always at this site during the migration periods.

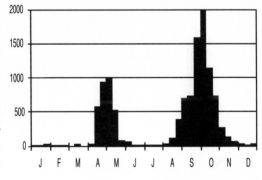

Peak counts

Spring:	300	7 May 1995	Migrant Trap
Fall:	282	11 Nov 1990	Port of Indiana

Status

The Double-crested Cormorant is a spring and fall transient, occasionally lingering through winter. Immature birds, with the buffy throat and breast, are frequently noted. Numbers of this species have increased dramatically over the past two decades. Prior the 1985 the maximum single party count was 30 birds; currently, daily counts exceeding 100 are made annually. Disregarding summer and winter records, migration data are:

	EARLIEST	ARRIVE	PEAK	DEPART	LATEST	N
Spring	1 Mar 91	14 Apr	2 May	31 May	3 May 81	130
Fall	6 Aug 94	1 Sep	4 Oct	6 Nov	- -	467

FAMILY FREGATIDAE: Frigatebirds

MAGNIFICENT FRIGATEBIRD (*Fregata magnificens*)

Finding Code = 9, three records in the Dunes, though one (the October 1988 adult male) was identified only as frigatebird species. The earliest report occurred 27 and 28 April 1957 at Michigan City Harbor (AFN 11:349). Ray Grow (pers. comm.) described the sighting as follows: "Upon arriving at the harbor parking lot on 27 April, both myself and Jim Landing (in another automobile) spotted a huge bird being mobbed by a large number of gulls. As we jumped from the cars the bird rose above the mobbing flock and I immediately identified it as a frigatebird." On 28 April Grow (unpub. notes) wrote, "It was a young bird with the white head, breast, etc. (and it) stayed for about one hour, the last we saw it was winging toward Chicago." Two additional frigatebirds appeared at the same location following Hurricane Gilbert in 1988. The first, an immature, was photographed 30 September and the second, an adult male, appeared 4 October (Brock, 1989).

FAMILY ARDEIDAE: Bitterns and Herons

Ten members of the bittern-heron family, four of which are currently active nesters, occur in the Dunes area. Nesting species include Least Bittern, Great Blue Heron, Green-backed Heron, and Black-crowned Night Heron. The American Bittern, Great Egret, and Cattle Egret are regular transients. Visitants and/or vagrants include the Little Blue Heron, Snowy Egret, and Yellow-crowned Night Heron.

AMERICAN BITTERN (*Botaurus lentiginosus*)

Finding data

Finding Code = 7, mid-April until mid-May. The bittern has a penchant for cattail marshes and is rarely found far from the concealment of this habitat. Spring birds are often flushed from cattails of the interdunal marshes; especially good locations include Cowles Bog and along Beverly Drive near Beverly Shores.

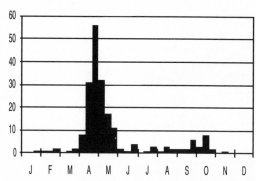

Peak counts

Spring:	6	20 Apr 1986	West Beach
Fall:	2	20 Aug 1952	Northern Porter County

Status

The "stake-driver," as it is locally named, is a spring and fall transient that formerly nested in the Dunes. Smith (1936) reportedly found a nest of this secretive species at Wolf Lake, 14 June 1933. On 22 June 1950, Mumford (unpub. notes) located a nest containing three young at George Lake. There is no recent nesting evidence. A few winter records also exist. Migration data:

	EARLIEST	ARRIVE	PEAK	DEPART	LATEST	N
Spring	28 Jan 59	11 Apr	26 Apr	17 May	- - -	127
Fall	- - -	29 Jul	27 Sep	19 Oct	13 Nov 49	33

Observations

The presence of January and February records of this marsh dweller is quite curious. Apparently the bittern can accommodate winter cold providing food is available. During the winter of 1959 Reuter-skiold (unpub. letter) observed an American Bittern, between 28 January and 21 February, stationed at a hole in the ice (in a swamp near Baileytown) where about 100 fish were gulping for air just below the surface.

LEAST BITTERN (*Ixobrychus exilis*)

Finding data

Finding Code = 5, mid-May through August. The Least Bittern is difficult to see; usually only a brief glimpse is obtained as flying birds skim the cattails in moving from one section of the marsh to another. Areas inhabited in recent summers include Cowles Bog, and Long Lake.

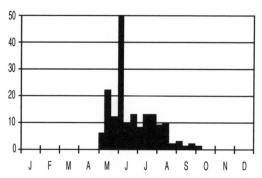

Peak counts

Spring:	4	17 May 1951	Wolf Lake
Summer:	20	2 Jun 1916	Long Lake
Fall:	2	12 Aug 1975	Cowles Bog

Status

The Least Bittern is a summer resident of the cattail marshes. Although this diminutive species still breeds in the Calumet Region, it is considerably less common than in former years. Stoddard (unpub. notes) reported about 20 adults plus nests and eggs on a 2 June 1916 trip to Long Lake.

	EARLIEST	ARRIVE	PEAK	DEPART	LATEST	N
Spring	8 May 17	11 May	30 May	11 Jun	- - -	51
Fall	- - -	- -	15 Aug	- -	2 Oct 83	26

GREAT BLUE HERON (*Ardea herodias*)

Finding data

Maximum Finding Code = 2 from April through mid-August. Nesting birds arrive in the Dunes by mid-March. Large numbers often appear in late summer in conjunction with the post-nesting dispersal. Foraging birds frequently appear along Lake Michigan beaches in summer.

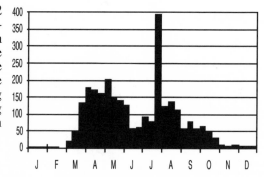

Peak counts

Spring:	60	25 May 1996	Miller Beach
Fall:	150	28 Jul 1980	Cowles Bog

Status

This large heron is a summer resident and late summer transient in the Dunes; it occasionally lingers into winter. A well established Great Blue Heron rookery is located in the Heron Rookery unit of the National Lakeshore. This rookery is at least sixty years old. The first birds return to the rookery in mid-March; young birds are present by early May; and fledging occurs in late July. Fledging correlates with the increased numbers of Great Blue Herons noted in the late summer post-nesting dispersal. Apparently, not all birds appearing in the Dunes during the dispersal period are local herons. For example, a color tagged bird observed at Long Lake 25 August 1977 was, according to the Ohio Cooperative Wildlife Research Unit, "Banded as a nestling in a rookery at Winous Point Shoot Club on Sandusky Bay, Ohio, on 28 May 1977." Migration data are:

	EARLIEST	ARRIVE	PEAK	DEPART	LATEST	N
Spring	- - -	23 Mar	24 Apr	5 Jun	- - -	410
Fall	- - -	15 Jul	24 Aug	15 Oct	- - -	443

GREAT EGRET (*Ardea albus*)

Finding data

Maximum Finding Code = 3, throughout the summer. The recent establishment of a breeding colony at nearby Lake Calumet, Illinois, has greatly increased the numbers of this species in the Dunes area, especially on the lacustrine plain. Locations frequented by this species include Roxana Pond, Long Lake, and George Lake.

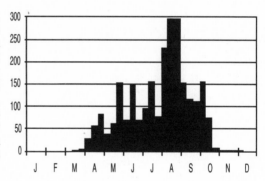

Peak counts

Spring:	22	26 May 1989	Northern Lake County
Summer:	90	15 Jun 1996	Northern Lake & Porter Counties
Fall:	68	31 Aug 1952	Northern Porter County

Status

This elegant heron is primarily a forager and post-breeding wanderer in the Dunes area; however, in 1996, several birds built unsuccessful nests in a Little Calumet River swamp south of the entrance to the Port of Indiana. Migration data are:

	EARLIEST	ARRIVE	PEAK	DEPART	LATEST	N
Spring	14 Mar 96	14 Apr	14 May	17 Jun	- -	178
Fall	- -	23 Jul	27 Aug	7 Oct	1 Dec 84	262

Observations

1952 must be regarded as the year of the Great Egret. During that year this species was present at several locations between 15 June and 12 October, and groups exceeding 50 birds were reported on four occasions.

SNOWY EGRET (*Egretta thula*)

Finding data

A total of eight records; Finding Code = 8. Among the herons recorded in the Dunes area, the Snowy Egret is by far the rarest. Recent sightings have been in a flooded field in Gary, at Michigan City Harbor, and at the Gary Dump. The earliest arrival was 19 April 1986 and the latest departure 26 August 1959.

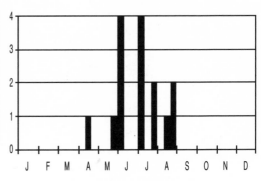

Peak counts

Spring:	1		All spring records are singletons
Summer:	4	1 Jul 1996	Gary, in a flooded field
Fall:	1	31 Aug 1952	All fall records are singletons

LITTLE BLUE HERON (*Egretta caerulea*)

Finding data

Finding Code = 8. Although a majority of the records are from late summer, many recent sightings have occurred in spring. Recent reports have come from Cowles Bog and the Gary Dump. This species was far more common earlier this century.

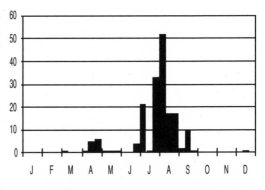

Peak counts

Spring:	20	? Jul 1924	Indiana Dunes (R. Mumford notes)
Fall:	30	1 Aug 1956	Baileytown (Reuter-skiold notes)

Status

The Little Blue Heron is primarily a spring and fall visitant to the Dunes. On 17 December 1982 a yearling, in the pied blue and white plumage, was observed flying across U.S. Highway 6 near Westville (IAQ 61:162). Migration data:

	EARLIEST	ARRIVE	PEAK	DEPART	LATEST	N
Spring	5 Mar 83	- -	23 Apr	- -	26 May 83	14
Fall	25 Jun 85	30 Jun	8 Aug	11 Sep	17 Dec 82	30

CATTLE EGRET (*Bubulcus ibis*)

Finding data
Finding Code = 7. Cattle Egrets have occurred at sites across the entire Dunes area, but a majority of the records come from Gleason Park. Surprisingly, the reports of this invading species have not increased over the past decade. It is occasionally discovered foraging in grass roadsides along the highway right-of way.

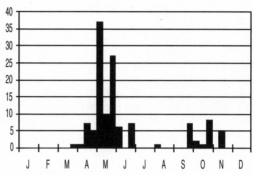

Peak counts
Spring:	17	23 May 1981	Wolf Lake (IAQ 60:57)
	17	8 May 1993	N. Porter County
Fall:	7	27 Oct 1979	Long Lake

Status
This small egret was first reported in the Dunes 11 November 1970 (AB 25:65). The Cattle Egret is a spring and fall transient through the Dunes area. Migration data are:

	EARLIEST	ARRIVE	PEAK	DEPART	LATEST	N
Spring	24 Mar 82	- -	8 May	- -	9 Jun 89	23
Fall	25 Jun 85	- -	16 Oct	- -	15 Nov 88	9

GREEN HERON (*Butorides striatus*)

Finding data
Finding Code = 3, during the migration peaks in early May, and August. This widespread species is found at almost any location providing both water and cover; good sites include the interdunal marsh near Beverly Shores, Cowles Bog, Long Lake, and Gleason Park.

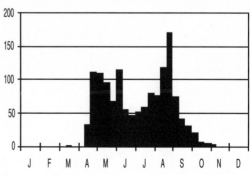

Peak counts
Spring:	19	14 May 1975	Cowles Bog
Fall:	30	31 Aug 1974	Cowles Bog

Formerly known as the "Green-backed Heron," this well established breeding species is widespread throughout the Dunes. Migration data are:

	EARLIEST	ARRIVE	PEAK	DEPART	LATEST	N
Spring	17 Mar 74	23 Apr	9 May	6 Jun	- - -	262
Fall	- -	21 Jul	24 Aug	26 Sep	15 Nov 88	242

BLACK-CROWNED NIGHT HERON (*Nycticorax nycticorax*)

Finding data

Finding Code = 5, from mid-April through July. A majority of recent records have come from the Hammond (foraging birds from the Lake Calumet, Illinois colony), Port of Indiana, and Long Lake.

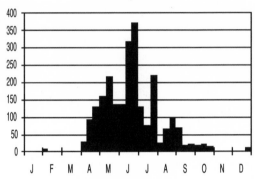

Peak counts

Spring:	100	13 May 1978	Gary rookery (see below)
	100	29 May 1997	Michigan City Harbor
Fall:	50	30 Aug 1981	Gleason Park

Status

This striking species is a summer resident of the Lacustrine Plain; some individuals winter. In June 1976, George Pyle detected a colony in a wooded swamp immediately north of the Kaiser Refractory plant in Gary. On 13 May 1978 100 birds were present in the rookery. A survey of the site on 25 April 1979, prior to development of dense foliage and the arrival of the herons, revealed 110 nests from the previous season. The nesting season appeared normal in 1980, but the rookery was entirely abandoned in 1981. An explanation for the abrupt departure of the colony is lacking, but it is likely the Gary birds joined the enormous colony at Lake Calumet, Illinois.

Interestingly, substantial numbers of Black-crowned Night-Herons have appeared at Long Lake during the nesting season. In 1995, 68 birds were present 28 April and 31 were seen 13 May; however, no nests have been located. Migration data are:

	EARLIEST	ARRIVE	PEAK	DEPART	LATEST	N
Spring	1 Mar 86	14 Apr	9 May	- -	- -	103
Fall	- -	- -	25 Aug	17 Oct	- -	102

YELLOW-CROWNED NIGHT HERON (*Nycticorax violaceus*)

Finding data

Finding Code = 8, from late April through early June. Virtually all of the previous records occurred in spring; almost half of these were made at Baileytown, a site now destroyed. Juveniles were found on six occasions during fall of 1995, suggesting the possibility of nesting on the lacustrine plain.

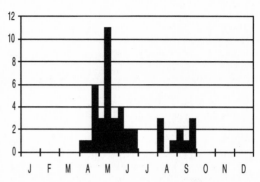

Peak counts

Spring:	4	24 Apr 1960	Baileytown
Fall:	1		All fall records are singletons

Status

The Yellow-crowned Night Heron is a visitant to the Dunes. An attempted nesting in a Munster woodlot is especially interesting. In May 1976 the construction of three nests was observed in the residential woodlot, and eggs were noted; however, by 2 June the eggs were destroyed and the nests abandoned. Migration data are:

	EARLIEST	ARRIVE	PEAK	DEPART	LATEST	N
Spring	1 Apr 86	- -	19 May	- -	22 Jun 77	16
Fall	1 Aug 95	- -	5 Sep	- -	30 Sep 95	9

FAMILY THRESKIORNITHIDAE:
Ibises and Spoonbills

PLEGADIS IBIS (either Glossy or White-faced Ibis)

An unidentified Plegadis ibis was observed flying westward along the lakefront at the Port of Indiana 27 October 1979 (IAQ 59:14).

FAMILY ANATIDAE: Swans, Geese, and Ducks

Three swan species have occurred in the Dunes area. Of these the Mute Swan is a permanent resident, the Tundra Swan a transient, and the Trumpeter Swan is extirpated. Among the Dunes area's four geese, the Greater White-fronted and Brant are vagrants, the Snow is a transient, and the Canada is a permanent resident.

TUNDRA SWAN (*Cygnus columbianus*)

Finding data

Finding Code = 6, throughout November. Most records consist of small flocks observed flying along the lakefront; rarely small groups land on the lake. Occasionally, one or two birds settle in a small lake or pond (e.g., George Lake or Long Lake) and remain for a few days. Tundra Swans are quite rare in spring.

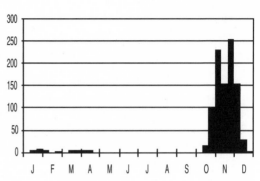

Peak counts

Spring:	3	19 Mar 1988	George Lake
Fall:	108	1 Dec 1985	Marquette Lagoon

Status

The Tundra Swan is a fall transient that occasionally winters in the Dunes. Bellrose (1976) shows the primary migration corridor passing northeast of Indiana; thus Tundra Swans appearing in the Dunes are slightly south of the central migratory track. The latest spring record is 19 April 1979. Fall migration data are:

	EARLIEST	ARRIVE	PEAK	DEPART	LATEST	N
Fall	11 Oct 94	26 Oct	15 Nov	2 Dec	- -	73

TRUMPETER SWAN (*Cygnus buccinator*)

This species was extirpated from the entire state by the end of the last century. Butler (1898) indicates that a specimen was taken in Lake County during spring 1882 and another in Porter County on 22 February 1894.

MUTE SWAN (*Cygnus olor*)

Finding data

Finding Code = 2, on Wolf Lake and George Lake where birds are permanent residents. If George Lake freezes, resident swans move to Wolf Lake. Transitory birds are occasionally seen along the lakefront, especially following the first winter freeze which eliminates preferred habitat on small ponds.

Peak counts

Spring:	30	4 May 1991	Northern Lake County
Fall:	29	23 Nov 1991	George Lake
Winter:	136	14 Jan 1996	Wolf Lake

Status
This species has been expanding significantly in recent years. The first Dunes area record was 4 November 1961; numbers have increased dramatically since the mid-1980s. Nesting has occurred on both Wolf and George Lakes.

GREATER WHITE-FRONTED GOOSE (*Anser albifrons*)

Finding Code = 9. Smith (1936) indicated that this species was observed 24 March 1934 (no specific location given), one was observed flying past Miller Beach 29 October 1989 (IAQ 68:179), seven were seen at Long Lake 19 February 1997, and 33 were counted at the Highway 49 borrow pit in Chesterton 22 February 1997. At least 22 birds were still present at the latter site 1 March.

SNOW GOOSE (*Chen caerulescens*)

Finding data
Finding Code = 6, during the final half of October. Few land in the Dunes; most are observed from Lake Michigan's shores as southbound flocks migrate down the lake. Most flocks are mixed snow and blue forms. Rarely, an immature of the blue form lands with other water-fowl; these birds comprise most of the December records.

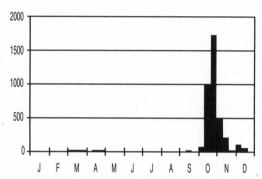

Peak counts
Spring:	18	27 Mar 1978	Chesterton
Fall:	400	24 Oct 1962	Baileytown

Status
The Snow Goose is primarily a fall transient, although a few spring and winter records exist. Fall migration data are:

	EARLIEST	ARRIVE	PEAK	DEPART	LATEST	N
Spring	2 Mar 55	- -	27 Mar	- -	2 May 80	13
Fall	18 Sep 93	12 Oct	26 Oct	13 Nov	28 Dec 78	83

Observations
Bellrose (1976) states that migrating Snow Geese fly virtually nonstop from the James Bay staging area to the Louisiana wintering grounds. The Dunes lie almost directly on the track between these areas, strongly suggesting that October Snow Goose flocks are enroute on their trans-continental marathon.

BRANT (*Branta bernicla*)

Finding data
Finding Code = 8; October through December. Most are observed on or near Lake Michigan, especially at Michigan City Harbor. Inland sightings include singletons at Long Lake and George Lake.

Peak counts
Spring:	1		All spring reports consist of singletons
Fall:	9	9 Oct 1993	Port of Indiana
Winter	75	14 Dec 1975	Beverly Shores

Status
The Brant is primarily a fall transient; however, numbers appear to be increasing. Indiana's first record of this small goose was established at Michigan City Harbor, where three birds were seen 19 October 1957 and a wounded individual was taken as a specimen 26 October 1957. In 1983 a bird lingered in the Michigan City yacht basin until 22 May. Fall migration data are:

	EARLIEST	ARRIVE		PEAK	DEPART		LATEST	N
Fall	9 Oct 93	-	-	3 Nov	-	-	21 Dec 83	14

CANADA GOOSE (*Branta canadensis*)

Finding data
Finding Code = 1. Large semi-tame, but free flying flocks are permanent residents throughout the Dunes area. These birds are becoming a nuisance at many locations. Disregarding permanent residents, the largest single party count is 220 observed along the lakefront on 16 October 1982.

Status
A permanent resident. Nests in local ponds and lakes. The existence of local populations makes migration assessment difficult, but data suggest that spring migration occurs between mid-February and April and the fall flight is in late October and early November.

SUBFAMILY ANATINAE: Ducks

Of the 29 duck species occurring in the Dunes, only three, the Mallard, Wood Duck, and Blue-winged Teal, are regular summer residents. The remaining species are winter residents, transients, and vagrants.

WOOD DUCK (*Aix sponsa*)

Finding data
Finding Code = 2, July through September. Although this species nests in wooded swamps, late summer birds often gather on open ponds, such as Long Lake and Roxana Pond, in preparation for migration; they are most easily observed during this flocking period.

Peak counts

Spring:	61	24 May	96	Gary
Fall:	2000	6 Oct	1986	Dunes State Park

Status

Although a few winter records of this handsome duck exist, it is primarily a summer resident. Wood Ducks are well established as a breeding species in the Dunes area. Recent nesting reports have come from Dunes State Park.

GREEN-WINGED TEAL (*Anas crecca*)

Finding data

Finding Code = 3, during the fall flight in October when large migrating flocks appear on the lakefront. This small teal also associates with flocks of ducks on most shallow ponds and lakes; it is often seen at Long Lake, Roxana Pond, and George Lake.

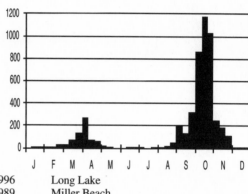

Peak counts

Spring:	34	13 Mar	1996	Long Lake
Fall:	600	17 Oct	1989	Miller Beach

Status

The Green-winged Teal is a spring and fall transient through the Dunes. Although a dozen summer records exist, there is no evidence of breeding.

	EARLIEST	ARRIVE	PEAK	DEPART	LATEST	N
Spring	- -	13 Mar	6 Apr	25 Apr	- -	112
Fall	- -	6 Sep	17 Oct	18 Nov	- -	269

AMERICAN BLACK DUCK (*Anas rubripes*)

Finding data

Finding Code = 2, from October through February when wintering birds join local Mallard flocks. Black Ducks invariably occur with any large gathering of winter dabblers; a few winter at Michigan City Harbor each year. Numbers have declined in recent years.

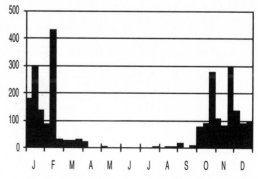

Peak counts

Spring:	8	5 May 1917	West Beach
Fall:	175	29 Nov 1958	Michigan City Harbor
Winter:	260	12 Feb 1966	Michigan City Harbor

Status

Records of this species occur in every month; however, it must be considered primarily a winter resident. On 17 May 1952 Mumford (unpub. notes) found a Black Duck nest containing seven eggs near Schererville, in Lake County.

Observations

Ford (1956) writes that in 1920 the Black Duck was almost as common as the Mallard in the Dunes area. If this was true, then a marked decrease in the Black Duck has taken place in the past sixty years, as the current ratio is about 40 Mallards per Black Duck. Keller et al. (1979) suggest that interbreeding with the Mallard may be diluting the Black Duck strain.

MALLARD (*Anas platyrhynchos*)

Finding data

Finding Code = 1, throughout most of the year; somewhat less common in summer. Present throughout the region wherever water is found. Many winter on Trail Creek.

Peak counts

Spring:	375	1 Mar 1993	Wolf Lake
Fall:	690	23 Nov 1993	Gleason Park
Winter:	971	30 Dec 1995	Roxana Pond & adjacent river

Status

The Mallard is a permanent resident and the most common breeding duck in the Dunes. Females with downy young have been observed as early as 24 April. Migration periods are obscured by records of resident birds.

NORTHERN PINTAIL (*Anas acuta*)

Finding data

Finding Code = 5, during the fall migration peak in October. The largest counts are recorded along the lakefront during fall migration. This elegant duck also occurs with other dabblers on ponds and small lakes (e.g., Long Lake and George Lake).

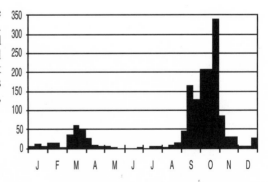

Peak counts

Spring:	30	18 Mar 1979	Dunes State Park
Fall:	105	24 Oct 1995	Miller Beach

Status

The Pintail is a spring and fall transient through the Dunes, but it has been reported in all winter months. Migration data are:

	EARLIEST	ARRIVE	PEAK	DEPART	LATEST	N
Spring	3 Mar 55	8 Mar	23 Mar	19 Apr	12 May 51	52
Fall	18 Jul 77	10 Sep	17 Oct	21 Nov	- -	182

BLUE-WINGED TEAL (*Anas discors*)

Finding data

Finding Code = 2, from mid-August through mid-October. In fall large flocks are frequently seen flying along the lakefront during the migration peak. Also found on ponds and wetlands throughout the region; it is especially common at Long Lake, Gleason Park, and Roxana Pond.

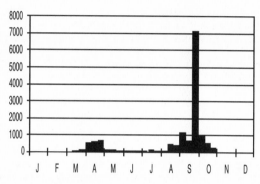

Peak counts

Spring:	100	22 Apr 1953	Miller Beach
Fall:	3900	23 Sep 1993	Miller Beach

Status

The Blue-winged Teal is a summer resident and seasonal transient. It does not winter. Nests and young birds have been observed in May and June.

	EARLIEST	ARRIVE	PEAK	DEPART	LATEST	N
Spring	7 Mar 76	31 Mar	19 Apr	14 May	- - -	265
Fall	- - -	18 Aug	18 Sep	17 Oct	22 Nov 86	253

CINNAMON TEAL (*Anas cyanoptera*)

Finding Code = 10; only one record. Brodkorb (1926) lists this species from Hammond 10 August 1926. This extraordinary record is described as follows. "Mrs. H. L. Baldwin reports that on August 10 she and a friend obtained a close view of 10 or 12 Cinnamon Teal near Hammond, Ind. As two of the birds were adult males, there seems to be no possibility of mistaken identity." Except for occasional reports of pairs, all other sightings in Indiana and surrounding states have consisted of singletons; consequently, this report must be viewed with skepticism.

NORTHERN SHOVELER (*Anas clypeata*)

Finding data

Finding Code = 3, during the migration peaks: late March through April and late October. During the fall flight migrant flocks are frequently noted flying along the lakefront. Gleason Park, Long Lake, and Roxana Pond provide fine locations to observe this species.

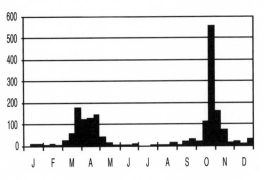

Peak counts

Spring:	36	24 Mar 1994	Gleason Park
Fall:	326	24 Oct 1995	Miller Beach

Status

The Shoveler is primarily a spring and fall transient through the Dunes, but several nesting records exist. The average spring migration peak is 8 April, whereas the average fall peak is 11 October. Smith (1936) mentions a nest containing nine eggs on 14 July 1935 and Blake (1936) reports a nest with eight eggs 26 June 1936; both at George Lake. On 28 June 1965 a female and eight young were found in a marsh remnant west of Gleason Park (Mumford, 1966).

	EARLIEST	ARRIVE	PEAK	DEPART	LATEST	N
Spring	- - -	12 Mar	11 Apr	2 May	- - -	163
Fall	- - -	23 Sep	26 Oct	29 Nov	- - -	124

GADWALL (*Anas strepera*)

Finding data

Finding Code = 3, during both spring (mid-March through mid-April) and fall (mid-October through November) migrations. The most reliable locations are Long Lake, Roxana Pond, and Gleason Park. In addition, migrants frequently accompany the puddle duck flocks seen on the lakefront.

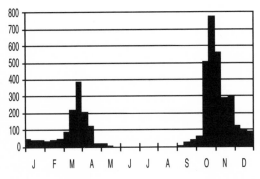

Peak counts

Spring:	93	8 Apr 1989	Long Lake
Fall:	122	9 Nov 1996	Long Lake

Status

The Gadwall is a spring and fall transient that occasionally winters; it is absent during the summer. Migration data are:

	EARLIEST	ARRIVE	PEAK	DEPART	LATEST	N
Spring	- -	8 Mar	27 Mar	24 Apr	16 May 96	98
Fall	5 Sep 81	12 Oct	2 Nov	5 Dec	- -	209

EURASIAN WIGEON (*Anas penelope*)

Finding Code = 9; only three records. Ford (1956) gives two records for Wolf Lake: 17 April 1930 and 20 April 1949. The only recent record was an adult male, seen at Long Lake on 3 April 1981 (IAQ 60:60).

AMERICAN WIGEON (*Anas americana*)

Finding data

Finding Code = 2 during the fall migration peak, from mid-October through early November. Fall migrants are regular members of the dabbler flocks seen on the lakefront. Inland, birds often land on shallow ponds (e.g., Long Lake or Roxana Pond) with other migrant waterfowl.

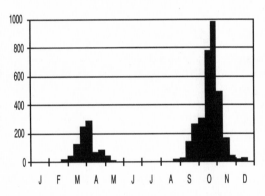

Peak counts

Spring:	50	6 Apr 1958	Baileytown
Fall:	179	24 Oct 1995	Miller Beach

Status

The "baldpate" is a spring and fall transient through the Dunes. Spring birds have lingered into early June, but there is no evidence of nesting. Migration data are tabulated below.

	EARLIEST	ARRIVE	PEAK	DEPART	LATEST	N
Spring	12 Feb 66	14 Mar	4 Apr	2 May	5 Jun 50	158
Fall	7 Aug 95	19 Sep	21 Oct	15 Nov	- -	256

CANVASBACK (*Aythya valisineria*)

Finding data
Maximum Finding Code = 3, during the fall flight in late October, when migrants are detected among the large scaup flocks on Lake Michigan. Finding Code = 5, in winter. Recent winter records are from Michigan City Harbor, Port of Indiana, and Long Lake.

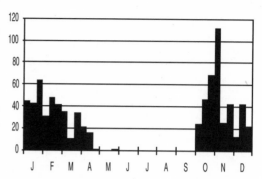

Peak counts

Spring:	18	1 Apr 1979	George Lake
Fall:	30	19 Oct 1996	Miller Beach & Michigan City Harbor
Winter:	30	16 Feb 1957	Michigan City Harbor

Status
The Canvasback is a winter resident of the Dunes; however, a very early spring migration (mid-January to mid-April) probably occurs, suggesting that many late winter Canvasbacks are in fact spring migrants. According to Mlodinow (1984) one summered near Michigan City in 1966.

	EARLIEST	ARRIVE	PEAK	DEPART	LATEST	N
Spring	- - -	- - -	-	1 Apr	23 May 30	30
Fall	7 Oct 89	15 Oct	3 Nov	25 Nov	- - -	70

REDHEAD (*Aythya americana*)

Finding data
Finding Code = 2, during the fall migration: late October through mid-November. Redheads ac-company the large autumn flocks of scaup on Lake Michigan.   This duck also occurs on inland waters, such as the Michigan City yacht basin, Long Lake, Wolf Lake, and George Lake.

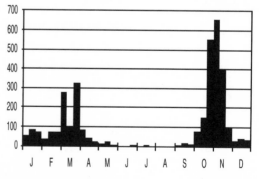

Peak counts

Spring:	150	24 Mar 1967	Gary Harbor
Fall:	175	6 Nov 1989	Port of Indiana

Status

The Redhead is a spring and fall transient, but a few often winter. Smith (1950) reports an anomalous summer male 15 July 1934 near the Illinois state line. Migration data are:

	EARLIEST	ARRIVE	PEAK	DEPART	LATEST	N
Spring	- -	4 Mar	24 Mar	8 May	25 May 90	96
Fall	10 Sep 87	17 Oct	4 Nov	10 Dec	- -	175

RING-NECKED DUCK (*Aythya collaris*)

Finding data

Finding Code = 2, during spring migration from March through mid-April; it is less numerous in the fall. Spring flocks appear as soon as the ice breaks, marking the end of winter's grip on the Dunes. The Ring-necked Duck prefers inland lakes, ponds and borrow pits; it can almost always be found at Long Lake during migration.

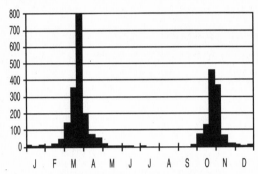

Peak counts

Spring:	200	22 Mar 1950	Baileytown
Fall:	120	3 Nov 1995	Long Lake

Status

This handsome species is a spring and fall transient through the Dunes; however, it is considerably more abundant in spring than in fall. A 1953 nesting record was reported at George Lake (AFN 7:311), and in 1962 a pair lingered at Baileytown from late May into June. In 1995 a male summered in the yacht basin at Michigan City Harbor. Migration data are:

	EARLIEST	ARRIVE	PEAK	DEPART	LATEST	N
Spring	- - -	8 Mar	29 Mar	26 Apr	9 Jun 90	127
Fall	21 Sep 95	7 Oct	30 Oct	22 Nov	- -	120

GREATER SCAUP (*Aythya marila*)

Finding data
Finding Code = 2, in winter, late December through mid-February. Most are observed on Lake Michigan near the warm water outlets of power plants; in recent years concentrations have appeared off the Migrant Trap. This species may well have benefited from the accidental introduction of zebra mussels into Lake Michigan.

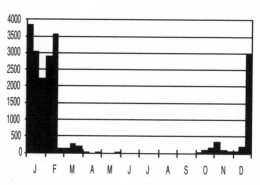

Peak counts
Spring:	113	28 Mar 1955	Gary Harbor
Fall:	71	1 Nov 1994	Miller Beach
Winter:	2760	9 Feb 1996	Lakefront

Status
Difficulties in separating this species from the Lesser Scaup raise questions about the validity of data for both species. In October legions of scaup fly along the lakeshore; hundreds are often seen in a single day. Most observers feel that these flocks consist dominantly of Lessers, but exact ratios have not been established. The Greater Scaup is primarily a winter resident in the Dunes, but a spring flight may occur in March. In 1939 this species lingered until 1 June (Boyd notes) and a male was at Baileytown 21 May 1962 (Reuterskiold notes).   Migration data are:

	EARLIEST	ARRIVE	PEAK	DEPART	LATEST	N
Winter	22 Sep 90	25 Oct	- -	24 Apr	1 Jun 39	145

LESSER SCAUP (*Aythya affinis*)

Finding data
Maximum Finding Code = 1, from late October through mid-November.   Large autumn flocks on Lake Michigan are mainly this species. Enormous rafts are frequently observed swimming well offshore on the lake (especially at Miller Beach) during the height of fall migration.   The high autumn daily totals consist of counting migrating flocks along the lakefront.

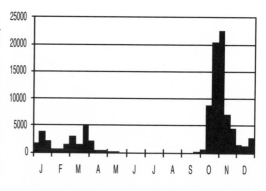

Peak counts
Spring:	2000	27 Mar 1992	Port of Indiana
Fall:	5000	2 Nov 1986	Michigan City Harbor

56

Status
Probably a fall transient and winter resident (but see comments under Greater
Scaup). Records exist for June, July, and August.

	EARLIEST			ARRIVE	PEAK	DEPART	LATEST			N
Spring	-	-	-	20 Feb	24 Mar	25 Apr	-	-	-	242
Fall	-	-	-	16 Oct	2 Nov	2 Dec	-	-	-	283

KING EIDER (*Somateria spectabilis*)

Finding data
Finding Code = 8, November
through mid-December. All
modern records come from Lake
Michigan where birds appear at
harbor facilities. Recent
sightings come from Michigan
City Harbor and the Port of
Indiana. An immature male
lingered at the latter site from 28
November through 24
December, 1985.

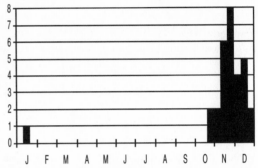

Peak counts
    Spring: No spring records
    Fall: 6   11 Nov 1983   Michigan City Harbor (AB 40:286)

Status
Indiana's first record was a female or immature collected on George Lake 6
November 1936 (Smith, 1950). King Eiders are fall transients that occasionally
linger into mid-winter.

	EARLIEST	ARRIVE	PEAK	DEPART	LATEST	N
Fall	22 Oct 59		28 Nov		16 Jan 86	19

HARLEQUIN DUCK (*Histrionicus histrionicus*)

Finding data

Finding Code = 7, November through March. The vast majority of the records come from Michigan City Harbor, but it also occurs regularly at the Port of Indiana. This species is usually seen diving along rocky portions of the breakwaters; it is inconspicuous and can be easily overlooked.

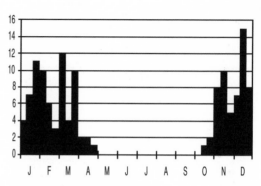

Peak counts

Spring:	3	2 Mar 1996	Michigan City Harbor
Fall:	4	2 Nov 1989	Michigan City Harbor
Winter:	4	16 Dec 1995	Michigan City Harbor

Status

The Harlequin Duck is a winter resident along harbor facilities on Lake Michigan's shores. Most birds arrive in November, but, upon finding a suitable site, often remain throughout the winter. Virtually all possess the brownish female or immature plumage. Several of the male reports involved lingering immatures that gradually molted into male plumage; the white "shoulder patches" were visible by late December. One male, in full adult plumage, arrived at Whiting Park 24 October 1996. Migration data are:

	EARLIEST	ARRIVE	PEAK	DEPART	LATEST	N
Winter	17 Oct 72	2 Nov	- -	6 Apr	27 Apr 92	54

OLDSQUAW (*Clangula hyemalis*)

Finding data

The current Finding Code = 6, between November and March. This species was far more common (perhaps Code 2) in the 1950s. All records come from Lake Michigan. The largest single party count was an incredible 31,539 on the 1955 Michigan City Christmas Bird Count. The latter tally was excluded from the Occurrence Histogram.

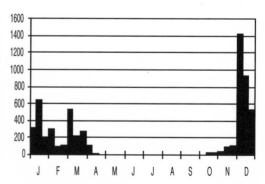

Peak counts

Spring:	300	3 Mar 1957	Michigan City Harbor
Fall:	30	28 Nov 1952	Northern Porter County
Winter:	31,539	26 Dec 1955	Michigan City Harbor

Status

The Oldsquaw is a winter resident on Lake Michigan; however, numbers have declined dramatically in recent decades. Throughout the 1970s only a few birds were reported annually. From 1985 through 1995 an average of ten birds per year were reported. In contrast, Oldsquaws were reported daily in the 1950s. Migration data are:

	EARLIEST	ARRIVE	PEAK	DEPART	LATEST	N
Winter	10 Oct 96	2 Nov	- -	4 Apr	17 May 93	123

BLACK SCOTER (*Melanitta nigra*)

Finding data

Finding Code = 5, during fall migration: mid-October through mid-November. Within this period flocks of migrating scoters (all three species) are frequently seen flying low over Lake Michigan. Look for scoters on the windy days immediately following passage of a cold front.

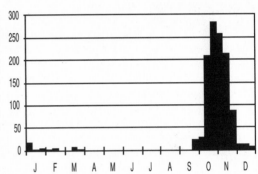

Peak counts

Spring:	6	19 Mar 1986	Port of Indiana
Fall:	100	13 Nov 1982	Beverly Shores

Status

The Black Scoter is a fall transient that occasionally winters. Fall migration data are:

	EARLIEST	ARRIVE	PEAK	DEPART	LATEST	N
Spring	- -	- -	- -	- -	21 Mar 78	3
Fall	29 Sep 84	15 Oct	2 Nov	28 Nov	29 Dec 53	197

Observations

Virtually all of the "dark-winged" scoters are in the drab female or immature plumage (only three adult males have been reported); thus many distant flying birds cannot be identified with certainty.

SURF SCOTER (*Melanitta perspicillata*)

Finding data

Finding Code = 5. See previous species for finding information. Although scoters occasionally land sufficiently close for observation on the water, more often they are simply observed in flight. Accordingly, many dark-winged scoters are not identified. Adult males are rare; only 17 have been reported.

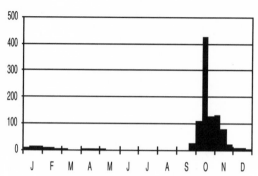

Peak counts

Spring:	1		All spring record are singletons
Fall:	178	11 Oct 1987	Beverly Shores

Status

The status of this species is the same as the Black Scoter; however, the Surf Scoter is slightly less common. Migration data are:

	EARLIEST	ARRIVE	PEAK	DEPART	LATEST	N
Spring	- -	- -	- -	- -	8 May 76	14
Fall	25 Sep 93	6 Oct	26 Oct	23 Nov	- -	147

WHITE-WINGED SCOTER (*Melanitta fusca*)

Finding data

Finding Code = 5. See Black Scoter for finding information. Unlike the other scoters White-wings are easily identified in flight (even at great distance) by their flashing white wing patches. Field reports suggest a decline in the numbers of this species over the past decade.

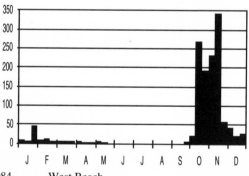

Peak counts

Spring:	3	7 May 1984	West Beach
Fall:	115	18 Nov 1995	Beverly Shores

Status

The White-winged Scoter is primarily a fall transient, but winters more frequently than the other scoters. Migration data are:

	EARLIEST	ARRIVE	PEAK	DEPART	LATEST	N
Spring	- -	- -	- -	- -	17 May 56	23
Fall	27 Sep 93	16 Oct	4 Nov	1 Dec	- -	194

COMMON GOLDENEYE (*Bucephala clangula*)

Finding data
Finding Code = 1, from mid-December through mid-March when this species winters along the lakeshore. Flocks of 20-100 feed on Lake Michigan at many locations; Beverly Shores and West Beach are especially good sites. When ice covers the lake, Goldeneye concentrate around the warm-water outlets of the power plants.

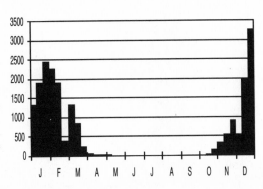

Peak counts

Spring:	500	4 Mar 1949	Northern Porter Co.
Fall:	150	28 Nov 1987	Miller Beach
Winter:	600	29 Dec 1955	Michigan City Harbor

Status
The Common Goldeneye is a winter resident on Lake Michigan. Migration data are:

	EARLIEST	ARRIVE	PEAK	DEPART	LATEST	N
Winter	2 Oct 51	7 Nov	- -	14 Apr	7 Jun 91	394

BARROW'S GOLDENEYE (*Bucephala islandica*)

Finding data
Finding Code = 10, only one acceptable record. A carefully described female was observed on Lake Michigan adjacent to the Illinois state line 5-7 March 1993 (IAQ 71:4).

BUFFLEHEAD (*Bucephala albeola*)

Finding data
Finding Code = 1, from mid-November through February. This small duck shares the Common Goldeneye's winter habitat.

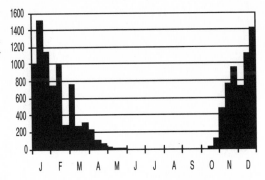

Peak counts

Spring:	200	8 Mar 1956	Michigan City Harbor
Fall:	150	28 Nov 1952	Northern Porter County
Winter:	500	27 Jan 1955	Michigan City Harbor

Status

The Bufflehead is primarily a winter resident on Lake Michigan; three summer records exist. Migration data, excluding the summer records, are:

	EARLIEST	ARRIVE	PEAK	DEPART	LATEST	N
Winter	10 Oct 93	2 Nov	- -	25 Apr	26 May 84	394

HOODED MERGANSER (*Lophodytes cucullatus*)

Finding data

Finding Code = 3, in March and November. During migration this colorful species can usually be found at Long Lake, Marquette Lagoon, or George Lake. One or two often winter in Trail Creek. In fall migrant flocks are often noted flying along the lakefront.

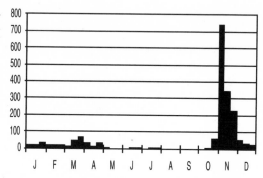

Peak counts

Spring:	11	4 Apr 1954	Chesterton
Fall:	247	4 Nov 1995	Long Lake, Miller Beach & Michigan City

Status

The Hooded Merganser is a spring and fall transient; however, a few usually winter and eleven summer records exist. Migration data are:

	EARLIEST	ARRIVE	PEAK	DEPART	LATEST	N
Spring	- -	11 Mar	30 Mar	29 Apr	- -	74
Fall	- -	1 Nov	14 Nov	10 Dec	- -	154

COMMON MERGANSER (*Mergus merganser*)

Finding data
Finding Code = 2, in January and February. This large duck occurs almost exclusively on Lake Michigan, often gathering in large winter flocks near power plant outlets. If open water is present a few usually winter at the Port of Indiana.

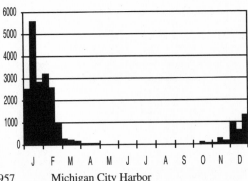

Peak counts

Spring:	70	3 Mar 1957	Michigan City Harbor
Fall:	100	11 Nov 1959	Gary Harbor
Winter:	3000	11 Jan 1953	Michigan City Harbor

Status
A winter resident on Lake Michigan. Migration data are:

	EARLIEST	ARRIVE	PEAK	DEPART	LATEST	N
Winter	16 Oct 77	19 Nov	- -	6 Apr	30 Apr 62	213

RED-BREASTED MERGANSER (*Mergus serrator*)

Finding data
Finding Code = 1, during migration periods (late March through mid-April and early November). This species is most easily seen on Lake Michigan. A tour along Lake Front Drive at Beverly Shores, during migration, will surely reveal scores, perhaps hundreds.

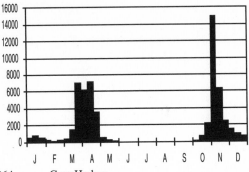

Peak counts

Spring:	1000	31 Mar 1964	Gary Harbor
Fall:	3000	9 Nov 1957	Gary Harbor

Status
This merganser is a seasonal transient and winter resident; however, in winter, it is less common than the previous species. A mixed flock of males and females (up to eight birds) summered on Wolf Lake in 1984. Migration data are:

	EARLIEST	ARRIVE	PEAK	DEPART	LATEST	N
Spring	- -	18 Mar	8 Apr	7 May	9 Jun 90	332
Fall	19 Jul 87	21 Oct	10 Nov	14 Dec	- -	381

RUDDY DUCK   (*Oxyura jamaicensis*)

Finding data

Finding Code = 4, during spring migration: late March through April. This small duck is occasionally seen swimming on Lake Michigan, but is more often found on inland lakes or harbors. Long Lake, Wolf Lake, and the George Lake yield frequent records.

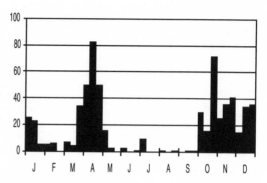

Peak counts

Spring:	30	14 Apr 1990	Wolf Lake
Fall:	26	30 Oct 1957	Miller Beach

Status

The Ruddy Duck is a spring transient and winter resident; it occasionally lingers in summer to breed. Mumford (1966) reported three adult males, two females, and six young birds in a marsh pond west of Gleason Park on 28 June 1965. On 2 July 1980 a female and seven downy young were observed at Gleason Park (IAQ 60:17). No distinct migration peak is evident in fall. Disregarding the summer reports, migration data are:

	EARLIEST	ARRIVE	PEAK	DEPART	LATEST	N
Spring	- -	22 Mar	14 Apr	1 May	3 Jun 83	71
Fall	2 Aug 89	10 Oct	20 Nov	24 Dec	- -	105

FAMILY CATHARTIDAE: Vultures

BLACK VULTURE (*Coragyps atratus*)

Finding Code = 10. Only one acceptable record. Raymond Grow (unpub. letter) reported observing this southerly species at West Beach, 25 July 1953: "He circled nearby then flew south and out of sight, only to return 20 minutes later for another close view and then headed south west...(I) got all the markings, the flap-and-soar flight, (and) the vulture head." The observation occurred at 5:30 p.m. DST.

TURKEY VULTURE (*Cathartes aura*)

Finding data
Finding Code = 3, from late March through early May. Vultures are usually observed soaring over Dunes State Park or the Beverly Shores area. Oddly, this species is rarely seen in western portions of the Calumet Region; 95 percent of all records are from Porter County. It is seen daily during the spring migration at the Johnson Beach hawk-watch.

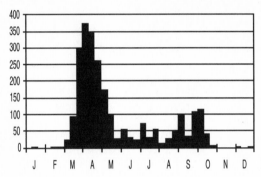

Peak counts
Spring:	46	6 Apr 1989	Johnson Beach hawk-watch
Fall:	52	6 Sep 1996	at a LaPorte Co. roost

Status
The Turkey Vulture is presently a spring transient and summer resident; sporadic winter reports have occurred in recent years. Its abundance has apparently increased in recent decades. Eifrig (1918), for example, describes this species as: "A rare accidental visitor, though one would expect it to be more common." A nest tree was discovered near Mt. Baldy 22 May 1986 and was still occupied 17 June. Migration data are:

	EARLIEST	ARRIVE	PEAK	DEPART	LATEST	N
Spring	12 Jan 93	22 Mar	13 Apr	13 May	- - -	406
Fall	- - -	30 Jul	14 Sep	9 Oct	5 Dec 93	152

Observations
The vulture serves on the lakeshore clean-up crew by scavenging along the beach. On 13 May 1967, Baxter (1967) reported a dozen birds feeding on dead alewives along the beach at Beverly Shores. A similar foraging behavior was observed 9 July 1981 when 14 vultures were noted along the eastern beach of Dunes State Park.

SUPERFAMILY ACCIPITROIDEA: Hawks and Falcons

Fourteen representatives of this superfamily occur more or less regularly in the Dunes, and five more have appeared as vagrants. Tabulated below are abundance rankings (based on total numbers recorded in the Dunes Area) and seasonal tallies for each species.

NUMBERS OF HAWKS THROUGH DECEMBER 1996

	Rank	Spring	Summer	Fall	Winter
Osprey	10	271	4	85	-
Swallow-tailed Kite	16	2	1	-	-
Mississippi Kite	18	1	1	-	-
Bald Eagle	11	123	5	43	22
Northern Harrier	5	1,617	31	101	59
Sharp-shinned Hawk	2	4,899	2	139	22
Cooper's Hawk	7	674	24	87	80
Northern Goshawk	13	58	-	14	12
Red-shouldered Hawk	6	1,267	45	92	67
Broad-winged Hawk	3	2,843	145	601	-
Swainson's Hawk	15	4	-	-	-
Red-tailed Hawk	1	9,926	61	714	331
Ferruginous Hawk	17	-	-	1	1
Rough-legged Hawk	8	231	-	177	69
Golden Eagle	14	32	1	5	-
American Kestrel	4	1,441	99	297	254
Merlin	12	68	-	40	2
Peregrine Falcon	9	57	37	240	49
Gyrfalcon	19	-	-	1	-

Spring hawk flights constitute an impressive spectacle in the Dunes. When conditions are right, usually a warm day with brisk winds from a southerly quadrant, scores, even hundreds of hawks can be seen from good vantage points (hawk-watch sites) along the dune-crests (see section on raptor migration, page 7).

FAMILY ACCIPITRIDAE: Hawks

OSPREY (*Pandion haliaetus*)

Finding data

Finding Code = 4, during the last two-thirds of April at the hawk-watch sites. Ospreys are most often observed near Lake Michigan and are frequently seen during spring hawk watches. A few are recorded at inland lakes such as Cowles Bog, Wolf Lake, or George Lake.

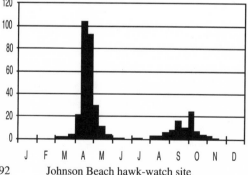

Peak counts

| Spring: | 15 | 19 Apr 1992 | Johnson Beach hawk-watch site |
| Fall: | 5 | 5 Oct 1986 | West Beach |

Status

The "fish hawk" is primarily a spring and fall transient, but several summer records exist. Migration data are:

	EARLIEST	ARRIVE	PEAK	DEPART	LATEST	N
Spring	5 Mar 91	9 Apr	21 Apr	7 May	9 Jun 84	153
Fall	4 Aug 84	27 Aug	26 Sep	21 Oct	11 Nov 94	70

SWALLOW-TAILED KITE (*Elanoides forficatus*)

Finding Code = 10; only two records. Ford (1956) gives the following, "Miss Belle Wilson observed this species at Tremont, Porter County, Indiana, 5 April 1921. It was observed again in the same locality, 6 June 1948 (Ford, 1956)."

MISSISSIPPI KITE (*Ictinia mississippiensis*)

Finding Code = 10; only two records. The first was seen by several members of the Chicago Ornithological Society 3 June 1973 in the High Dunes (AB 27:875).   The second, an adult, flew over the Johnson Beach hawk-watch site 23 April 1992 (AB 46:430).

BALD EAGLE (*Haliaeetus leucocephalus*)

Finding data

Finding Code = 5, in the last two-thirds of March. Numbers have increased in conjunction with re-introduction programs throughout the Midwest. Bald Eagles are most often seen flying near the lakeshore; any vantage point near the lake allowing a wide view should serve. A majority of the recent records are from the Johnson Beach hawk-watch site.

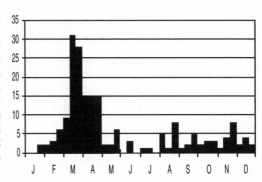

Peak counts

Spring:	10	14 Mar 1990	Johnson Beach hawk-watch site
Fall:	5	8 Aug 1897	Miller Beach (at nest site, Woodruff, 1907)

Status

This noble raptor nested in the Dunes during the last century (Woodruff, 1907), but was subsequently decimated by man. Eifrig (1918) writes, "Up to twenty years ago this great bird was almost a common sight in the Dunes, nesting regularly." The fall flight is poorly defined. Spring migration data are:

	EARLIEST	ARRIVE	PEAK	DEPART	LATEST	N
Spring	- -	11 Mar	30 Mar	27 Apr	9 Jun 84	153

NORTHERN HARRIER (*Circus cyaneus*)

Finding data
Current Finding Code = 3, late March through April, formerly more common. The Harrier is usually seen flying along the Dunes or above the interdunal marshes. Spring migrants are seen frequently from the hawk-watch sites where it is not unusual to count a dozen birds per day.

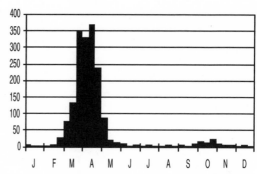

Peak counts
Spring:	50	29 Mar 1960	Baileytown
Fall:	3	28 Oct 1916	Indiana Dunes

Status
Today the "Marsh Hawk" is a primarily spring and fall transient through the Dunes; however, in past years it was a summer resident and common nesting species. Eifrig (1918) believed it was the most common hawk in the Dunes and provided breeding data near Mineral Springs. The last recorded nesting occurred 13-26 July 1954 when Reuter-skiold (unpub. notes) reported, "Four immature, but full grown, marsh hawks" in a marsh near Baileytown. This species appears sporadically during the winter months. Migration data are:

	EARLIEST	ARRIVE	PEAK	DEPART	LATEST	N
Spring	4 Feb 53	11 Mar	6 Apr	2 May	8 Jun 83	425
Fall	5 Aug 89	18 Aug	14 Oct	11 Nov	29 Nov 91	80

SHARP-SHINNED HAWK (*Accipiter striatus*)

Finding data
Maximum Finding Code = 2, on "hawk flight days" in April; Finding Code = 3, at other times during spring migration in April. "Sharpies" are most easily seen migrating along the Dunes; the Johnson Beach hawk-watch site and Mt. Baldy provide excellent observation sites.

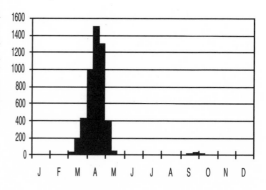

Peak counts
Spring:	223	19 Apr 1992	Johnson Beach hawk-watch site
Fall:	6	19 Sep 1981	Lakefront

Status

This small accipiter is primarily a spring and fall transient, being far more common in spring. Although Butler (1898) reported eggs from Lake County, 17 April 1886, recent nesting evidence is lacking. Fall migration data suggest two peaks: one in late September and the other in late November. A few apparently linger into winter. Migration data are:

	EARLIEST	ARRIVE	PEAK	DEPART	LATEST	N
Spring	20 Feb 91	19 Mar	15 Apr	5 May	20 Jun 81	385
Fall	24 Jul 58	9 Sep	5 Oct	27 Nov	27 Dec 64	121

COOPER'S HAWK (*Accipiter cooperii*)

Finding data

Finding Code = 4, during the peak of spring migration, late March through late April. This accipiter is most easily seen from one of the hawk observation sites such as Mt. Baldy or Johnson Beach. It also harasses passerines at winter feeders.

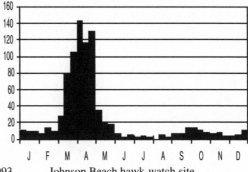

Peak counts

Spring:	19	7 Apr 1993	Johnson Beach hawk-watch site
Fall:	2	-	Recorded on three occasions

Status

Cooper's Hawk is both a permanent resident and transient. The average spring migration peak is 9 April; the fall flight is more diffuse, but a weak peak appears near 6 October. In former years the Cooper's Hawk commonly nested in the Dunes. Nesting records span the interval 1914 to 1943. On 25 May 1914, Stoddard (unpub. notes) collected four partly incubated eggs from a nest 45 feet up in a tamarack at Mineral Springs. This observer also reported a nest at Tremont (13 July 1915) containing four young Cooper's Hawks "just about the age when they leave the nest." Recent nesting has been reported at Marquette Park and Gibson Woods.

NORTHERN GOSHAWK (*Accipiter gentilis*)

Finding data
Finding Code = 8; however, records are strongly correlated with invasion years.
Clear evidence of the invasionary character of this species was provided in 1982-83 when 12 sightings (involving 23 individuals, 22 of which were adults) were recorded. Most records come from the hawk-watch sites. A majority of the records are in spring (March through late April).

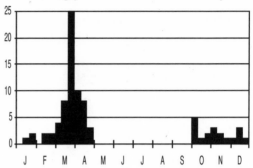

Peak counts
Spring:	5	12 Apr 1983	Johnson Beach hawk-watch site
Fall:	3	3 Oct 1982	Cowles Bog

Status
In view of its irregular occurrence and rarity, the Goshawk's status is difficult to assess. It is probably a periodic transient and winter resident. The fall flight is poorly defined. Migration data are:

	EARLIEST	ARRIVE	PEAK	DEPART	LATEST		N
Spring	- - -	11 Mar	30 Mar	12 Apr	27 Apr	93	42
Fall	3 Oct 82	- -	7 Nov	- -	- -	-	15

RED-SHOULDERED HAWK (*Buteo lineatus*)

Finding data
Finding Code = 3, during the spring flight peak, which occurs in the last two-thirds of March. Red-shouldered Hawks are most often seen from the hawk-watch sites. A few birds winter in wooded swamps at Dunes State Park and along the Little Calumet River.

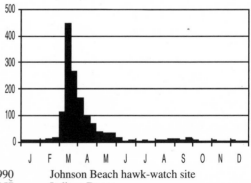

Peak counts
Spring:	75	14 Mar 1990	Johnson Beach hawk-watch site
Fall:	5	4 Sep 1957	Indiana Dunes

Status
This buteo is a permanent resident and transient. At least a half-dozen nesting pairs breed in the High Dunes; one territory in Dunes State Park has been occupied for more than a decade. Peak of the well defined spring migration occurs in mid-March.

BROAD-WINGED HAWK (*Buteo platypterus*)

Finding data
Finding Code = 4, during the spring flight in late April, but numbers vary considerably from year to year. Most Broad-wings are seen migrating along the Dunes in spring; they are quite rare in fall. The vast majority of spring migrants pass through during the last ten days in April.

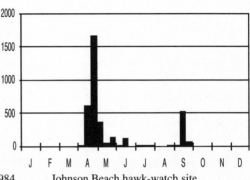

Peak counts
Spring:	421	26 Apr 1984	Johnson Beach hawk-watch site
Fall:	250	17 Sep 1986	Indiana Dunes State Park

Status
This small buteo is a spring transient and summer resident in the Dunes. Southbound Broad-wingeds are apparently deflected away from the Dunes area by Lake Michigan; accordingly, they are surprisingly rare during the autumn flight. A significant exception to this rule occurred during September 1986, where daily counts of 250 and 220 were logged in the High Dunes. Migration data are:

	EARLIEST	ARRIVE	PEAK	DEPART	LATEST	N
Spring	4 Mar 61	18 Apr	25 Apr	14 May	- - -	202
Fall	- - -	- -	18 Sep	- -	22 Nov 58	26

On 20 June 1979 a nest was discovered in the climax forest of Dunes State Park. The nest, some 17 meters above the ground, was in an oak; it contained a single downy nestling on 27 June. Another nest, near Cowles Bog, contained two downy young on 20 June 1981.

Observations
An unusual summer Broad-winged Hawk flight occurred 20 June 1981 at Beverly Shores. Between 9:00 and 11:00 a.m. a total of 110 Broad-winged Hawks soared westward along the dune crests. Most were immatures and all had the "ragged" appearance of molting birds (AB 35:944).

SWAINSON'S HAWK (*Buteo swainsoni*)

Finding data
Finding Code = 9; four records. Landing (pers. comm.) observed this species near the prison farm on 3 May 1958 (AFN 12:357). An immature was seen at the Johnson Beach Hawk-watch site 5 May 1991 (AB 45:452), an adult light-morph was seen near Dunes State Park 19 April 1994 (IAQ 72:198), and a light-morph adult was seen over Dunes State Park 25 May 1996 (AFN 50:288).

RED-TAILED HAWK (*Buteo jamaicensis*)

Finding data
Finding Code = 2, from late March through April (spring migration). Mt. Baldy and the Johnson Beach Hawk-watch site are the best locations to observe spring migrants. Perhaps one bird in two or three hundred is a dark morph, having entirely dark chestnut-brown plumage except for the tail. Both the dark "Harlan's" and the pale "Krider's Red-tail" have been reported on several occasions.

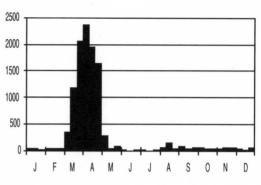

Peak counts
Spring:	274	25 Apr 1955	Baileytown
Fall:	58	4 Sep 1957	Indiana Dunes

Status
The Red-tailed Hawk is a permanent resident and transient. This is the most frequently observed buteo in the Dunes; it is especially common during the spring migration. Nests are seen regularly in Lake and Porter Counties. A poorly defined fall migration probably occurs in August and September. Spring migration data are:

	EARLIEST	ARRIVE	PEAK	DEPART	LATEST	N
Spring	- - -	13 Mar	7 Apr	1 May	- - -	440

Observations
The two common winter buteos in the Dunes are this species and the Rough-legged Hawk. Both raptors have a penchant for resting in bare trees, and, although this is not infallible, they can often be identified by their selected perch sites; the Rough-legged usually sits atop the highest branch, whereas the Red-tailed prefers an outer branch about 1/3 of the way down.

FERRUGINOUS HAWK (*Buteo regalis*)

Finding Code = 10. Only two acceptable records. Ford (1956) reports that an injured bird, found 25 September 1934 in Porter County, was taken to the Chicago Natural History Museum where it was banded and released. On 31 December 1952 and again on 8 January 1953, Reuter-skiold (AFN 7:215) observed this species near Baileytown. Dr. Reuter-skiold (unpub. notes) described the bird as having: "Back color similar to dead oak leaves, a light rusty brown with some splotches of white showing while the bird was sitting. In flight the underparts were snowy white from chest to legs; the legs were rusty." Large white patches were visible on upper surfaces of the wings (near tips) during flight. The tail seemed grayish at tip, but white toward the base. These reports apparently constitute the first Indiana records for this raptor.

ROUGH-LEGGED HAWK (*Buteo lagopus*)

Finding data
Finding Code = 5, during the migration peaks: mid-April and mid-November. A few usually winter in agricultural areas. Rarely, distinct fall flights have been observed in November; these consist of three to twenty-two south-westerly bound birds, flying almost single file, separated by perhaps half a kilometer.

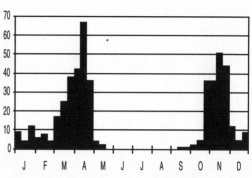

Peak counts
Spring:	18	17 Apr 1985	Over downtown Gary
Fall:	22	18 Nov 1988	Indiana Dunes

Status
The Rough-legged Hawk is a winter resident and transient. Migration data are:

	EARLIEST	ARRIVE	PEAK	DEPART	LATEST	N
Spring	- - -	12 Mar	7 Apr	24 May	13 May 96	125
Fall	12 Sep 59	24 Oct	11 Nov	24 Nov	- - -	95

GOLDEN EAGLE (*Aquila chrysaetos*)

Finding data
Finding Code = 8, during the first two-thirds of April. Most occurrences of this western raptor consist of individuals observed soaring over the Dunes during the spring hawk flights. A majority of the records come from the Johnson Beach Hawk-watch site. Among the 25 birds that were aged, 19 were immatures and six were adults.

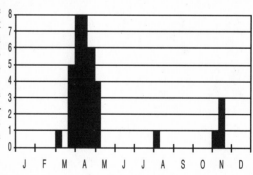

Peak counts
Spring:	3	18 Apr 1992	Johnson Beach Hawk-watch site
Fall:	1	-	All fall observations consist of singletons

Status
The Golden Eagle, far less common than the Bald Eagle, is mainly a spring transient. Extreme spring records are 2 March 1988 and 9 May 1993. Most fall birds appear during the first half of November.

FAMILY FALCONIDAE: Falcons

AMERICAN KESTREL (*Falco sparverius*)

Finding data
Finding Code = 2, from mid-March through April. Migrants are frequently observed at the hawk-watch sites. This species is also commonly seen along the interstate highways.

Peak counts
Spring:	88	7 Apr 1993	High Dunes
Fall:	7	25 Nov 1978	Cowles Bog

Status
The "Sparrow Hawk," as it was formerly known, is a permanent resident and spring transient through the Dunes. Spring flights, consisting of easterly bound birds paralleling the lakeshore along the dune-crests, are often noted when winds are from a southerly direction. The spring migration peak is near 8 April.

MERLIN (*Falco columbarius*)

Finding data
Finding Code = 6, during spring migration (late March through April). Sightings of this falcon have increased markedly over the past decade. Since 1988 it has been recorded annually at the Johnson Beach hawk-watch site and seven were recorded there in spring 1993. Merlins are occasionally seen at other locations along the lakefront but no particular site is reliable.

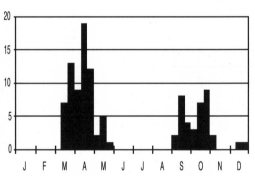

Peak counts
Spring:	3	-	Recorded on three occasions
Fall:	2	13 Oct 1956	Baileytown

Status
The Merlin is a spring and fall transient through the Dunes; a few December records exist. Migration data are:

	EARLIEST	ARRIVE	PEAK	DEPART	LATEST	N
Spring	11 Mar 16	18 Mar	16 Apr	5 May	22 May 54	58
Fall	2 Sep 52	14 Sep	3 Oct	29 Oct	6 Nov 93	36

PEREGRINE FALCON (*Falco peregrinus*)

Finding data
Finding Code = 3, at the nesting sites. The establishment of nesting birds has drastically increased the likelihood of finding Peregrines. This species is now encountered with regularity along the lakefront, especially on windy days.

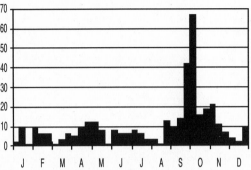

Peak counts

Spring:	2	-	Recorded on four occasions
Fall:	11	8 Oct 1983	Miller Beach (10) and Michigan City Harbor (1)

Status
The Peregrine is a permanent resident and transient through the Dunes. In 1996 four Peregrine nests in the Dunes area produced eight young. The presence of resident birds throughout the year now masks the passage of migrants; however, the spring peak is in late April and the fall flight peaks in early October.

GYRFALCON (*Falco rusticolus*)

Finding data
Finding Code = 10, only one acceptable record. A dark-morph bird was seen harassing gulls at Miller Beach 16 September 1986 (AB 41:95).

FAMILY PHASIANIDAE: Pheasants, Grouses, and Quails

RING-NECKED PHEASANT (*Phasianus colchicus*)

Finding data
Finding Code = 3, during spring (late March through May) when birds call. Pheasants are most often seen and heard in agricultural areas, the interdunal marsh at Beverly Shores, and Oak Ridge Prairie Park.

Peak count

Maximum	9	12 Jan	94	Northern LaPorte County

Status
The first report of this introduced species, which is now a permanent resident in the Dunes, consisted of three birds at Miller, 29 October 1943 (Boyd, unpub. notes). Mumford (unpub. notes) observed a female on a nest containing 12 eggs in northern Lake County, 22 May 1974.

RUFFED GROUSE (*Bonasa umbellus*)

Extirpated as a breeding species. Despite Eifrig's (1918) optimistic statement, "This fine species still holds its own in the dense cover of scrubby oak, juniper, sumac, etc., between the middle dunes and in the woods on the southern fringe of them," the Ruffed Grouse is no longer a resident of the Dunes. On 16 May 1920 Stoddard (unpub. notes) discovered a nest, containing ten eggs, on a hike from West Beach to Cowles Bog. Wandering birds apparently occasionally stray into the Dunes, as there have been three reports over the past decade.

GREATER PRAIRIE-CHICKEN (*Tympanuchus cupido*)

Extirpated from the state of Indiana. An indication of the previous abundance of this once widespread bird is given by Ford (1956): "In 1850 there were 6,000 in one shipment from Michigan City, Indiana." Woodruff (1907) describes this species as "Formerly abundant, but now fast disappearing....still occasionally found in....Lake County, Indiana." Eifrig (1918) classifies the Prairie Chicken as very rare (in the Dunes).

WILD TURKEY (*Meleagris gallopavo*)

Finding Code = 10; only two records. This species has been reintroduced at locations outside the Dunes area. Birds released at these new sites occasionally wander into the Dunes area. The two reports include one seen flying across a roadway in the High Dunes 24 November 1995, and fresh tracks in snow found at Moraine Nature Preserve 9 March 1996.

NORTHERN BOBWHITE (*Colinus virginianus*)

Finding data
Currently the Finding Code = 4. This species was formerly more common, but populations have suffered greatly during recent hard winters. Almost all recent reports are from West Beach and Miller Woods. The largest single party count was 25, on 25 November 1951, at Baileytown.

Status
The Bobwhite is a permanent resident of agricultural and grassland portions of the Dunes. Castrale (unpub. statewide whistle count) detected an incredible 91 percent decline in the quail population in the northern third of Indiana between 1981 and 1982. Populations in the Dunes have followed a similar pattern.

FAMILY RALLIDAE: Rails

Knowledge of these secretive species is quite limited due to their furtive nature. Recent surveys by the National Biological Survey reveal that at least the Sora and Virginia Rail are more common than normal observations suggest.

YELLOW RAIL (*Coturnicops noveboracensis*)

Finding data
Finding Code = 8. Several recent records come from Cowles Bog where birds answered taped calls at dawn. The appearance of 14 dead Yellow Rails on Lake Michigan's beaches on 16 April 1960, following a severe thunderstorm, attests to the fact that the vast majority pass through the Dunes undetected.

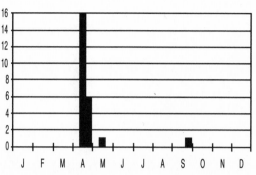

Peak counts
Spring:	14	16 Apr 1960	Kill on Lake Michigan (Segal, 1960)
	3	22 Apr 1988	Inland Marsh (AB 42:441)
Fall:	1	24 Sep 1919	Northern Porter County

Status
The furtive habits of this species render status assessment difficult. Present data suggest that this small rail is a transient through the Dunes; however, Woodruff (1907) referred to it as a common summer resident of the Chicago area. In mid-April 1980, calling rails, believed to be this species, were heard at Cowles Bog. The single fall record comes from Stoddard's unpub. notes, dated 24 September 1919: "(I) saw a fine yellow rail and shot at him but missed- out in the high grass and weeds well back from the Little Calumet." This observation was made on a trek from Miller to Cowles Bog.

BLACK RAIL (*Laterallus jamaicensis*)

Finding data
Finding Code = 9, only three records. In September 1951, Raymond Grow (pers. comm.) observed this species in a Gary marsh, in early May 1976 a dead bird was found in the window well of a home in Gary (Simon, 1977), and a Black Rail was caught in a snake trap at Oak Ridge Prairie Park 5 August 1996 (Dancey in press).

KING RAIL (*Rallus elegans*)

Finding data
Finding Code = 8, from mid-April through May. The King Rail is found in cattail marshes; in recent years the most reliable location is the cattail marsh along the east edge of George Lake. Like many other wetland species, this species has suffered from loss of breeding habitat.

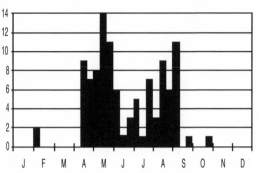

Peak counts

Spring:	5	18 Apr 1917	Wolf Lake
Fall:	5	2 Sep 1933	Near Chesterton

Status
This large rail is a transient and summer resident of the Dunes; however, it is apparently far less common than in previous years. Nests were found at Long Lake 2 June 1916 (Stoddard notes) and at George Lake 3 June 1935 (Smith, 1936). On 11 August 1984, an adult and three downy young were observed at the latter site (IAQ 63:116). Eifrig (1918) describes this species as more common than the Virginia Rail, a situation certainly untrue at present. Migration data are:

	EARLIEST	ARRIVE	PEAK	DEPART	LATEST	N
Spring	13 Apr 10	18 Apr	11 May	25 May	- - -	33
Fall	- - -	- - -	24 Aug	- -	21 Oct 16	22

Observations
Two winter King Rail records are provided by Ford (1956) and Reuter-skiold (unpub. notes). The former consisted of a bird found dead in Whiting, 4 February 1935. The latter was seen walking along a stream near Baileytown 10 February 1956; identification was confirmed by measurements of tracks ("Middle toe— 75 to 80 mm").

VIRGINIA RAIL (*Rallus limicola*)

Finding data
Finding Code = 3 during the late April migration. As with the other rails, this species is more often heard than seen. The rapid two-note "tick!-tick!" call is heard most frequently. The interdunal marshes along Beverly Drive (Beverly Shores) and Mineral Springs Road (crossing Cowles Bog) provide excellent sites for finding this rail.

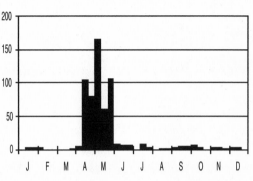

Peak counts

Spring:	31	18 Apr 1994	National Lakeshore survey in Great Marsh
Fall:	3	4 Oct 1975	Cowles Bog

Status
The Virginia Rail is a transient and summer resident. Some years, perhaps most, it winters. At least 21 birds were found dead along Lake Michigan beaches following a powerful thunderstorm, 16 April 1960 (Segal, 1960). Mumford (unpub. notes) found two nearly complete nests at the Hoosier Prairie, 22 May 1974. A fully grown immature was seen at Gleason Park, 24 July 1980. The fall migration is poorly defined (see Occurrence Histogram), but suggests a peak in early October; spring data are:

	EARLIEST	ARRIVE	PEAK	DEPART	LATEST	N
Spring	28 Mar 92	18 Apr	7 May	22 May	- - -	130

Observations
The first winter observations of this species were made by Reuter-skiold (unpub. notes) 21 January 1958 near Baileytown. On 11 January 1976 a single bird was discovered at Cowles Bog and two were observed on the 18th. In subsequent years they have regularly answered taped calls on the Christmas Bird Counts, suggesting that at least a few are regular winter residents. A glimpse of one of these denizens of the cattails, scurrying across a snowdrift, constitutes a most extraordinary sight.

SORA (*Porzana carolina*)

Finding data

Finding Code = 2, from mid-April through mid-May when calling birds are heard from almost every cattail marsh. Good locations include Cowles Bog, Gleason Park, Roxana Pond, and the Beverly Shores interdunal marsh. On rare occasions migrants occur in the lakefront parks.

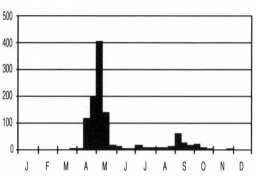

Peak counts

Spring:	54	10 May 1994	National Lakeshore survey in Great Marsh
Fall:	15	8 Sep 1976	Chesterton

Status

As the most common rail in the Dunes, the Sora is a transient and summer resident. The anomalous fall record on 28 November 1950 consisted of an injured bird that was captured and sustained on chicken feed (Boyd, unpub. notes). Otherwise the latest fall record was 21 October 1991 at George Lake. Mumford (unpub. notes) found a nest at the Hoosier Prairie 22 May 1974. The Occurrence Histogram reveals only a weak fall migration peak; migration data are:

	EARLIEST	ARRIVE	PEAK	DEPART	LATEST	N
Spring	27 Mar 58	18 Apr	4 May	14 May	- - -	200
Fall	- - -	17 Aug	10 Sep	8 Oct	28 Nov 50	76

PURPLE GALLINULE (*Porphyrula martinica*)

Finding Code = 10, only two records. Ford (1956) quotes second-hand information from an unpublished paper by Gadd indicating that a specimen noted in a Chicago taxidermist's shop in 1868 was from Tolleston (Lake County, Indiana). On 5 June 1985 a single bird was seen at close range near the Wilson Shelter footbridge in Dunes State Park (IAQ 64:70).

COMMON MOORHEN (*Gallinula chloropus*)

Finding data
Finding Code = 5, during the nesting and migration period (May through September). The Moorhen has declined signifi-cantly over the past decade (in 1986 the Finding Code was 2). Traditionally, the best site for Moorhens was Roxana Pond, but it is now difficult to find at that location.

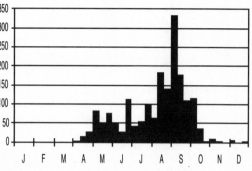

Peak counts
Spring:	34	31 May 1986	Roxana Pond
Fall:	90	4 Sep 1980	Roxana Pond

Status
The "Common Gallinule," as this species was formerly known, is a summer resident and transient through the Dunes. Nests or young have been observed at five different locations throughout the Calumet Region. On 23 July 1981 a Moorhen was observed sitting on a nest at Gleason Park. A subsequent observation on the 26th revealed six very small downy chicks, accompanied by an adult, swimming near the nest. A few birds occasionally linger into early winter. Migration data are as follows:

	EARLIEST	ARRIVE	PEAK	DEPART	LATEST	N
Spring	8 Apr 86	23 Apr	14 May	2 Jun	- - -	120
Fall	- - -	12 Aug	7 Sep	8 Oct	27 Dec 86	151

AMERICAN COOT (*Fulica americana*)

Finding data
Finding Code = 1, throughout fall migration: October through mid-November. Coots are widely distributed throughout the small lakes and ponds; in fall hundreds usually gather on Wolf Lake, George Lake, and Long Lake.

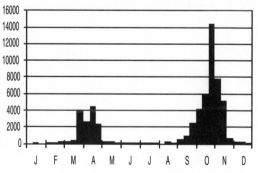

Peak counts
Spring:	1200	30 Mar 1996	Long Lake
Fall:	3300	27 Oct 1994	George Lake

Status

The Coot is a transient and summer resident; a few often winter. The Coot has nested at Gleason Park and Roxana Pond. Juveniles were observed at the latter site in 1985, 1986, and 1990. Migration data are:

	EARLIEST	ARRIVE	PEAK	DEPART	LATEST	N
Spring	- - -	17 Mar	11 Apr	18 May	- - -	251
Fall	- - -	8 Sep	18 Oct	25 Nov	- - -	300

Observations

In late May 1985 a coot possessing an enlarged frontal shield and entirely lacking any trace of the red callus on the shield was observed at Roxana Pond. The white-shielded individual lingered into June and nested. It was mated with a normal American Coot.

FAMILY GRUIDAE: Cranes

SANDHILL CRANE (*Grus canadensis*)

Finding data

Finding Code = 3, from mid-March through early April. Over the past decade the number of Dunes area sightings has increased along with the regional population. The gravely calls of migrating flocks are usually heard long before the birds are seen. Migrating Cranes are frequently seen at the Johnson Beach hawk-watch site, but the largest counts come from northern Lake County, especially the Gibson Woods Preserve.

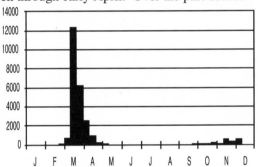

Peak counts

Spring:	2050	12 Mar 1996	Gibson Woods Preserve
Fall:	325	13 Nov 1992	Northern Lake Co.

Status

The Sandhill Crane is a spring transient through the Dunes; most fall records come from western Lake County. Migration data are:

	EARLIEST	ARRIVE	PEAK	DEPART	LATEST	N
Spring	11 Feb 89	11 Mar	24 Mar	18 Apr	3 Jun 87	302
Fall	19 Sep 81	4 Oct	2 Nov	24 Nov	9 Dec 92	30

ORDER CHARADRIIFORMES: Plovers, Avocets, and Shorebirds

Four members of this order currently nest in the Dunes: Killdeer, Spotted Sandpiper, Upland Sandpiper, and American Woodcock. Thirty-five additional species are either transients or vagrants. The total number of individuals observed in the Dunes Area and their relative abundance rankings, are tabulated below. The column headed "Nos." includes all data available through December 1996.

ABUNDANCE RANKINGS AND NUMBERS OF DUNES AREA SHOREBIRDS

Rank	Nos.	Species	Rank	Nos.	Species
12	1054	Black-bellied Plover	7	3303	Semipalmated Sandpiper
17	572	American Golden-Plover	32	43	Western Sandpiper
37	2	Snowy Plover	6	3460	Least Sandpiper
7	1295	Semipalmated Plover	30	57	White-rumped Sandpiper
27	108	Piping Plover	23	185	Baird's Sandpiper
4	7240	Killdeer	3	8617	Pectoral Sandpiper
36	2	Black-necked Stilt	29	60	Purple Sandpiper
24	175	American Avocet	5	5168	Dunlin
13	1001	Greater Yellowlegs	39	1	Curlew Sandpiper
2	8859	Lesser Yellowlegs	18	496	Stilt Sandpiper
15	926	Solitary Sandpiper	31	54	Buff-breasted Sandpiper
16	850	Willet	38	1	Ruff
11	1238	Spotted Sandpiper	14	972	Short-billed Dowitcher
20	247	Upland Sandpiper	22	186	Long-billed Dowitcher
28	78	Whimbrel	10	1244	Common Snipe
34	18	Hudsonian Godwit	19	431	American Woodcock
33	34	Marbled Godwit	25	141	Wilson's Phalarope
8	1450	Ruddy Turnstone	35	14	Red-necked Phalarope
21	189	Red Knot	26	137	Red Phalarope
1	12473	Sanderling			

Other than the few species that display a preference for the sandy expanses of Lake Michigan's beaches, the appearance of migrant shorebirds depends heavily upon the availability of suitable habitat. Although shorebirds are markedly opportunistic, taking full advantage of scarce mudflats at even the most unlikely locations, in many years limited habitat greatly restricts their numbers.

The fall shorebird migration actually consists of two flights: the adults pass through first and are followed by the young birds born during the summer nesting season. For many species the field data allow resolution of these two flights. In these cases the migration envelope is modified to provide information on both adults and juveniles. When this additional information is provided, it is denoted by (all) for all fall migrants, (ad.) for adults only, and (juv.) for juveniles. Similar notation is used to designate Peak Count values.

FAMILY CHARADRIIDAE: Plovers

BLACK-BELLIED PLOVER (*Pluvialis squatarola*)

Finding data

Finding Code = 3, during the fall flight; late September through October. The best site in recent years has been a large open beach west of the Lake Street parking lot at Miller Beach where juveniles often rest on the sand. A few birds also appear along other Lake Michigan beaches in the fall.

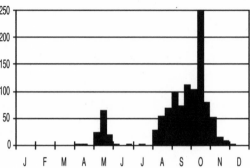

Peak counts

Spring:	33	17 May 1952	Northern Lake County
Fall: (all)	65	12 Oct 1953	Northern Lake County
Fall: (ad.)	6	6 Aug 1986	Wolf Lake
Fall: (juv.)	14	17 Oct 1992	George Lake

Status

The Black-bellied Plover is a spring and fall transient through the Dunes. Migration data are:

	EARLIEST	ARRIVE	PEAK	DEPART	LATEST	N
Spring	6 Apr 63	6 May	16 May	25 May	6 Jun 55	37
Fall (all)	15 Jul 52	19 Aug	28 Sep	1 Nov	6 Dec 80	290
Fall (ad.)	3 Aug 84	8 Aug	19 Aug	6 Sep	23 Sep 94	44
Fall (juv.)	24 Aug 96	13 Sep	7 Oct	31 Oct	21 Nov 92	118

AMERICAN GOLDEN-PLOVER (*Pluvialis dominicus*)

Finding data

Finding Code = 6, during the spring flight when breeding plumed birds are occasionally observed in plowed fields. Migrant flocks are rarely noted from the spring hawk-watch sites. The presence of this species is limited by habitat; it is far more common a few miles further south, on the Kankakee River floodplain.

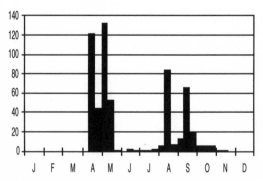

Peak counts

Spring:	50	7 May 1976	Rural northern Porter County
Fall:	81	20 Aug 1995	Miller Beach (migrating flock)

84

Status
This colorful species is a spring and fall transient through the Dunes; no doubt most simply over-fly, without landing. Migration data are:

	EARLIEST	ARRIVE	PEAK	DEPART	LATEST	N
Spring	12 Apr 82	- -	6 May	- -	15 Jun 88	27
Fall (all)	29 Jun 87	9 Aug	15 Sep	15 Oct	23 Sep 94	60

SNOWY PLOVER (*Charadrius alexandrinus*)

Finding Code = 10; only two acceptable records. Keller et al. (1979) discredit a specimen (now missing) that was reportedly collected at Miller on 4 September 1887. On 19 May 1980 a single bird appeared along the shoreline between Miller Beach and West Beach and was studied at close range by four observers (IAQ 59:130). A bird, believed to be molting from juvenile into first-winter plumage, was seen at the same location 15 September 1990 (AB 45:110).

SEMIPALMATED PLOVER (*Charadrius semipalmatus*)

Finding data
Finding Code = 2, in August. One or two are usually on the beaches at Michigan City Harbor and Miller Beach during the fall migration peak; also found on mudflats with other shorebirds where habitat is available.

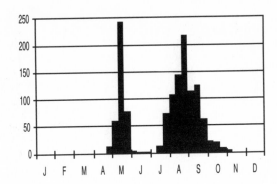

Peak counts
Spring:	49	13 May 1991	Gleason Park
Fall: (all)	26	28 Aug 1986	Gary sewage pond
Fall: (ad.)	18	11 Aug 1995	Miller Brach
Fall: (juv.)	23	23 Sep 1995	At two Dunes area ponds

Status
The Semipalmated Plover is a spring and fall transient through the Dunes. Migration data are:

	EARLIEST	ARRIVE	PEAK	DEPART	LATEST	N
Spring	27 Apr 63	7 May	15 May	25 May	19 Jun 96	85
Fall (all)	19 Jun 96	30 Jul	24 Aug	24 Sep	3 Nov 92	351
Fall (ad.)	24 Jul 96	27 Jul	12 Aug	24 Aug	24 Sep 93	39
Fall (juv.)	11 Aug 81	17 Aug	6 Sep	1 Oct	31 Oct 92	118

PIPING PLOVER (*Charadrius melodus*)

Finding data
Current Finding Code = 7, but this endangered species was far more common in former years. All recent records consist of migrants along Lake Michigan beaches, primarily at Michigan City Harbor and Miller Beach. The peak count of 10 on 22 April 1917 included breeding birds.

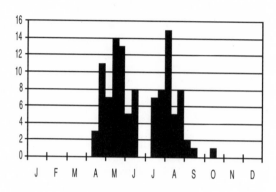

Peak counts
Spring:	10	22 Apr 1917	Lakefront
Fall:	6	24 Aug 1919	West Beach

The peak modern count consisted of an adult and juvenile at Miller Beach 24 August 1994.

Status
Today the Piping Plover is a transient through the Dunes; however, in the early 1900s it nested along Lake Michigan's beaches. Breeding records span the interval from 1897 through 1955. Undoubtedly this reclusive plover was gradually displaced as the Dunes became popular after the turn of the century. Eifrig (1918) suggested that this species suffered overrunning of its breeding grounds by "campers, bathers, dune prowlers, ecology classes and others." Migration data, based solely on post-1959 records, are:

	EARLIEST	ARRIVE	PEAK	DEPART	LATEST	N
Spring	26 Apr 97	- -	- -	- -	31 May 96	3
Fall	15 Jul 92	- -	8 Aug	- -	16 Oct 79	16

KILLDEER (*Charadrius vociferus*)

Finding data
Finding Code = 2, between March and October. This widespread plover appears throughout the region. Although it prefers drier areas, the Killdeer can almost always be found among gatherings of shorebirds. In early March migrants are seen regularly at the hawk-watches.

Peak counts
Spring:	120	14 Mar 1989	Johnson Beach hawk-watch
Fall:	163	7 Jul 1980	Gleason Park

Status
The Killdeer is a summer resident and transient; a few occasionally winter. The mean spring arrival is 7 March and the average fall departure is 24 October. Numbers peak in July when post-nesting wanderers gather before migration. Downy young were observed at Wolf Lake 23 May 1981.

FAMILY RECURVIROSTRIDAE: Stilts and Avocets

BLACK-NECKED STILT (*Himantopus mexicanus*)

Finding data
Finding Code = 10, only one record. Two were seen at Miller Beach 7 April 1995, where they landed briefly on the beach (AFN 49:258).

AMERICAN AVOCET (*Recurvirostra americana*)

Finding data
Finding Code = 6, during late summer, mid-July through mid-September; it is quite rare in spring. Most Avocets are seen on Lake Michigan beaches or flying along the lakefront. A majority of the records are from Michigan City Harbor and Miller Beach.

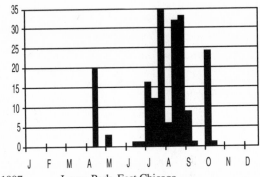

Peak counts

Spring:	19	26 Apr 1997	Jeorse Park, East Chicago
Fall:	20	20 Oct 1984	Miller Beach

Status
This stately wader is primarily a late summer transient through the Dunes; however, four spring records exist. Migration Data are:

	EARLIEST	ARRIVE	PEAK	DEPART	LATEST	N
Spring	23 Apr 90	- -	- -	- -	13 May 78	5
Fall	21 Jun 89	19 Jul	25 Aug	12 Oct	28 Oct 95	36

FAMILY SCOLOPACIDAE: Shorebirds

GREATER YELLOWLEGS (*Tringa melanoleuca*)

Finding data
Finding Code = 4, during the spring migration peak: late April and early May. The Greater Yellowlegs prefers larger, more open shorebird habitats. In recent years the cinder-fill in Hammond (141st and Columbia streets) has attracted this species. It also occurs in flooded fields.

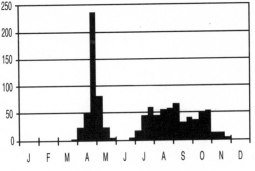

Peak counts

Spring:	30	24 Apr 1993	Near Chesterton
Fall: (all)	11	22 Sep 1984	George Lake
Fall: (ad.)	6	6 Aug 1986	Wolf Lake
Fall: (juv.)	10	28 Oct 1989	Michigan City Harbor

Status

The Greater Yellowlegs is a spring and fall transient; migration data are:

	EARLIEST	ARRIVE	PEAK	DEPART	LATEST	N
Spring	29 Mar 94	8 Apr	25 Apr	13 May	29 Jun 87	99
Fall (all)	26 Jun 86	17 Jul	31 Aug	26 Oct	25 Nov 88	256
Fall (ad.)	9 Jul 89	13 Jul	2 Aug	26 Aug	18 Sep 89	43
Fall (juv.)	7 Aug 93	23 Aug	26 Sep	28 Oct	25 Nov 88	51

Observations

Excluded from the Peak Count was a remarkable report from Stoddard's notes. Regarding this observation he states, "Near Dune Park (now the West Beach area) along the Grand Calumet are some wonderful snipe grounds and there are literally thousands of Snipe, Pectoral Sandpipers, Greater & Lesser Yellowlegs, and a few Solitary Sandpipers."

LESSER YELLOWLEGS (*Tringa flavipes*)

Finding data

Finding Code = 3, in late April-early May and mid-July through August. This species, the most numerous of the mudflat shorebirds, is found in flooded fields and shallow ponds. Numbers have declined in recent years, perhaps in response to limited habitat. If water levels are appropriate, Gleason Park and Roxana Pond invariably have this yellowlegs.

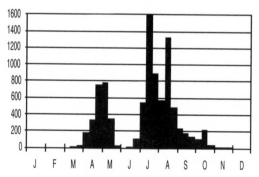

Peak counts

Spring:	208	7 May 1982	Roxana Pond
Fall: (all)	300	18 Jul 1920	Cowles Bog
Fall: (ad.)	274	12 Jul 1988	Roxana Pond
Fall: (juv.)	145	17 Oct 1984	Roxana Pond

Status

The Lesser Yellowlegs is a spring and fall transient through the Dunes. Migration data are:

	EARLIEST	ARRIVE	PEAK	DEPART	LATEST	N
Spring	14 Mar 86	7 Apr	29 Apr	14 May	30 May 78	188
Fall (all)	15 Jun 87	10 Jul	14 Aug	2 Oct	25 Nov 78	400
Fall (ad.)	15 Jun 87	11 Jul	31 Jul	22 Aug	21 Sep 89	94
Fall (juv.)	2 Aug 86	14 Aug	9 Sep	15 Oct	19 Nov 90	104

SOLITARY SANDPIPER (*Tringa solitaria*)

Finding data
Finding Code = 3, during the spring migration peak: late April-early May. This sandpiper shows a greater preference for marshes than most other shorebirds. When water levels are low migrants can usually be found at Gleason Park and Roxana Pond.

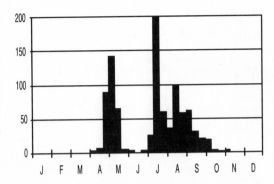

Peak counts
Spring:	16	27 Apr 1986	Near Chesterton
Fall:	100	18 Jul 1920	Cowles Bog

Status
This graceful wader is a spring and fall transient through the Dunes. Migration data are:

	EARLIEST	ARRIVE	PEAK	DEPART	LATEST	N
Spring	2 Apr 94	24 Apr	5 May	14 May	4 Jun 77	150
Fall	29 Jun 80	13 Jul	16 Aug	20 Sep	1 Nov 86	232

The Solitary Sandpiper lingers into early June and returns in late June; consequently, early ornithologists believed that it nested locally. Close examination of the Occurrence Histogram reveals a distinct break, albeit only of one week duration, between the two migrations.

Observations
The largest single party count of this species, which is anomalously large on the Occurrence Histogram, also comes from Stoddard's notes. On an expedition to Mineral Springs (now Cowles Bog area) Stoddard commented, "Noted about 100 Solitary Sandpipers, hundreds of L. Yellowlegs, (and) a few Killdeer." Solitary counts approaching this magnitude have not been recorded subsequently.

WILLET (*Catoptrophorus semipalmatus*)

Finding data

Finding Code = 6, during late summer. Virtually all records come from Lake Michigan, where birds are seen flying along the lakefront or resting on the beach. Flocks exceeding 20 individuals have been recorded eleven times, suggesting that migrants are quite gregarious. On several occasions individuals have been noted standing on the outer breakwater at Michigan City Harbor.

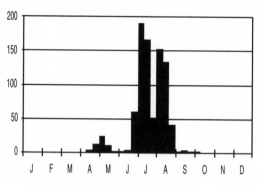

Peak counts

Spring:	6	25 Apr 1995	Michigan City Harbor
Fall:	67	9 Jul 1994	Michigan City Harbor

Status

Although a handful of spring records exist, the Willet is primarily a late summer transient through the Dunes. Migration data are:

	EARLIEST	ARRIVE	PEAK	DEPART	LATEST	N
Spring	15 Apr 54	- -	7 May	- -	7 Jun 83	27
Fall	15 Jun 96	30 Jun	26 Jul	20 Aug	2 Oct 88	124

SPOTTED SANDPIPER (*Actitis macularia*)

Finding data

Finding Code = 2, during the spring and fall migrations: late April through May and mid-July until September. Migrants are usually found in habitat attracting other shorebirds and especially along the breakwaters on Lake Michigan.

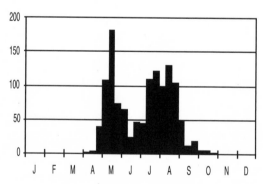

Peak counts

Spring:	52	8 May 1997	Lakefront
Fall:	15	8 Aug 1995	Miller Beach

Status

The Spotted Sandpiper is a summer resident and transient. June nests have been found in marram grass along the beaches. Migration data are:

	EARLIEST	ARRIVE	PEAK	DEPART	LATEST	N
Spring	6 Apr 86	28 Apr	12 May	2 Jun	- - -	155
Fall	- - -	3 Jul	10 Aug	8 Sep	25 Oct 89	307

UPLAND SANDPIPER (*Bartramia longicauda*)

Finding data

Finding Code = 4, at the Gary Airport nesting site. Limited habitat availability restricts the appearance of Upland Sandpipers in the Dunes Area. This species is only rarely noted in agricultural areas, but during the nesting season it is found regularly in grassy areas adjacent to the Gary Airport.

Peak counts

Spring:	9	30 Apr 1987	Gary Airport
Summer:	19	28 Jun 1986	Gary Airport (includes three young)
Fall:	3	15 Aug 1951	Northern Porter County

Status

The Upland Sandpiper is a transient and summer resident with a small nesting population at the Gary Airport. The earliest spring record is 15 April and the latest fall date is 17 August.

WHIMBREL (*Numenius phaeopus*)

Finding data

Finding Code = 8, in late summer and fall (July through September). Virtually all records come from Lake Michigan, where this large bird is usually seen flying along the shore. Occasionally birds are observed on the beach. Most records are from Michigan City Harbor.

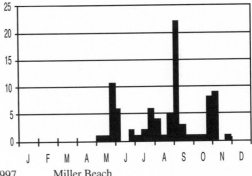

Peak counts

Spring:	8	25 May 1997	Miller Beach
Fall:	12	1 Sep 1952	Michigan City Harbor

Status

At present no distinctive migration pattern exists for the Whimbrel. Migration data are:

	EARLIEST	ARRIVE	PEAK	DEPART	LATEST	N
Spring	10 May 80	- -	- -	- -	5 Jun 83	8
Fall	29 Jun 96	21 Jul	3 Sep	1 Nov	22 Nov 87	37

Observations

In 1987 a juvenile, with a growth on its toe, was discovered at Miller Beach 4 October; the bird remained throughout October, gradually wandering eastward to West Beach where it was last seen 22 November.

HUDSONIAN GODWIT (*Limosa haemastica*)

Finding Code = 8, in May and late August through September. Most records come from large mudflat areas in northern Lake County, especially Roxana Pond and George Lake. A few have been observed flying along the lakefront.

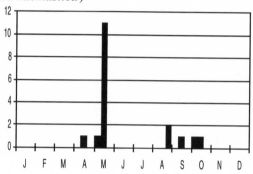

Peak counts

Spring:	8	11 May 1978	Roxana Pond
Fall:	1		All fall records are singletons

	EARLIEST	ARRIVE	PEAK	DEPART	LATEST	N
Spring	18 Apr 95	- -	- -	- -	15 May 95	5
Fall	23 Aug 84	- -	- -	- -	14 Oct 89	5

MARBLED GODWIT (*Limosa fedoa*)

Finding data

Finding Code = 8. A majority of records are in late June and July. Most reports are from the lakefront, especially Michigan City Harbor, but this species has also occurred at Gleason Park and Roxana Pond.

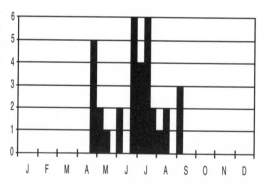

Peak counts

Spring:	1		All spring records consist of singletons
Fall:	3	6 July 1996	Michigan City Harbor

Status

The Marbled Godwit is a spring and fall transient through the Dunes. The earliest spring date is 24 April 1947 and the latest record is 9 September 1948. An exceptional year occurred in 1996 when ten birds were reported in the Dunes area.

RUDDY TURNSTONE (*Arenaria interpres*)

Finding data

Finding Code = 3, during migration peaks: late May and August through early September. The Turnstone prefers rocky beaches and breakwaters. Most records are in autumn, but more individuals occur in the spring, when large flocks occasionally appear in eastern Lake County. Whihala Beach is especially good in spring; fall birds usually occur on the piers at Michigan City Harbor.

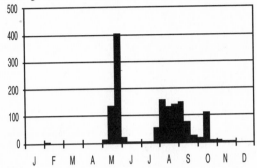

Peak counts

Spring:	70	22 May 1954	Wolf Lake
Fall: (all)	100	15 Oct 1976	Bailly Generating Station
Fall: (ad.)	53	4 Aug 1994	Miller Beach
Fall: (juv.)	8	17 Aug 1994	Miller Beach

Status

This colorful shorebird is primarily a transient, but birds have been reported throughout the summer and one winter record (2 February 1980) exists. Migration data are:

	EARLIEST	ARRIVE	PEAK	DEPART	LATEST	N
Spring	1 May 86	13 May	22 May	30 May	9 Jun 96	93
Fall (all)	18 Jun 86	2 Aug	26 Aug	29 Sep	28 Nov 85	292
Fall (ad.)	18 Jun 86	27 Jul	11 Aug	27 Aug	13 Sep 88	84
Fall (juv.)	14 Aug 94	20 Aug	6 Sep	29 Sep	2 Nov 85	74

RED KNOT (*Calidris canutus*)

Finding data

Finding Code = 7, from late August through early September. Knots are usually observed among the mixed shorebird flocks on Lake Michigan's beaches; most records come from Michigan City Harbor and Miller Beach. Virtually all fall birds are in the distinctive juvenile plumage, displaying silvery gray backs adorned with pearly scales.

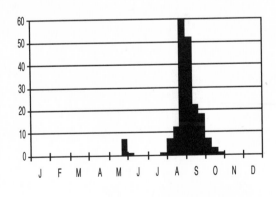

Peak counts

Spring:	3	23 May 1976	Michigan City Harbor
Fall:	21	21 Aug 1920	Beach between Gary & Dunes State Park

Status

This plump shorebird is a transient through the Dunes, being far more common in the fall. Migration data are:

	EARLIEST	ARRIVE	PEAK	DEPART	LATEST	N
Spring	21 May 86	- -	- -	- -	2 Jun 17	5
Fall	30 Jul 40	18 Aug	3 Sep	30 Sep	24 Oct 79	89

SANDERLING (*Calidris alba*)

Finding data

Finding Code = 1, from mid-August through early October. Darting flocks of these pale sandpipers abound on Lake Michigan beaches during the fall. This species is rarely found away from the lake. Sanderlings can usually be found on any beach; Michigan City Harbor and Miller Beach are especially good.

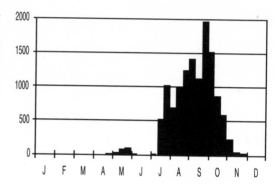

Peak counts

Spring:	50	27 May 1951	Northern Lake County
Fall: (all)	535	23 Sep 1980	West Beach
Fall: (ad.)	150	20 Jul 1996	Lakefront
Fall: (juv.)	210	10 Sep 1988	Miller Beach

Status

A few spring records exist; however, the Sanderling is primarily a fall transient. Sanderlings occasionally linger into winter; West (1954) reported a bird on the beach near Gary, 16 January 1954. Migration data are:

	EARLIEST	ARRIVE	PEAK	DEPART	LATEST	N
Spring	28 Apr 95	7 May	20 May	31 May	3 Jun 83	39
Fall (all)	28 Jun 94	27 Jul	7 Sep	23 Oct	23 Dec 80	733
Fall (ad.)	10 Jul 93	18 Jul	7 Aug	25 Aug	10 Sep 85	173
Fall (juv.)	26 Jul 96	24 Aug	20 Sep	23 Oct	12 Dec 90	217

Observations

Two fall Sanderlings displayed color leg-bands indicating that they were banded along the Pacific Coasts of Peru and Chile.

SEMIPALMATED SANDPIPER (*Calidris pusilla*)

Finding data
Finding Code = 2, in late August. This "peep" is seen most often on the sandy beaches of Lake Michigan's shores. A few are invariably present at Michigan City Harbor (often scurrying among fishermen on the jetty). The largest counts, however, come from inland mudflats.

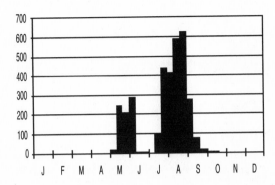

Peak counts
Spring:	110	1 Jun 1953	Northern Lake County
Fall: (all)	132	10 Aug 1996	Flooded field in Gary
Fall: (ad.)	86	26 Jul 1986	Gary sewage pond
Fall: (juv.)	83	14 Aug 1996	Flooded field in Gary

Status
The Semipalmated Sandpiper is a spring and fall transient through the Dunes. Migration data are:

	EARLIEST	ARRIVE	PEAK	DEPART	LATEST	N
Spring	3 May 58	12 May	22 May	4 Jun	21 Jun 86	77
Fall (all)	11 Jul 96	24 Jul	18 Aug	8 Sep	19 Oct 86	352
Fall (ad.)	11 Jul 96	17 Jul	29 Jul	12 Aug	5 Sep 96	73
Fall (juv.)	26 Jul 96	14 Aug	23 Aug	10 Sep	19 Oct 86	132

WESTERN SANDPIPER (*Calidris mauri*)

Finding data
Finding Code = 7. This species is surprisingly difficult to find in the Dunes area. It has been observed in a variety of habitats; recent records have come from Wolf Lake, Miller Beach, and Michigan City Harbor.

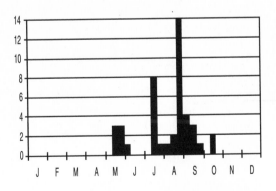

Peak counts
Spring:	2	11 May 1961	Gary
Fall:	6	25 Aug 1956	Michigan City Harbor
	6	18 Jul 1982	Hammond

Status

The Western Sandpiper is a transient through the Dunes, but its rarity renders exact migration dates uncertain. Migration data are:

	EARLIEST	ARRIVE	PEAK	DEPART	LATEST	N
Spring	11 May 61	- -	- -	- -	1 Jun 93	6
Fall	11 Jul 81	- -	25 Aug	- -	14 Oct 89	24

LEAST SANDPIPER (*Calidris minutilla*)

Finding data

Finding Code = 2, during the migrations: May and July through August. This minute sandpiper prefers the mudflats, but is also regularly seen along the lakefront. Almost every August at least one brightly colored and remarkably tame juvenile is found on the Michigan City jetty.

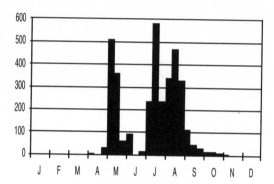

Peak counts

Spring:	198	7 May 1982	Roxana Pond
Fall: (all)	106	14 Aug 1996	Flooded field in Gary
Fall: (ad.)	74	12 Jul 1988	Roxana Pond
Fall: (juv.)	106	14 Aug 1996	Flooded field in Gary

Status

The Least Sandpiper is a spring and fall transient through the Dunes. Migration data are:

	EARLIEST	ARRIVE	PEAK	DEPART	LATEST	N
Spring	7 Apr 82	3 May	12 May	23 May	6 Jun 55	96
Fall (all)	25 Jun 88	11 Jul	9 Aug	7 Sep	3 Nov 91	367
Fall (ad.)	25 Jun 88	9 Jul	17 Jul	9 Aug	25 Aug 92	99
Fall (juv.)	15 Jul 95	2 Aug	20 Aug	18 Sep	30 Oct 89	140

WHITE-RUMPED SANDPIPER (*Calidris fuscicollis*)

Finding data
Finding Code = 7, during spring migration in the last half of May. A few recent records have occurred in early June. It is quite rare in fall. This species prefers mudflats, but is occasionally found on Lake Michigan beaches.

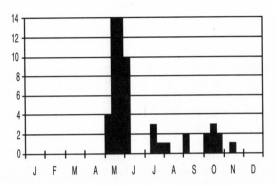

Peak counts
Spring:	4	4 Jun	1983	Michigan City Harbor
Fall:	2	20 Jul	1950	Wolf Lake

Status
The White-rumped Sandpiper is a transient through the Dunes. Fall records are rather dispersed with no obvious peak. Migration data are:

	EARLIEST	ARRIVE	PEAK	DEPART	LATEST	N
Spring	8 May 49	- -	23 May	- -	10 Jun 52	28
Fall	14 Jul 50	- -	- -	- -	23 Oct 82	11

BAIRD'S SANDPIPER (*Calidris bairdii*)

Finding data
Finding Code = 5, during the narrow migration window between mid-August and mid-September. Almost all recent records are from the beaches and breakwaters of Lake Michigan; it has been observed along the entire lakefront, but more reports are from Michigan City Harbor than any other single location.

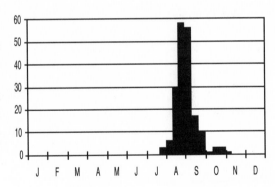

Peak counts
Spring:			There are no spring records
Fall:	20	2 Sep 1951	Wolf Lake

Status
Baird's Sandpiper is exclusively a fall transient through the Dunes. Most records involve birds in the "scaly-backed" juvenile plumage; indeed, only five adults have been identified. Migration data are:

	EARLIEST	ARRIVE	PEAK	DEPART	LATEST	N
Fall	25 Jul 95	15 Aug	29 Aug	21 Sep	4 Nov 78	98

Observations

This handsome sandpiper often associates with mixed flocks of Sanderlings and Semipalmated Sandpipers on the beach. It is detected in these flocks by its intermediate size and long-bodied appearance. The latter characteristic comes from the unusually long wings; they extend well beyond the tail (typically 2-3 cm), forming a scissors-like V-shape.

PECTORAL SANDPIPER (*Calidris melanotos*)

Finding data

Finding Code = 3, in late April and in early August. Occurrence is strongly related to habitat availability during the migration periods. Shows a strong habitat preference for mudflats or flooded fields. When water levels are right, Gleason Park and Roxana Pond are good locations.

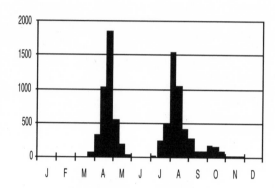

Peak counts

Spring:	810	22 Apr 1980	Gleason Park
Fall: (all)	700	8 Aug 1988	Roxana Pond
Fall: (ad.)	210	12 Aug 1988	Roxana Pond
Fall: (juv.)	44	9 Oct 1991	Gleason Park & Roxana Pond

Status

The Pectoral Sandpiper is a spring and fall transient through the Dunes. The bimodal character of the fall flight is evident on the histogram. Migration data are:

	EARLIEST	ARRIVE	PEAK	DEPART	LATEST	N
Spring	26 Mar 88	6 Apr	24 Apr	11 May	2 Jun 84	139
Fall (all)	9 Jul 80	19 Jul	22 Aug	12 Oct	22 Nov 91	294
Fall (ad.)	12 Jul 88	21 Jul	9 Aug	10 Sep	13 Oct 89	60
Fall (juv.)	20 Aug 87	10 Sep	9 Oct	31 Oct	16 Nov 91	38

PURPLE SANDPIPER (*Calidris maritima*)

Finding data

Finding Code = 7, during late November. Indeed, this species is often referred to by hopeful observers as the "Thanksgiving Day" bird. This sandpiper frequents breakwaters and jetties. Its habit of remaining motionless among the boulders, even when closely approached, renders it easily overlooked.

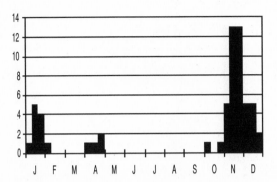

Peak counts

Spring:	2	24 Apr 1977	Michigan City Harbor
Fall:			Two were recorded on 5 occasions

Status

This maritime species is mainly a late fall and early winter visitant; however, records also exist for January, February, and April. Presumably, the April birds represent spring migrants, but the January peak shown on the histogram raises the possibility that some northbound birds pass through in mid-winter.

	EARLIEST	ARRIVE	PEAK	DEPART	LATEST	N
Spring	2 Apr 77	- -	- -	- -	22 Apr 77	3
Fall	9 Oct 77	2 Nov	23 Nov	12 Dec	6 Feb 54	55

DUNLIN (*Calidris alpina*)

Finding data

Finding Code = 3, during the fall migration in late October. Spring birds frequent mudflats and flooded fields, whereas fall migrants are commonly found on the beaches or in flocks migrating along the shoreline. Good locations are Michigan City Harbor and Miller Beach.

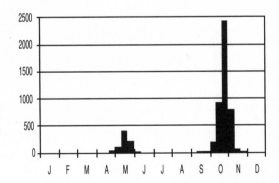

Peak counts

Spring:	93	15 May 1982	Roxana Pond
Fall:	753	23 Oct 1991	Miller Beach

Status

The "Red-backed Sandpiper," as it was formerly known, is a spring and fall transient through the Dunes. Spring birds are in the colorful "red-backed" plumage, but autumn migrants are in winter dress. Keller (1958) lists a summer record (4 July 1952) for Lake County. Migration data are:

	EARLIEST	ARRIVE	PEAK	DEPART	LATEST	N
Spring	23 Apr 82	2 May	17 May	28 May	13 Jun 52	119
Fall	5 Aug 51	8 Oct	22 Oct	5 Nov	4 Dec 82	214

CURLEW SANDPIPER (*Calidris ferruginea*)

Finding Code = 10; only one record. On 23 May 1980 a single bird, believed to be a female in breeding plumage, was observed and photographed at Wolf Lake (Brock, 1980). Photographs are on file at Earlham College.

STILT SANDPIPER (*Calidris himantopus*)

Finding data
Finding Code = 6, during the fall migration: mid-July through August. This sandpiper occurs almost exclusively on mudflats or in shallow pond habitat; consequently, almost all records come from the Lacustrine Plain portions of Lake County. Recent records are from Gleason Park and Roxana Pond. Migrating birds do not stop if suitable habitat is unavailable.

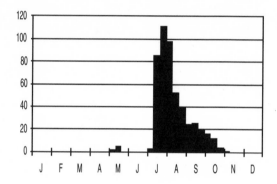

Peak counts
Spring:	3	19 May 1980	Gleason Park
Fall: (all)	41	25 Jul 1978	Gleason Park
Fall: (ad.)	13	11 Jul 1989	Roxana Pond
Fall: (juv.)	5	21 Aug 1994	Miller Beach

Status
The Stilt Sandpiper is primarily a fall transient; however, a few May records also exist. Migration data are:

	EARLIEST	ARRIVE	PEAK	DEPART	LATEST	N
Spring	7 May 82	- -	- -	- -	19 May 80	5
Fall (all)	9 Jul 89	17 Jul	12 Aug	6 Oct	2 Nov 36	107
Fall (ad.)	9 Jul 89	11 Jul	26 Jul	12 Aug	22 Aug 92	31
Fall (juv.)	10 Aug 96	- -	13 Sep	- -	6 Oct 90	19

BUFF-BREASTED SANDPIPER (*Tryngites subruficollis*)

Finding data
Finding Code = 7, from the last of August through late September. Limited habitat restricts the occurrence of this pert sandpiper; no reliable sites are known within the Dunes area. Most recent sightings have been on lakefront beaches at Miller Beach and Michigan City Harbor. It is a regular fall migrant at sod farms in southern Lake and LaPorte Counties (outside the Calumet Region).

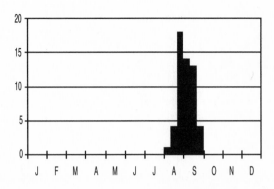

Peak counts
Spring:			There are no spring records
Fall:	10	18 Sep 1980	Gleason Park golf course

Status
The Buff-breasted Sandpiper is a fall transient through the Dunes. Migration data are:

	EARLIEST	ARRIVE	PEAK	DEPART	LATEST	N
Fall	7 Aug 95	- -	1 Sep	- -	21 Sep 91	29

Observations
A most unusual record of this prairie species occurred 26-27 August 1977 when a bird was observed feeding on insects along the top of the jetty at Michigan City Harbor. As is normally the case with shorebirds on the jetty, this displaced wanderer was remarkably tame, allowing observers to approach to within 2 meters.

RUFF (*Philomachus pugnax*)

Finding data
Finding Code = 10, only one record. On 8 and 9 August 1986, a female was seen at the large settling pond immediately north of the Gary Sanitary District (AB 41:96).

SHORT-BILLED DOWITCHER (*Limnodromus griseus*)

Finding data
Finding Code = 5, during the fall migration, July through August. This species prefers the mudflat or shallow pond habitat. In recent years it has become more difficult to find. If water levels are appropriate Short-billeds regularly occur at Roxana Pond and Gleason Park.

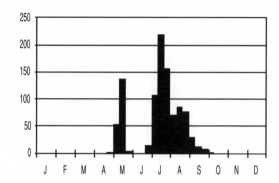

Peak counts
Spring:	30	12 May 1986	Chesterton
Fall: (all)	81	17 Jul 1978	Gleason Park
Fall: (ad.)	34	10 Jul 1982	Roxana Pond
Fall: (juv.)	24	22 Aug 1981	Gleason Park

Status
A few May records exist; however, the Short-billed Dowitcher is primarily a late summer and fall transient. Migration data are:

	EARLIEST	ARRIVE	PEAK	DEPART	LATEST	N
Spring	29 Apr 86	7 May	13 May	17 May	28 May 90	38
Fall (all)	26 Jun 89	10 Jul	1 Aug	5 Sep	6 Oct 90	172
Fall (ad.)	28 Jun 80	9 Jul	19 Jul	8 Aug	29 Aug 80	79
Fall (juv.)	30 Jul 87	8 Aug	22 Aug	14 Sep	24 Sep 83	60

LONG-BILLED DOWITCHER (*Limnodromus scolopaceus*)

Finding data
Finding Code = 8, in October; it is almost never reported in spring. In past years the only reliable location for this species has been Roxana Pond, but water-levels at that site have been too high in recent years; consequently, this species is extremely difficult to find in the Dunes area.

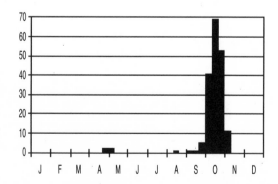

Peak counts
Spring:	2	1 May 1991	Gleason Park
Fall:	38	16 Oct 1982	Roxana Pond

102

Status

Primarily a fall transient; only three spring records exist. Summer records are suspect. Smith (1950) reports a specimen taken at Lake George on 17 July 1936. The skin is now at the National Museum of Natural History. After recently examining this specimen, Dr. Ralph Browning (pers. comm.) indicated: "Although identified by Oberholzer 193? and R. C. Laybourne in 1972 I cannot agree and have determined the specimen to be a representative of hendersoni" (the inland race of the Short-billed Dowitcher). Thus, it is unclear that any July Long-billed Dowitcher records exist. Migration data are:

	EARLIEST	ARRIVE	PEAK	DEPART	LATEST	N
Spring	23 Apr 82	- -	- -	- -	1 May 91	3
Fall	17 Aug 74	- -	14 Oct	- -	3 Nov 90	24

Observations

Long-billed Dowitchers passing through the Dunes in late fall do not display breeding plumage. In contrast to the adult Short-billed Dowitchers observed in July and August, adult Long-billed Dowitchers have already taken on their somber winter plumage. Birds in juvenile plumage are noted with the winter adults.

COMMON SNIPE (*Gallinago gallinago*)

Finding data

Finding Code = 3, during the spring flight in April. Snipes prefers wet meadows or mudflats with peripheral vegetation and are often observed at Gleason Park and Roxana Pond. In spring large numbers often congregate at choice feeding locations.

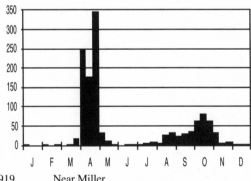

Peak counts

Spring:	100	27 Apr 1919	Near Miller
Fall:	15	12 Aug 1978	Gleason Park

Status

The Common Snipe, a species recorded every month, is primarily a transient through the Dunes. A summer record of 20 June 1978 was made at Gleason Park. Much confusion exists regarding current nesting patterns of this species. Spring birds are often observed giving their winnowing display flight and there are a few summer records; however, no firm evidence of breeding has been brought forth. A few have wintered and Butler (1898) reports breeding in Lake County. Migration data are:

	EARLIEST	ARRIVE	PEAK	DEPART	LATEST	N
Spring	- - -	3 Apr	19 Apr	3 May	22 May 77	136
Fall	20 Jun 78	19 Aug	9 Oct	1 Nov	- - -	159

AMERICAN WOODCOCK (*Scolopax minor*)

Finding data
Finding Code = 2, for those visiting display areas at twilight in late March through May; otherwise this species is much more difficult to locate. Display areas are widespread throughout the Dunes; the most accessible are along margins of the interdunal marshes on Mineral Springs Road, Kemil Road (east end of the State Park), and Beverly Drive.

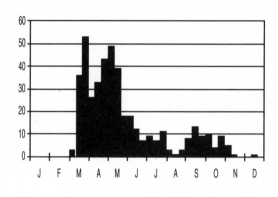

Peak counts
Spring:	7	7 May 1988	High Dunes
Fall:	4	11 Sep 1993	George Lake

Status
The Woodcock is a summer resident and transient through the Dunes. The "pinnt!" call of displaying birds can be heard soon after arrival in early March; nests have been located as early as 1 April (an active nest containing four eggs was found at Cowles Bog in 1975, Cutright, 1976). Most nesting records occur in late April and May, but nests and young have also been noted in June and early July.

	EARLIEST	ARRIVE	PEAK	DEPART	LATEST	N
Spring	5 Mar 83	17 Mar	25 Apr	31 May	- - -	180
Fall	- - -	4 Sep	28 Sep	31 Oct	20 Dec 74	56

WILSON'S PHALAROPE (*Phalaropus tricolor*)

Finding data
The current Finding Code = 7, in early May, but this species was more common in former years when it nested. Even as recent as the 1970s, this elegant wader was seen regularly on mudflats with other shorebirds. Numbers have decreased dramatically in the last two decades. Almost all records come from the Lacustrine Plain habitats of Lake County.

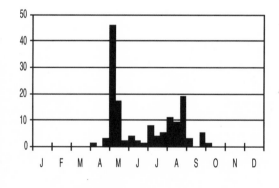

Peak counts
Spring:	28	9 May 1978	Roxana Pond (AB 32:1014)
Fall:	10	24 Aug 1977	Roxana Pond

Status
Currently this phalarope is a transient through the Dunes; however, migration data are somewhat obscured by records of former summer residents. Boyd (unpub. notes) reported nesting at Wolf Lake (5 July 1924) and Smith (1950) found nests at Lake George as follows: 30 May 1936 (4 eggs); 5 June 1936 (4 eggs); and 5 June 1937 (4 eggs). Bognar (1951) extends nesting records at the latter site through 1941, which constitutes the last known nesting date. During the fall flight, the earliest juvenile record is 12 July 1988 and the latest adult is 17 August 1987. Migration data are:

	EARLIEST	ARRIVE	PEAK	DEPART	LATEST	N
Spring	7 Apr 95	- -	9 May	- -	22 Jun 78	26
Fall	11 Jul 80	21 Jul	19 Aug	24 Sep	3 Oct 84	35

RED-NECKED PHALAROPE (*Phalaropus lobatus*)

Finding data
Finding Code = 8, in August and September. This species, which is the rarest phalarope in the Dunes area, has not been recorded in more than a decade. The most recent records were at Gary Sanitary Landfill, Gleason Park, and Roxana Pond. All records consist of single birds.

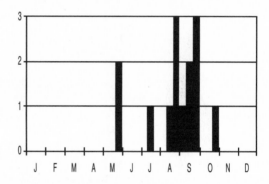

Peak counts

Spring:	all records consist of singletons
Fall:	all records consist of singletons

Status
The "Northern Phalarope," as it was formerly known, is a late summer and fall transient through the Dunes; however, one spring record (30 May 1950) exists. The October record (IAQ 41:65) follows the next latest record by more than a month. Migration data are:

	EARLIEST	ARRIVE	PEAK	DEPART	LATEST	N
Spring	23 May 86	- -	- -	- -	30 May 50	2
Fall	15 Jul 82	- -	1 Sep	- -	28 Oct 62	11

RED PHALAROPE (*Phalaropus fulicaria*)

Finding data
Finding Code = 7, during the fall peak: late October through mid-November. This pelagic shorebird is observed on Lake Michigan, mainly at Michigan City Harbor where it is usually seen swimming buoyantly in the harbor. Birds occasionally land on the beach and feed in debris piles at the water's edge.

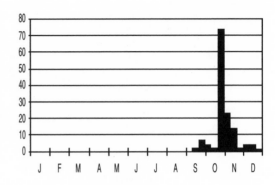

Peak counts
Spring:			No spring records
Fall:	25	28 Oct 1959	Along the Indiana lakefront

Status
The Red Phalarope is a late fall transient through the Dunes. Migration data are:

	EARLIEST	ARRIVE	PEAK	DEPART	LATEST	N
Fall	18 Sep 54	26 Sep	28 Oct	8 Dec	27 Dec 53	41

Observations
In 1959, what can only be described as a major Red Phalarope invasion occurred in the Dunes. During that year eight records, involving 68 individuals (almost half of all recorded birds), were observed along Indiana's lakefront.

SUBFAMILY STERCORARIINAE: Jaegers

For many birders the most salient characteristic of the Dunes Area birdlife is the fall jaeger flight. More than a dozen of these pelagic marauders are reported annually along the Indiana lakefront. Accordingly, following every autumn storm, birders gather at lake-watch sites in hopes of seeing these maritime birds. However, the regular fall passage of jaegers through southern Lake Michigan was not discovered until the mid-twentieth century.

The first published account of a jaeger on southern Lake Michigan described an adult Pomarine seen near the Illinois-Indiana state line October 9, 1876 (Nelson, 1876). In that era it was hypothesized that Pomarine Jaegers might winter on Lake Michigan. Six decades later Ford, Sandborn, and Coursen (1934) listed specimens of the other two species and, most interestingly, deemed the Long-tailed the most common jaeger in the Chicago Region. In 1956, Ford published a substantial list of Parasitic Jaeger records, thereby establishing that species as the most common jaeger on Lake Michigan.

The following footnote, attributed to Charles T. Clark, was appended to Ford's Parasitic Jaeger summary, "Intensive field work in recent years has shown that jaegers–species unknown– are uncommon, but regular fall migrants between Michigan City and Miller, Ind..." This comment is the first published acknowledgment that a regular jaeger flight occurs on Lake Michigan. It was also a prolog for the astonishingly large flights that occurred in the mid 1950's. The maximum annual count during that remarkable decade consisted of 76 birds seen in 1957. The latter total includes the all-time single day record of 61 birds, observed by Raymond Grow. Of the identified birds, the Parasitic is most commonly reported, but many jaegers are unidentified.

As suggested by Ford (1956), the Parasitic is still widely believed to be Lake Michigan's most common jaeger. This conclusion, however, is based on limited sampling. A typical sighting consists of a blackish appearing juvenile seen at more than 200 meters; the view is often brief and made in dim light while the observer is buffeted by strong wind. As a result, about three-fourths of the jaegers are not identified. The large number of unidentified birds obscures the exact ratio of the three species; however, based on those identified, about 75% are Parasitic, 17% are Pomarine, and 8% are Long-tailed. A majority of the jaegers, perhaps as many as 90%, are juveniles, which contributes to the great number of unidentified birds, as juvenile jaegers are notoriously difficult to identify. Jaeger numbers through 1996 are as follows:

Unidentified jaeger	400
Parasitic Jaeger	104
Pomarine Jaeger	23
Long-tailed Jaeger	11
Total	538

Unfortunately, the large number of unidentified birds obscures the true ratios of the three jaeger species. Many of the older records were simply reported as "jaegers," and others were routinely called Parasitics based on the assumption that most Lake Michigan jaegers were indeed that species.

In view of the identification problem with these maritime wanderers, a discussion of jaegers in general, including all records of both identified and unidentified birds, provides the most reliable information base.

Composite Jaeger Records

Finding data
The current Finding Code = 6. The primary flight period occurs between mid-September and mid-November. October is the traditional "jaeger month" in the Dunes. Virtually all birds are observed flying over Lake Michigan; very rarely a bird is noted swimming on the lake or standing on the beach. Jaegers are reported from many points along the lakeshore, but most records come from Miller Beach and Michigan City Harbor. Flying birds often glide low through wave troughs, rendering them remarkably difficult to see; others are noted soaring high above the water, and a few have even been seen flying over the beach or parking lots. Most jaegers are reported on raw autumn days, when northerly winds sweep in from the lake. These conditions normally prevail immediately after passage of a strong cold front. Despite the many observations on the bitter "jaeger days," a fair number of

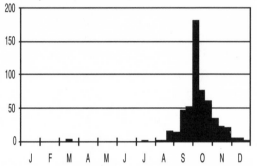

sightings are also made on warm sunny days when winds are calm. The standard jaeger-watching technique consists of establishing a vigil, immediately after passage of a cold front, and simply watching the lake. In recent years the single most productive site is adjacent to the Marquette Park concession stand at Miller Beach. In addition to modest elevation for better viewing, the building shields birders from the strong north winds.

Peak counts
Spring:	1		Only two spring records, both singletons
Fall:	61	6 Oct 1957	Miller Beach

Status
Jaegers are late summer, fall, and early winter transients through the Indiana lakefront. Two spring records, 17 March 1923 (Mumford, pers. comm.) and 11 March 1953 (Reuter-skiold notes), both along the Porter County beach, are quite unusual. The 1950s were the golden era for jaeger watching on Lake Michigan. In those days scores of jaegers were recorded on a single day. For example, an incredible 61 birds were observed 6 October 1957 at Miller Beach (AFN 12:35) and 34 were logged at the same location 7 October 1956 (AFN 11:30). Composite migration data for all jaeger records are:

	EARLIEST	ARRIVE	PEAK	DEPART	LATEST		N
Fall (all)	16 Jul 92	12 Sep	10 Oct	10 Nov	21 Dec	40	220
Fall (ad.)	7 Sep 96	- -	24 Sep	- -	11 Nov	84	14
Fall (juv.)	10 Sep 93	- -	18 Oct	- -	10 Dec	94	29

Generally, Long-taileds migrate earliest and Pomarines latest. As suggested by the Migration Envelope, adults precede the juveniles.

Landing (1966), noting that most jaegers are observed flying westward along the lakeshore and that there are few reports from Illinois and Wisconsin, concluded that these pelagic interlopers migrate down the eastern side of Lake Michigan. Presumably after reaching its southern tip (near Miller Beach) they fly overland to the Gulf of Mexico. Although this scenario may be correct, few birds have actually been observed flying inland; instead most simply pass quickly from view while maintaining a heading parallel to the lakefront. The total number of jaegers reported annually is tabulated below (no reports exist for omitted years).

ANNUAL JAEGER COUNTS ALONG THE INDIANA LAKEFRONT

1876	1	1950	3	1959	11	1983	3	1985	15	1993	21
1915	1	1952	18	1972	1	1976	1	1986	8	1994	26
1917	2	1953	20	1960	8	1977	6	1987	5	1995	14
1918	2	1954	14	1961	6	1978	8	1988	4	1996	43
1923	1	1955	44	1965	25	1979	6	1989	15		
1929	1	1956	45	1966	1	1980	1	1990	18		
1940	1	1957	76	1970	1	1981	1	1991	16		
1948	8	1958	7	1971	1	1984	10	1992	19		

Pomarine Jaeger (*Stercorarius pomarinus*)

Finding data
Finding Code = 8. Pomarine records span virtually the entire autumn migration period, but most occur in November and December. The 8 August 1981 bird was an adult (or near adult) light-morph individual. There is no evidence the juvenile Pomarines appear before the third week of September.

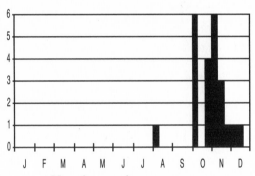

Peak counts
Spring:			No spring records
Fall:	5	9 Oct 1965	Michigan City Harbor

Status
The Pomarine was the first jaeger to be reported in Indiana (Butler, 1898, gives an observation on 9 October 1876, near the Illinois state line). On 10 November 1987 a juvenile Pomarine spent the day perched on the sand at Miller Beach. The bird was also present the following morning, allowing photographers to obtain physical evidence of this species occurrence in the state. Fall migration data are:

	EARLIEST	ARRIVE		PEAK	DEPART		LATEST		N
Fall	8 Aug 81	-	-	2 Nov	-	-	15 Dec	79	17

PARASITIC JAEGER (*Stercorarius parasiticus*)

Finding data

Based on records from the last decade the Finding Code = 6. This is generally believed to be the most common jaeger on Lake Michigan. The latest adult Parasitic was recorded 11 November and the earliest juvenile 13 September.

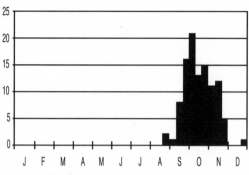

Peak counts

Spring:			No spring records
Fall:	11	8 Oct 1955	Miller Beach (AFN 10:28)

Status Migration data for the Parasitic Jaeger are:

	EARLIEST	ARRIVE	PEAK	DEPART	LATEST		N
Fall	31 Aug 94	17 Sep	14 Oct	13 Nov	21 Dec	40	70

LONG-TAILED JAEGER (*Stercorarius longicaudus*)

Finding data

Finding Code = 8. Between 1989 and 1996 intense observation at Miller Beach produced six Long-tailed Jaegers, suggesting that this species is more common than past records indicate. Of these three were adults, two were juveniles, and one was in second-year plumage.

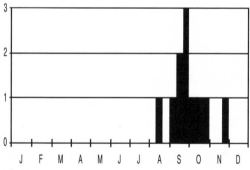

Peak counts

Spring:	No records
Fall:	All records consist of singletons

Status An adult was collected 20 August 1917; the specimen is in the Chicago Field Museum of Natural History. The 30 November bird, a juvenile, was also collected. Migration data are:

	EARLIEST	ARRIVE	PEAK	DEPART	LATEST		N
Fall	20 Aug 17	-	-	-	-	-	-	30 Nov	18	11

SUBFAMILY LARINAE: Gulls

Eighteen gull species have been reported in the Dunes. Large numbers of Herring and Ring-billed Gulls are observed throughout the year and Bonaparte's Gull is a regular migrant. The remaining species are winter visitors, irregular transients, or vagrants. The numbers of most gull species have increased dramatically over the past two decades. Total numbers and relative abundance rankings of Dunes Area gulls (Ring-billed and Herring Gull numbers are greatly under counted), through December 1996, are tabulated below :

NUMBERS AND ABUNDANCE RANK OF DUNES AREA GULLS

Species	No.	Rank	Species	No.	Rank
Laughing	96	9	Thayer's	198	7
Franklin's	336	5	Iceland	58	12
Little	83	10	Lesser Black-backed	80	11
Black-headed	3	16	Slaty-backed	1	17
Bonaparte's	76K	3	Kelp	1	18
Mew	5	15	Glaucous	345	4
Ring-billed	243K	1	Great Black-backed	269	6
California	6	14	Sabine's	40	13
Herring	204K	2	Black-leg Kittiwake	104	8
K = thousands					

LAUGHING GULL (*Larus atricilla*)

Finding data
Finding Code = 6, mid-May through June. All observations are from Lake Michigan; 80 percent are from Michigan City Harbor. This species is usually noted among the mixed gull flocks resting on the beaches or breakwaters. Stragglers linger into late November.

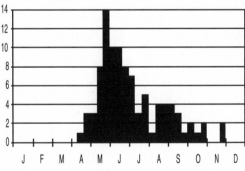

Peak counts
Spring:	4	13 May 1996	Michigan City Harbor
Fall:	2	15 Sep 1984	Michigan City Harbor

Status
The Laughing Gull is primarily a spring transient that lingers through the summer and fall. A majority of the spring birds are breeding-plumed adults. Six juveniles have been identified, all between 15 August and 9 October. Migration data are:

	EARLIEST	ARRIVE	PEAK	DEPART	LATEST	N
Spring	19 Apr 96	12 May	7 Jun	14 Jul	- - -	62
Fall	- - -	- - -	6 Sep	- -	28 Nov 95	22

FRANKLIN'S GULL (*Larus pipixcan*)

Finding data
Finding Code = 6, from late September through mid-November. Most records come from Michigan City Harbor or other points along the lakefront. This small Larid occasionally occurs in migrating flocks, but more often one or two are seen on the beach among the more common gulls.

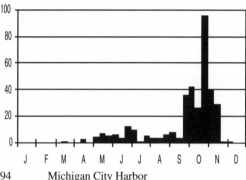

Peak counts
Spring:	5	13 May 1994	Michigan City Harbor
Fall:	54	24 Oct 1994	Miller Beach

Status
The Occurrence Histogram suggests that Franklin's Gull is a visitor in the Dunes during all seasons except winter. Reported plumages include first-year and adult. Of the aged birds, 72 were adults and 15 were immatures. Considerably more birds are reported in fall than at other seasons.

	EARLIEST	ARRIVE	PEAK	DEPART	LATEST	N
Spring	14 Mar 64	- -	19 May	- -	- - -	18
Fall	- - -	28 Sep	18 Oct	3 Nov	8 Dec 56	106

LITTLE GULL (*Larus minutus*)

Finding data
Finding code = 7, in late October and November; it is quite rare in spring. All records come from Lake Michigan, primarily from Michigan City Harbor. The Little Gull is most often seen among the flocks of Bonaparte's Gulls migrating along the lakefront.

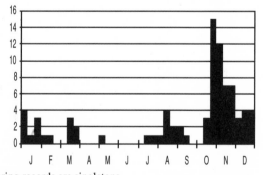

Peak counts
Spring:	All spring records are singletons
Fall:	Two birds have been recorded on three occasions

Status
Apparently the first Dunes record of this European gull was 24 January 1953; a specimen was obtained 22 December 1955 at Michigan City Harbor. Throughout the 1950s this small gull was a regular winter resident; it was recorded annually from 1953 through 1961. The current pattern is somewhat different. The last winter record was in 1987; most Little Gulls are now seen in late fall. The Histogram also reveals a small late summer flight that peaks in

mid-August. Of the reports that include plumage descriptions, 31 were adults and 14 were immatures. Migration data are:

	EARLIEST	ARRIVE	PEAK	DEPART	LATEST	N
Spring	- - -	- -	- -	- -	5 May 81	6
Fall	5 Aug 78	23 Aug	3 Nov	12 Dec	- - -	63

BLACK-HEADED GULL (*Larus ridibundus*)

Finding Code = 9, three records. Indiana's first record of this species, an adult in winter plumage, was discovered 20 August 1977 at Michigan City Harbor (Brock, Grube, and Hopkins, 1978).   At the same location an immature was seen on the beach 16 August 1980 (AB 35:189), and an adult flew past with a flock of Bonaparte's Gulls 20 April 1996 (AFN 50:288).

BONAPARTE'S GULL (*Larus philadelphia*)

Finding data
Finding Code = 3, during the migrations in April and November. A smaller migratory pulse is also evident in August. This graceful gull is most often observed along Lake Michigan's shores, but also occurs on inland ponds and lakes.

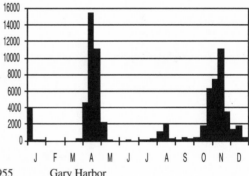

Peak counts
Spring:	8000	26 Apr 1955	Gary Harbor
Fall:	5000	14 Nov 1995	Michigan City Harbor

Status
This buoyant flyer has been recorded every month; however, it is primarily a spring and fall transient. Interestingly, the fall flight shows two peaks; these are designated Fall (1) and (2) in the migration envelope. In former years large numbers lingered into mid-winter. Migration data are:

	EARLIEST	ARRIVE	PEAK	DEPART	LATEST	N
Spring	- - -	2 Apr	19 Apr	5 May	- - -	173
Fall (1)	- - -	18 Jul	12 Aug	9 Sep	- - -	195
Fall (2)	- - -	11 Oct	4 Nov	1 Dec	- - -	380

MEW GULL (*Larus canus*)
Finding Code = 9, only five records; however, the rate of recent sightings suggests this species may be more common that previously believed.   The first Mew Gull ever found in Indiana was discovered at Michigan City Harbor 24 November 1987 (Brock and Jackson, 1988).   All five birds were adults observed at Michigan City Harbor. Dates of the subsequent sightings are: 14 January 1995, 29 March 1996, 14 December 1996, and 31 December 1996.

Mew Gulls associate with the extremely similar appearing Ring-billed Gulls; they are usually detected (with difficulty) by their slightly darker mantles and larger tertial crescents.

RING-BILLED GULL (*Larus delawarensis*)

Finding data
Finding Code = 1, except in late winter. Large numbers congregate at the ports and harbors along Lake Michigan. This species also frequents parks, garbage dumps, parking lots, and athletic fields. Ring-billeds are the most common gull during the summer months, when adults in full breeding plumage are often noted.

Peak counts
Spring:	4000	18 Mar 1989	Gary Sanitary Landfill
Summer:	7000	27 Jun 1992	Indiana Dunes
Fall:	3000	18 Aug 1990	LaPorte County

Status
The Ring-billed Gull is a permanent resident, whose numbers are reduced in late winter. Indiana's first Ring-billed Gull nesting was recorded 10 June 1991 at the Inland Steel landfill (Brock, 1991).   Young birds of the year, in crisp juvenile plumage, appear in June.   Migration peaks are late March and late November.

CALIFORNIA GULL (*Larus californicus*)

Finding Code = 8, only six records. All involved adult birds seen at Michigan City Harbor; five were reported in November and one in December.   Specific dates are: 10 November 1983, 18 November 1992, 20 November 1993, 20 November 1994, 9 November 1996, and 21 December 1996.

HERRING GULL (*Larus argentatus*)

Finding data
Finding Code = 1, from October through March. Large numbers gather at local garbage dumps, especially the Gary and LaPorte County Landfills. Herring Gulls are most numerous during the fall migration in late November and early December. This species also enjoys resting on the breakwaters and piers along Lake Michigan. On extremely bitter winters Herring Gulls move southward out of the Dunes Area.

Peak counts
Spring:	5000	16 Mar 1996	Gary Sanitary & LaPorte Co. Landfills
Fall:	3000	30 Nov 1996	Gary Sanitary Landfill

Status
The "sea gull" is a permanent resident, which becomes less common during the summer months. Other than the nesting season, when breeding birds are usually absent, the Herring Gull is the most common gull in the Dunes. On 2 June

1985, two Herring Gull nests were discovered on the outer breakwater at the Port of Indiana, providing Indiana's first breeding record (Brock, 1987).

THAYER'S GULL *(Larus thayeri)*

Finding data
Finding Code = 5, from mid-November through the first week of January. Most records come from the landfills, but this species is also observed along the lakefront, especially at Michigan City Harbor. It is usually found among the winter Herring Gull flocks.

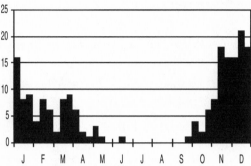

Peak counts

Spring:	2	21 Mar 1978	Gary Sanitary Landfill & Port of Indiana
Fall:	4	11 Nov 1989	Michigan City Harbor
Winter:	12	21 Dec 1996	Michigan City Harbor & LaPorte Landfill

Status
Thayer's Gull is a winter resident that occasionally lingers into spring; one summer record exists (20 June 1978). Of reports in which age was determined: 95 were adults; three were third-year; eleven were second-year; and 70 were first-year birds. Arrival and departure data are:

	EARLIEST	ARRIVE	PEAK	DEPART	LATEST	N
Winter	28 Sep 80	23 Oct	- -	7 Apr	17 May 85	170

ICELAND GULL *(Larus glaucoides)*

Finding data
Finding Code = 7. A slight majority of the records are clustered between late February and April; this is perhaps the best time to find this boreal species. It usually associates with the other large gulls; recent records have come from the Gary Sanitary Landfill and Michigan City Harbor.

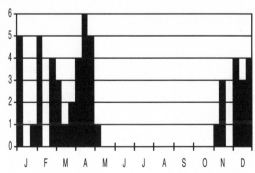

Peak counts

Spring:	3	1 May 1997	Michigan City Harbor
Fall:	1		All fall records are singletons.
Winter:	4	8 Jan 1997	LaPorte County Landfill.

Status

Many Dunes Area birds appear to be Kumlien's-Thayer's intergrades; consequently, identification difficulties cloud the status of the Iceland Gull. Current data suggest that more than three Thayer's are seen for every Iceland Gull. Virtually all of the adult birds show the gray Kumlien's type primaries. Forty-four records provided information on age: 23 adults; three third-year; five second-year; and 17 first-year birds. Arrival and departure data are:

	EARLIEST	ARRIVE	PEAK	DEPART	LATEST	N
Winter	5 Nov 89	18 Nov	- -	27 Apr	10 May 58	51

LESSER BLACK-BACKED GULL (*Larus fuscus*)

Finding data

Finding Code = 6. Reports of this species have increased dramatically over the past decade. It is most often seen among the landfill gull flocks, but also appears regularly along the lakefront. Records are more concentrated in late fall and winter, suggesting that this is the best time to find this species.

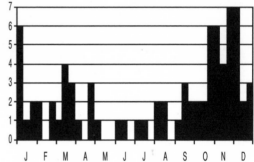

Peak counts

Spring:	2	17 Mar 1995	LaPorte County Landfill
Fall:	3	26 Oct 1996	Gary Sanitary Landfills
Winter:	2	12 Jan 1994	Gary Sanitary Landfill

Status

The Lesser Black-backed Gull has been reported every month but is most frequent in winter, when gulls concentrate at the landfills. Of the birds aged: 51 were adults; six were third-year; eleven were second-year; and nine were first-year birds. The low number of first-year birds suggests that observers are over looking birds in this plumage.

Observations

The first Lesser Black-backed Gull reported in Indiana was observed at Michigan City Harbor 2 October 1948. Lela Campbell (unpub. letter) explains that four observers examined the bird as it stood on the beach some 10 meters away, noting the black back, the small stature, and the yellow legs and feet.

KELP GULL (*Larus dominicanus*)

Finding Code = 10, only one record. A third-winter bird, believed to be this southern hemisphere species, was seen by two dozen observers at the Migrant Trap 19 October 1996; photographs and video were obtained. This bird was seen again at this location the following morning and 26 October at the Gary Dump. This constitutes Indiana's first record of this southern hemisphere gull.

SLATY-BACKED GULL (*Larus schistisagus*)

Finding Code = 10, only one record. Indiana's first Slaty-backed Gull, a winter-plumed adult, was seen by six observers at Michigan City Harbor 13 March 1993 (Brock, 1994a). The bird was perched on floating ice with 2000 Herring Gulls.

GLAUCOUS GULL (*Larus hyperboreus*)

Finding data
Finding Code = 4, mid-November through February. This large gull is most easily found with the Herring Gull flocks at garbage dumps. Most records are from the Gary and LaPorte County Landfills, but Glaucous Gulls also occur regularly along the lakefront.

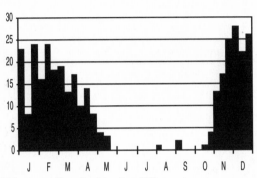

Peak counts
Spring:	5	1 Mar 1980	Gary Sanitary Landfill
Fall:	4	26 Nov 1996	LaPorte County Landfill
Winter:	7	2 Jan 1994	Gary Sanitary Landfill & Migrant Trap

Status
The "burgomaster," as this species was called in former years, is a winter resident of the Dunes. The anomalous summer record (8 August 1897) was a second-year bird collected on the beach at Millers, Indiana (Woodruff, 1907). Records containing age information are summarized as follows: adult, 58; third-year, 13; second-year, 52; and first-year, 178. Arrival and departure data are:

	EARLIEST	ARRIVE	PEAK		DEPART	LATEST		N
Winter	5 Aug 97	8 Nov	-	-	13 Apr	13 May	95	272

GREAT BLACK-BACKED GULL (*Larus marinus*)

Finding data
Finding Code = 5, in January, February, and March. Reports span the entire year, but are concentrated in late winter and early spring. Most records are from Michigan City Harbor and the Port of Indiana. Although this species occasionally appears at landfills, it apparently prefers the lakefront.

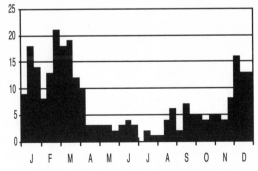

Peak counts

Spring:	5	17 Mar 1994	Port of Indiana
Fall:	2	20 Sep 1993	Michigan City Harbor
Winter:	7	27 Feb 1994	Port of Indiana

Status

The Great Black-backed Gull was formerly a casual vagrant in the Dunes; however, in recent years the number of reports has increased. It has been reported annually since 1974. Of the birds aged: 84 were adults; 20 were third-year; 32 were second-year; and 99 were first-year.

BLACK-LEGGED KITTIWAKE (*Rissa tridactyla*)

Finding data

Finding Code = 6, in November. All observations were made along the lakefront. Most appear on the following north winds of November gales. Many recent reports consist of birds observed flying past Miller Beach. Almost all birds are in fresh juvenile plumage.

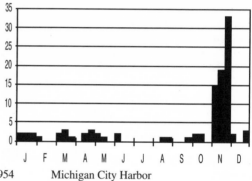

Peak counts

Spring:	2	6 Mar 1954	Michigan City Harbor
Fall:	11	21 Nov 1995	Miller Beach

Status

The Black-legged Kittiwake is a fall transient, but a few birds have wintered and two summer records exist. Of the birds aged, seven were adults, and 26 were listed as either first-year or immature. Fall migration data are:

	EARLIEST	ARRIVE	PEAK	DEPART	LATEST			N
Fall	15 Aug 53	15 Oct	16 Nov	30 Nov	-	-	-	47

Observations

On rare occasions non-breeding Kittiwakes linger along the lakefront. Examples include single birds seen 17 May 1951, 1 June 1996, and 9 Jun 1996. An unusually early Kittiwake was recorded at Wolf Lake 15 August 1953 (AFN 7:311).

SABINE'S GULL (*Xema sabini*)

Finding data
Finding Code = 8, from late September through mid-November. Most observations consist of immature birds (only two adults have been reported). All records are from Lake Michigan where this gull is usually observed flying along the lakeshore. It rarely lingers and seldom associates with other gulls. Many (perhaps most) observations are made on windy days.

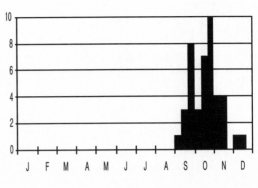

Peak counts
Spring:			No spring records
Fall:	4	23 Sep 1990	Miller Beach

Status
Sabine's Gull is a fall transient through the Dunes. Migration data are:

	EARLIEST	ARRIVE	PEAK	DEPART	LATEST	N
Fall	4 Sep 96	- -	18 Oct	- -	12 Dec 54	27

SUBFAMILY STERNINAE: Terns

Of the nine terns that have occurred in the Dunes, three species, the Common, Forster's, and Black Terns, have nested. The Caspian Tern is primarily a transient and the Gull-billed, Royal, Roseate, Least, and White-winged Terns are vagrants.

GULL-BILLED TERN (*Sterna nilotica*)

Finding data
Finding Code = 10, only one record. A single bird, in winter plumage, was seen with a large flock of migrating Common Terns at Miller Beach 31 August 1995 (AFN 50:63).

CASPIAN TERN (*Sterna caspia*)

Finding data
Finding Code = 2, in late April and during the "dog days" of summer in late August. Most records are from Lake Michigan where this large tern is frequently observed resting on beach and breakwaters with gulls. It is commonly found at Michigan City Harbor where 320 were counted 2 May 1995.

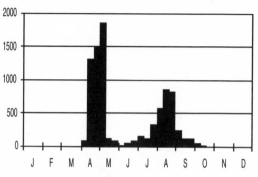

Peak counts
Spring:	495	2 May 1995	Miller Beach & Michigan City Harbor
Fall:	162	25 Aug 1989	Michigan City Harbor & Wolf Lake

Status
The Caspian Tern is a spring and fall transient; a few usually linger throughout the summer. Young birds, in the scaly-backed juvenile plumage, appear in late July; the earliest date is 21 July 1990. As this work was going to press a nesting colony of 137 adults, plus at least 64 eggs and 20 downy young, was discovered 24 June 1997, on the LTV Steel landfill. On 19 August 1960 Landing (unpub. letter) found a dead immature on the Michigan City beach that had been banded 5 July 1960 at Shoe Isle, Michigan.   Migration data are:

	EARLIEST	ARRIVE	PEAK	DEPART	LATEST	N
Spring	26 Mar 95	13 Apr	26 Apr	16 May	- - -	189
Fall	- - -	10 Jul	15 Aug	21 Sep	24 Oct 87	528

ROYAL TERN (*Sterna maxima*)

Finding data
Finding Code = 10; only one record. Indiana's first Royal Tern was discovered, and photographed, at Michigan City Harbor 29 June 1996 (AFN 50:956). This breeding-plumed bird was seen by a dozen observers.

ROSEATE TERN (*Sterna dougallii*)

Finding Code = 10; only one record. A specimen collected 14 August 1916 at Miller Beach proved to be this species (Stoddard, 1917a). The bird, which was standing along the water's edge, showed a "beautiful rosy tint on the breast" when examined in hand. This remains Indiana's only record of this tern.

COMMON TERN (*Sterna hirundo*)

Finding data

Finding Code = 3, during the fall flight in late August and September. Primarily observed along the shores of Lake Michigan; especially at Michigan City Harbor. This species is quite erratic in spring; many appear some years, but they are virtually absent in others.

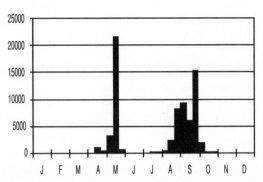

Peak counts

Spring:	10,000	20 May 1957	Gary Harbor (IAQ 35:63)
Fall:	7,930	24 Sep 1996	Michigan City Harbor

Status

Today the Common Tern is primarily a spring and fall transient; however, Smith (1950) reports that this species nested on four occasions near the Commonwealth Edison power plant at the Illinois state line. Three eggs were found 13 June 1934; five eggs on 23 June 1935; two eggs on 2 July 1935; and two eggs on 2 June 1936. Migrant juveniles, recognized by the black carpal bar on the upper wing coverts arrive in late July. Migration data are:

	EARLIEST	ARRIVE	PEAK	DEPART	LATEST	N
Spring	26 Mar 95	29 Apr	14 May	23 May	2 Jun 17	88
Fall	21 Jun 90	10 Aug	3 Sep	3 Oct	21 Nov 88	420

Observations

On the remarkably late dates of 16 and 17 October 1981, an adult Common Tern was observed feeding small fish to a juvenile at Michigan City Harbor. The youngster would perch on the outer breakwater, watching the adult fish in the harbor. As the adult approached with food, the young tern would beg and be fed by the adult.

ARCTIC TERN (*Sterna paradisaea*)

Finding Code = 10; only one record. An adult was discovered on the beach at Michigan City Harbor 15 July 1992. An excellent photograph of this bird was published (AB 46:1141)

FORSTER'S TERN (*Sterna forsteri*)

Finding data
Finding Code = 3, during the fall build-up; mid-August through mid-September. Forster's Terns are most often seen along the lakefront, but also appear regularly at inland ponds. Unlike, the Common Tern, it rarely appears in large migrating flocks.

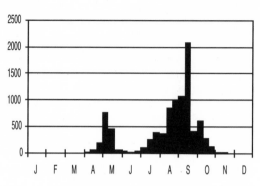

Peak counts
Spring:	220	18 May 1996	Michigan City Harbor
Fall:	1000	13 Sep 1956	Baileytown (Reuter-skiold notes)

Status
Today the Forster's Tern is a spring and fall transient, although a few birds usually summer. Birds of the year, showing a soft ginger-brown wash on the upper parts appear in late July. Landing (unpub. notes) reports an adult and immature standing at the nesting site in a Gary marsh on 21 July 1957. Keller et al. (1979) also give 1958 and 1962 nesting records for this area. Migration data are:

	EARLIEST	ARRIVE	PEAK	DEPART	LATEST	N
Spring	6 Apr 91	19 Apr	6 May	27 May	- - -	137
Fall	- - -	21 Jul	27 Aug	13 Oct	14 Nov 82	564

LEAST TERN (*Sterna antillarum*)

Finding Code = 9. The three known records are as follows: Smith (1936) gives an observation by A. F. Wilson: "A large flock of these birds observed the last week of August, 1933 at Waverly Beach, Porter Co."; on 5 August 1981, Henry West (pers. comm.) reported one at Michigan City Harbor; a first-year bird was at the latter site 11 July 1982 (IAQ 61:74-75), and an immature was seen at Miller Beach 5 October 1985 (IAQ 64:138). Large flocks of this species are uncharacteristic in the Midwest; consequently, the 1933 record must be viewed with skepticism.

WHITE-WINGED TERN (*Chlidonias leucopterus*)

Finding Code = 10; only one record. A single bird in nearly full breeding plumage was identified by five observers 19 July 1979 at Roxana Pond. Both the coal-black under-wing coverts and white rump were noted as the bird foraged with a small flock of Black Terns (Brock, 1983).

BLACK TERN (*Chlidonias niger*)

Finding data
Finding Code = 5, during the late summer migration on Lake Michigan; late August through mid-September. Migrants are sometimes seen flying offshore, often joining the Common Tern flocks. Occasionally, several individuals land on the boulders just inside the breakwater at Michigan City Harbor.

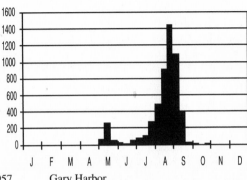

Peak counts

Spring:	100	20 May 1957	Gary Harbor
Fall:	650	5 Sep 1980	Michigan City Harbor

Status
The status of this species has changed drastically over the decades. In former years Black Terns were apparently common nesters in marshes and sloughs of the Lacustrine Plain. Gregory Jancich (pers. comm.), for example, reported several hundred nesting birds at George Lake during the early 1950s. Landing (unpub. notes) reported adults and young in Gary, 21 July 1957. During recent decades, however, industrial expansion and housing developments have encroached upon the nesting habitat of this species. If present trends continue, Black Terns will no longer be among Indiana's nesting avifauna. Migration data are:

	EARLIEST	ARRIVE	PEAK	DEPART	LATEST	N
Spring	27 Apr 57	5 May	18 May	2 Jun	- - -	65
Fall	- - -	10 Jul	19 Aug	13 Sep	27 Oct 54	189

BLACK SKIMMER (*Rynchops niger*)
Finding Code = 10; only one record. One was reported at Miller Beach 23 August 1913 (Mumford and Keller, 1984).

FAMILY ALCIDAE: Murrelets

MARBLED MURRELET (*Brachyramphus marmoratus*)

Finding Code = 10; only two records. On 2 December 1984 a winter plumed bird was discovered on Lake Michigan off Long Beach (Brock, 1986). Another bird flew past the Michigan City Harbor lighthouse 19 November 1994 (AFN 50:178).

ANCIENT MURRELET (*Synthliboramphus antiquus*)

Finding Code = 10; only one record. A dead bird was found on Miller Beach 8 November 1976. The skin is now in the Joseph Moore Museum at Earlham College (Mumford and Keller, 1984).

FAMILY COLUMBIDAE: Pigeons and Doves

ROCK DOVE (*Columba livia*)

Finding data
Finding Code = 1. Easily found near large bridges, grain elevators, refuse dumps, commercial buildings, or city parks. This introduced species is a permanent resident.

BAND-TAILED PIGEON (*Columbia fasciata*)

Finding Code = 10; only one record. During the interval 10-31 January 1981, a Band-tailed Pigeon regularly visited the feeder at a Beverly Shores residence, constituting Indiana's only record of this species (Brock and Cable, 1981).

MOURNING DOVE (*Zenaida macroura*)

Finding Code = 2, throughout the year. Widespread; frequently seen in agricultural areas and residential developments. The Mourning Dove is a permanent resident. Nesting records span the dates 22 April through 13 September.

PASSENGER PIGEON (*Ectopistes migratorius*)

Extinct. The last report of this formerly abundant species is given by Woodruff (1907) who states: "April 8, 1894, Mr. Edward J. Gekler saw a flock of about fifteen Wild Pigeons flying while in a woods near Liverpool, Indiana."

FAMILY CUCULIDAE: Cuckoos

BLACK-BILLED CUCKOO (*Coccyzus erythropthalmus*)

Finding Data
Finding Code = 5 from mid- to late May.   The populations of both cuckoos
show considerable annual
variation; in some years they
appear everywhere and in others
they are almost impossible to
find. The Black-billed usually
occurs along wood edges and in
scrubby second growth. Good
areas include margins of the
interdunal marsh at Beverly
Shores, Dunes State Park, and
Cowles Bog.

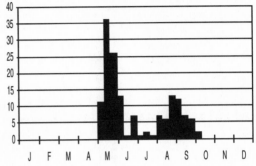

Peak counts
Spring:	3	16 May 1992	Northern Lake County
Fall:	2	2 Aug 1961	Baileytown

Status
The Black-billed Cuckoo is a transient and summer resident of the Dunes.
Smith (1936) found a nest containing five eggs at Lake George on 15 July
1935.   Migration data are:

	EARLIEST	ARRIVE	PEAK	DEPART	LATEST	N
Spring	3 May 55	10 May	20 May	5 Jun	- - -	78
Fall	- - -	1 Jul	28 Aug	24 Sep	10 Oct 16	61

YELLOW-BILLED CUCKOO (*Coccyzus americanus*)

Finding data
Finding Code = 4, during
migration peaks in late May and
mid-September, but numbers are
somewhat variable (see Black-
billed Cuckoo). Habitat similar
to former species, but prefers
slightly less wooded areas; it
frequents the interdunal marshes
of Dunes State Park and Beverly
Shores.   Migrants appear in
lakeside parks more often than
the Black-billed.

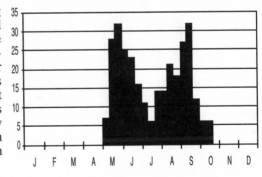

Peak counts
Spring:	4	15 May 1982	Dunes State Park
Fall:	5	16 Aug 1919	Miller Beach
Summer:	7	10 Jun 1979	Northern Porter County

Status

The Yellow-billed Cuckoo is a transient and summer resident. Stoddard (unpub. notes, 1919) found two nests near Cowles Bog 3 August 1919, and another, containing five "fresh eggs," near Miller on 16 August of the same year. Upon revisiting the latter nest a young bird "nearly ready to fly" was noted. Smith (1936) found young birds in a nest at Whiting on 9 July 1934. Migration data are:

	EARLIEST	ARRIVE	PEAK	DEPART	LATEST	N
Spring	4 May 86	11 May	25 May	13 Jun	- - -	83
Fall	- - -	1 Aug	5 Sep	26 Sep	20 Oct 57	136

GROOVE-BILLED ANI (*Crotophaga sulcirostris*)

Finding Code = 10; only one record. A single bird was observed on the Keammerer farm in northern Porter County, 16 and 18 November 1981 (Brock 1984). The bird was seen at close range (two meters) as it approached the feeding station immediately outside the house; grooves were noted on the bill.

ORDER STRIGIFORMES: Owls

Nine owl species are known to have occurred in the Dunes. Three of these, the Eastern Screech, Great Horned, and Barred, breed regularly. Evidence of nesting in previous years also exists for Barn, Long-eared, and Saw-whet Owls.

COMMON BARN-OWL (*Tyto alba*)

Finding Code = 9. During the 1950's Barn-Owls nested in the belfry of the old school house in Porter (now destroyed). Two eggs and a day-old bird were observed there 27 May 1951; three downy juveniles were noted 17 June of the same year. There are two recent records: one in the Migrant Trap 25 October 1993 and a dead bird found in Hammond 24 March 1994.

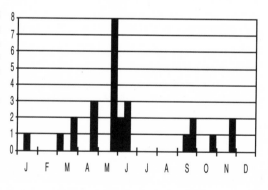

EASTERN SCREECH-OWL (*Otus asio*)

Finding Data

Finding Code = 4, (if taped calls are used at night). It seems to be most common in the scrubby oaks of the savannah complex and tangles in the interdunal marsh. The marsh in Beverly Shores, along Beverly Drive, is especially good. Birds occasionally respond to calls in mid-day (especially in August and September).

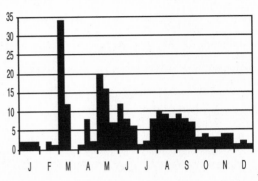

Peak counts

Spring:	23	8 Mar 1994	Beverly Shores (NBS census)
Fall:	3	7 Sep 1987	Beverly Shores

Status

The Screech-Owl is a permanent resident. Young birds have been found in Wood Duck nest boxes in May. The large early March "spike" on the Occurrence Histogram reflects census results of the National Biological Survey counts.

GREAT HORNED OWL (*Bubo virginianus*)

Finding data

Finding Code = 5. Widely distributed in wooded areas throughout the Dunes. Most easily detected in February and March when nesting birds are vocal. The deep, five-noted call is frequently heard just before dawn.

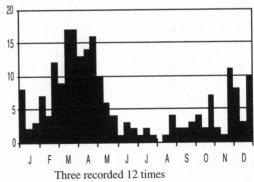

Peak counts

Spring:	3		Three recorded 12 times
Fall:	4	25 Nov 1916	Cowles Bog

Status

The Great Horned Owl is a permanent resident of the Dunes. More than nine nesting records, distributed throughout the region, exist. Eggs have been observed in late February and young birds by March. Stoddard (unpub. notes, 1914) found two nests near Miller on 15 March 1914; one was comprised of sticks about 12 meters up in a scrub pine and the other was about six meters high in a broken-off pine stub. Several nests have also been observed in recent years.

Observations

The dietary habits of this powerful predator are notorious. On 15 April 1914 Stoddard found a nest near Cowles Bog, which contained, in addition to a 3-week-old owlet, the remains of an American Crow and an American Bittern.

SNOWY OWL (*Nyctea scandiaca*)

Finding data

Finding Code = 7. November and December are the best months for this Arctic species; the average peak is 30 November. Snowy Owls are usually observed along the lakefront, often perched on piers or breakwaters. Many records have come from Michigan City Harbor, the Hammond Marina, and the Port of Indiana.

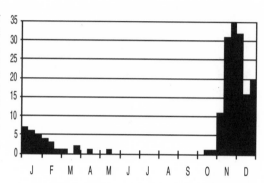

Peak counts

Spring:	1		All spring records are singletons
Fall:	5	30 Nov 1996	Lakefront

Status

This large owl is an occasional winter resident of the Dunes. Often several years pass with only meager reports, then birds may appear regularly for a few years. The April and May records consist of a lingering bird at Wolf Lake; it remained until 15 May 1950 (Mumford and Keller, 1984). In flight years most birds arrive in November, creating a distinct peak on the Occurrence Histogram. Interestingly, however, no similar peak exists for a return flight in the spring. Migration data are:

	EARLIEST	ARRIVE	PEAK		DEPART	LATEST		N
Winter	19 Oct 65	8 Nov	-	-	24 Mar	15 May	50	161

Observations

Dancey (1983) studied the feeding habits of a Snowy Owl at Michigan City Harbor and found, among other items, evidence that a Black Scoter, a Saw-whet Owl, and a snake were part of the owl's diet.

BURROWING OWL (*Athene cunicularia*)

Finding Code = 10; only two records. Indiana's first record of the Burrowing Owl was established 16 April 1924 when a specimen was collected near Dune Park, a station on the Chicago-South Shore located near the present site of the Burns Waterway (Hine, 1924). A second bird inhabited dry, grassy fields in Hammond from mid-June until 24 September 1980 (Brock, 1981).

BARRED OWL (*Strix varia*)

Finding data
Finding Code = 4, in late April and May when this species is especially vocal. The dense woods of Dunes State Park (east of Wilson Shelter) and the Little Calumet River floodplain are areas frequented by this species. It occasionally calls during the daylight hours. The eerie calls of young birds are heard in June.

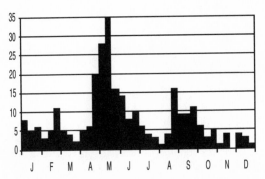

Peak counts
Spring:	15	8 May 1997	High Dunes (NBS census)
Fall:	3	12 Oct 1985	Dunes State Park

Status
The Barred Owl is a permanent resident of the Dunes. Stoddard (unpub. notes) found a nest, containing "newly hatched young," near Tremont on 25 April 1920. Two young owls were observed near Baileytown on 23 May 1954 (Reuter-skiold, unpub. notes) and a downy young, estimated to be less than a week old, was killed 30 April 1984 when strong winds destroyed a nest tree near Dunes State Park (IAQ 63:36). On 7 June 1994 a Barred Owl was observed catching downy Wood Duck young on the Little Calumet River floodplain (Brock, 1994b).

LONG-EARED OWL (*Asio otus*)

Finding data
Finding Code = 7; most reports are in late March and April. The Long-eared Owl was probably more common in former years when extensive tracts of pines were present. The most reliable location for this species is the jack pine grove at West Beach, where migrants occasionally land. In fall a few tardy migrants have been observed flying in off Lake Michigan at dawn.

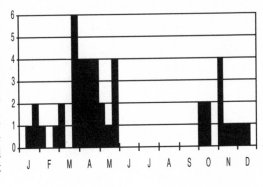

Peak counts
Spring:	5	26 Mar 1988	West Beach pinery
Fall:	2	5 Nov 1992	West Beach pinery

Status
The Long-eared Owl is a transient and winter visitant. Four birds, three young (about two weeks old) and an adult female, were collected by Stoddard (unpub. notes) 25 May 1914 near Cowles Bog. This species probably migrates through

the Dunes with regularity, but its secretive nature limits the number of observations.

	EARLIEST	ARRIVE	PEAK	DEPART	LATEST	N
Spring	- - -	- -	11 Apr	- -	12 May 62	20
Fall	5 Oct 85	- -	- -	- -	14 Dec 74	10

SHORT-EARED OWL (*Asio flammeus*)

Finding data

Finding Code = 6, during the migration peaks: late March through early April and late October through early November. In fall, migrants are often seen coming in off Lake Michigan. The largest single party count of five, was made at Michigan City Harbor during the Christmas Bird Count. All five owls were flying over the lake; one even landed briefly on the outer breakwater.

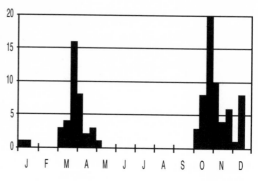

Peak counts

Spring:	4	25 Mar 1991	Mount Baldy
Fall:	4	5 Nov 1989	Michigan City Harbor & Miller Beach
Winter:	5	17 Dec 1977	Michigan City Harbor

Status

The Short-eared Owl is a transient and winter visitant. Eifrig (1918) suggested breeding: "It must nest, as adults were frequently seen during May and June, 1914, at Mineral Springs." Migration data are:

	EARLIEST	ARRIVE	PEAK	DEPART	LATEST	N
Spring	5 Mar 83	12 Mar	28 Mar	28 Apr	8 May 92	30
Fall	8 Oct 88	12 Oct	29 Oct	22 Nov	1 Dec 84	36

Observations

The perils of migration were clearly demonstrated on 12 March 1977 when observers at Michigan City Harbor noted a Short-eared Owl flying far out over the lake. A very strong south wind was blowing and the owl, apparently having overflown land's end, was fighting the wind trying to return to the shore. It alternately gained altitude (up to 10 meters) and then descended to within a meter of the wave crests. Despite these efforts the bird made virtually no progress toward land. Gradually the struggling owl drifted eastward along the shoreline, then back toward the west, without progressing toward the beach. After approximately an hour the bird encountered the lee of Mt. Baldy and in the dune's shelter finally reached shore, where it landed immediately. The owl was near exhaustion; it landed on the beach rather than flying another 30 meters where it could have found concealment in the tall dune grass. It surely would have perished in the lake had it not encountered Mt. Baldy's shelter.

NORTHERN SAW-WHET OWL (*Aegolius acadicus*)

Finding data
Finding Code = 8; a slight concentration of records occurs in March and April. There is no reliable location at which this small owl can be found; most are discovered by accident. No doubt this small owl is a regular migrant through the Dunes, but most pass through unseen.

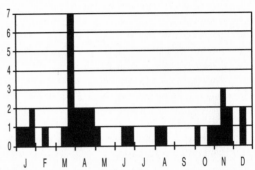

Peak counts

All observations consist of singletons

Status
The Saw-whet is so difficult to find that most birds surely slip through the Dunes undetected. Based on the limited records available it appears that this small owl is a transient and occasional winter resident.

Migration data are:

	EARLIEST	ARRIVE	PEAK	DEPART	LATEST	N
Spring	15 Feb 14	- -	30 Mar	- -	4 May 52	16
Fall	4 Oct 80	- -	- -	- -	20 Dec 86	12

The June records come from Butler (1898), who states, "Mr. B. T. Gault took a specimen in a grove at Sheffield (now part of Hammond)....June 14, 1889; another, June 28. They were in juvenile....stage. He thinks they undoubtedly were raised there." Both August records consist of calls (birds unseen); the first was 3 August 1954 near Baileytown and the second 19 August 1980 in Chesterton. In both cases the bird gave a series of "toots."

Observations
On the morning of 14 November 1981, a magnificent Snowy Owl was observed moving about Michigan City Harbor. A bit later a pile of owl feathers was discovered on the jetty, near the lighthouse. The feathers were collected and taken to Purdue University where they were identified as Saw-whet Owl feathers (T. Cable, pers. comm.). A fisherman mentioned that when he arrived the Snowy Owl was perched near the Saw-whet feathers. A few days later Dancey (1983) found a Snowy Owl pellet containing the tarsus of a Saw-whet Owl. These observations suggest that the following scenario may have unfolded at the harbor on that November morning: a Saw-whet Owl, migrating down the lake, was tardy in reaching the southern shore. Daylight broke as the little owl approached the southern shoreline. As the bird flew toward the nearest landfall (the lighthouse) it was sighted by the hungry Snowy Owl, who quickly dispatched the migrant, enjoying a leisurely meal on the jetty.

FAMILY CAPRIMULGIDAE: Goatsuckers

COMMON NIGHTHAWK (*Chordeiles minor*)

Finding data

Finding Code = 3, during evenings of the fall migration; late August and early September. On summer evenings its call can often be heard above the city lights, where it hawks flying insects. Migrating birds are observed throughout the region; autumn flights are often impressive.

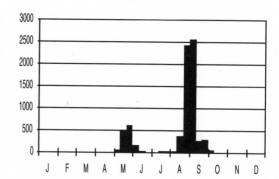

Peak counts

Spring:	286	25 May 1953	Baileytown
Fall:	450	30 Aug 1987	Northern Lake County

Status

The Common Nighthawk is a transient and summer resident of the Dunes. Migration data are:

	EARLIEST	ARRIVE	PEAK	DEPART	LATEST	N
Spring	2 May 88	11 May	20 May	4 Jun	- - -	149
Fall	- - -	20 Aug	1 Sep	19 Sep	11 Oct 91	159

CHUCK-WILL'S WIDOW (*Caprimulgus carolinensis*)

Finding data

The Finding Code currently = 4. In 1981 calling birds were discovered at Mount Baldy; subsequently, Chuck-will's-widows have been recorded annually at that location. Prior to discovery of the Mount Baldy population, this species was a vagrant in the Dunes area. On two occasions early May migrants have been discovered in dense vegetation at Michigan City NIPSCO.

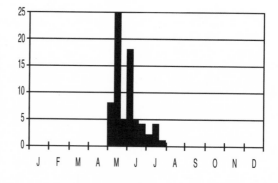

Peak counts

Spring:	3	5 May 1988	Mount Baldy
Summer:	7	7 Jun 1989	Mount Baldy and Beverly Shores
Fall:		No fall records.	

Status

This southern nightjar is a summer resident in the Mount Baldy area. Records prior to 1981 include: 1 June 1919 near Tremont (Brennan, 1923), 20 May 1934 at Whiting (Smith, 1936), and 14 May 1961 at Baileytown (AFN 15:415).

	EARLIEST	ARRIVE	PEAK	DEPART	LATEST	N
Summer	5 May 88	10 May	30 May	30 Jun	31 Jul 86	56

WHIP-POOR-WILL (*Caprimulgus vociferus*)

Finding data

Finding Code = 4, in spring when the birds actively call; late April through May. During this period calling birds can usually be heard at Beverly Shores, Cowles Bog, and the Inland Marsh. Most resident birds prefer the oak-savannah portion of the High Dunes. Fall migrants are occasionally flushed from tall weeds in the Migrant Trap.

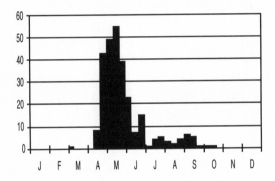

Peak counts

Spring:	9	10 May 1986	Beverly Shores
Fall:	2	5 Aug 1989	Baileytown

Status

The Whip-poor-will is a transient and summer resident of the Dunes; numbers are declining. Ford (1956) reports a nest containing a single egg 16 May 1920, in the Indiana Dunes. The fall flight is poorly defined. Migration data are (fall data from lakefront traps (*):

	EARLIEST	ARRIVE	PEAK	DEPART	LATEST	N
Spring	10 Mar 33	25 Apr	11 May	3 Jun	- - -	123
Fall*	29 Aug 81	- -	5 Sep	- -	12 Oct 85	22

ORDER APODIFORMES: Swifts and Hummingbirds

CHIMNEY SWIFT (*Chaetura pelagica*)

Finding data
Finding Code = 3, during the migrations in May and September. Summering birds are widespread throughout the Dunes and are often seen flying above urban areas. Migrating flocks frequently appear along the lakefront. Large spring flights are occasionally noted from the hawk-watch sites.

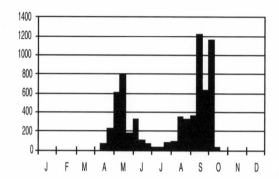

Peak counts

Spring:	300	20 May 1986	Hammond
Fall:	545	15 Sep 1989	Michigan City

Status
This fast flying species is a transient and summer resident. The Chimney Swift is almost certainly a common nester in towns and cities of the area; however, specific nesting data are lacking. Migration data are:

	EARLIEST	ARRIVE	PEAK	DEPART	LATEST	N
Spring	9 Apr 78	24 Apr	16 May	14 Jun	- - -	271
Fall	- - -	6 Aug	12 Sep	6 Oct	15 Oct 87	322

RUBY-THROATED HUMMINGBIRD (*Archilochus colubris*)

Finding data
Finding Code = 3, during the fall migration peak in late August and early September. Autumn migrants congregate around stands of jewel weed, which flourish along margins of the interdunal marshes. Thus, an early September trip along Beverly Drive usually produces this species.

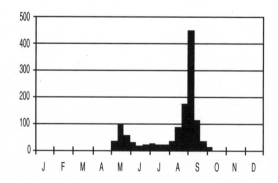

Peak counts

Spring:	16	17 May 1984	Dunes State Park
Fall:	100*	10 Sep 1919	Hike from Gary to Mineral Springs
			* see note under observations

Status

The Ruby-throated Hummingbird is a summer resident and transient through the Dunes. Nests have been observed in late June and July. Eifrig (1918) reports "what comes near to a nesting colony" along the creek at Tremont. Nine nests were found within a rather small radius (probably on 15 July 1917). Migration data are:

	EARLIEST	ARRIVE	PEAK	DEPART	LATEST	N
Spring	2 May 84	9 May	19 May	6 Jun	- - -	168
Fall	- - -	14 Aug	3 Sep	17 Sep	10 Oct 91	340

Observations

A remarkable count comes from Stoddard's unpub. notes. Following a 10 September 1919 hike from Gary to Mineral Springs (along the beach) Stoddard commented, "Literally <u>thousands</u> of hummingbirds in the swamps and surrounding territory, buzzing, and cheeping and fighting." A daily total of "thousands" of hummingbirds is absolutely unprecedented in the Dunes (twenty constitutes the second highest daily count); consequently the number was arbitrarily reduced to 100 for the Occurrence Histogram.

FAMILY ALCEDINIDAE: Kingfishers

BELTED KINGFISHER (*Ceryle alcyon*)

Finding data

Finding Code = 4, during migration; late March through April and September through October. This species is also present during both summer and winter but is more difficult to find. Invariably seen near water, especially shallow ponds or streams. Kingfishers are quite vocal and when present, can usually be detected by call.

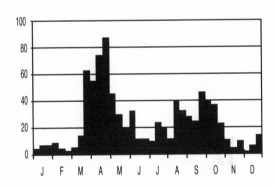

Peak counts

Spring:	6	27 Apr 1958	Michigan City Harbor
	6	17 Apr 1982	Lakefront
Fall:	4	16 Aug 1980	Roxana Pond
	4	12 Oct 1985	Northern Lake County

Status

The kingfisher is a permanent resident of the Dunes, but is more common during the migration periods. Although the Belted Kingfisher is undoubtedly a common nesting species in the Dunes, few nesting data are available. On 16 August 1919 Stoddard (unpub. notes) collected two "young or immature" birds along the Little Calumet River near Miller. Migration data are:

	EARLIEST	ARRIVE	PEAK	DEPART	LATEST	N
Spring	- - -	25 Mar	21 Apr	21 May	- - -	307
Fall	- - -	16 Aug	25 Sep	26 Oct	- - -	249

FAMILY PICIDAE: Woodpeckers

Eight representatives of this family have been reported in the Dunes. Of these, the Red-headed, Red-bellied, Hairy, Downy Woodpeckers, and Pileated Woodpecker, along with the Northern Flicker, are more or less permanent residents (although the latter is also strongly migratory). The Yellow-bellied Sapsucker is primarily a transient and the Black-backed is a vagrant.

RED-HEADED WOODPECKER (*Melanerpes erythrocephalus*)

Finding data
Finding Code = 2, between late April and mid-May. This strikingly marked species prefers the scrub oak-savannah habitat of the wooded dunes. Red-headed Woodpeckers can usually be located along the wooded dunes northeast of Wilson Shelter in Dunes State Park.

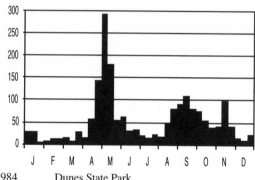

Peak counts
Spring:	30	5 May 1984	Dunes State Park
Fall:	100	15 Nov 1958	Dunes State Park

Status
The Red-headed Woodpecker is a permanent resident of the Dunes, but winter numbers vary widely from year to year. Nests have been discovered in June and newly fledged birds have been noted in early July. Migration data collected in the lakefront traps (*) are:

	EARLIEST	ARRIVE	PEAK	DEPART	LATEST	N
Spring*	26 Apr 86	27 Apr	6 May	21 May	2 Jun 33	37
Fall *	5 Sep 81	- -	21 Sep	- -	18 Oct 86	27

RED-BELLIED WOODPECKER (*Melanerpes carolinus*)

Finding data
Finding Code = 3, in May. This handsome woodpecker, which is most easily detected by call, prefers large trees of the forest interior. It can usually be found in Dunes State Park near the Nature Center feeders and Wilson Shelter. On eight occasions this species has been recorded in migrant traps along the lakefront.

Peak counts

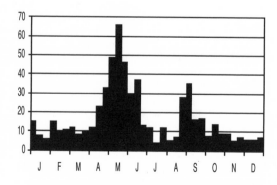

Spring:	10	21 May 1995	Dunes State Park and the Heron Rookery
Summer	11	14 Jun 1996	Dunes State Park and Beverly Shores
Fall:	6	31 Aug 1986	Dunes State Park

Status

The Red-bellied Woodpecker is a permanent resident of the Dunes. Strangely, Eifrig (1918) fails to mention this species in his listing of birds of the Dunes.

YELLOW-BELLIED SAPSUCKER (*Sphyrapicus varius*)

Finding data

Finding Code = 2, in lakefront traps during fall migration; late September and early October. Good sites include the Migrant Trap and Whiting Park. The largest single party count was the 141 dead birds found in the 16 April 1960 bird-kill on Lake Michigan (Segal, 1960).

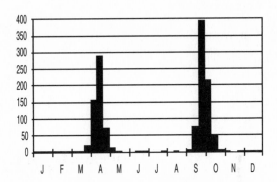

Peak counts

| Spring: | 141 | 16 Apr 1960 | Kill on lakefront beaches |
| Fall: | 35 | 24 Sep 1988 | Migrant Trap and Whiting Park |

Status

Although a few sapsuckers linger throughout the winter, and summer records exist, this species is primarily a spring and fall transient. Despite the summer records (26 June 1974 at Cowles Bog and 27 July 1975 at Cowles Bog) evidence of nesting in the Dunes is lacking. Migration data are:

	EARLIEST	ARRIVE	PEAK	DEPART	LATEST	N
Spring	- - -	3 Apr	13 Apr	25 Apr	11 May 96	218
Fall	17 Aug 20	19 Sep	29 Sep	11 Oct	- - -	283

DOWNY WOODPECKER (*Picoides pubescens*)

Finding data

Finding Code = 2, throughout the year. This small woodpecker is distributed widely throughout the Dunes, but is most often encountered along wood edges or in scrubby second growth. A few are invariably present in the Beverly Shores interdunal marsh.

Peak counts

| Spring: | 60 | 24 Mar 1917 | Near Cowles Bog |
| Fall: | 10 | 3 Oct 1977 | West Beach |

Status

The Downy Woodpecker is a permanent resident of the Dunes. Nests were reported 11 June 1914 (Stoddard notes) and 19 May 1934 in Dunes State Park (Smith, 1936).

HAIRY WOODPECKER (*Picoides villosus*)

Finding data

Finding Code = 3, during winter when birds visit suet feeders; the Dunes State Park feeders often attract this species. Otherwise Hairy Woodpeckers are difficult to locate.

Peak counts

Spring:	7	25 Apr 1917	West Beach
Fall:	2		Reported on numerous occasions.

Status

The Hairy Woodpecker is a permanent resident of the Dunes. A majority of the Hairy Woodpeckers on summer bird counts are found in Dunes State Park.

BLACK-BACKED WOODPECKER (*Picoides arcticus*)

Finding data

Finding Code = 9; nine records exist, only one of which occurred within the past 40 years. Stoddard (1917 and 1921) collected three specimens near West Beach (all within four miles); one 11 March 1917 and two on 24 October 1920. Eifrig (1922), in reporting a widespread 1920 invasion in the Chicago region, noted observing three at Millers on 26 November. The most recent occurrence was a sight record 13 November 1982 near Porter (IAQ 61:116)

NORTHERN FLICKER (*Colaptes auratus*)

Finding data

Maximum Finding Code = 2, during lakefront migrations in early April. On heavy flight days, scores of Flickers can be observed flying along the dune-crests parallel to the beach. Counts exceeding 100 migrating birds have been logged on at least ten occasions. During autumn migration Flickers are common in the lakefront traps.

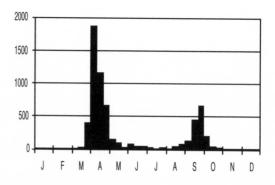

Peak counts

Spring:	500	6 Apr 1958	Migrating along the lakefront (AFN 12:358)
Fall:	50	23 Sep 1984	Lakefront traps

Status

The flicker is transient and summer resident, a few birds usually winter. Migration data from lakefront traps (*) are:

	EARLIEST	ARRIVE	PEAK	DEPART	LATEST	N
Spring*	21 Mar 95	6 Apr	19 Apr	5 May	25 May 91	62
Fall *	29 Jul 89	2 Sep	23 Sep	5 Oct	28 Nov 80	149

Observations

A nest-hole conflict between this species and a European Starling was once observed. Both birds entered the cavity attempting to take possession. In the ensuing struggle the flicker twice evicted the smaller starling, physically dragging it out by the wing. On each occasion the starling quickly returned. The ultimate resolution of this engagement is unknown.

PILEATED WOODPECKER (*Dryocopus pileatus*)

Finding data

The current Finding Code = 4, in April and May when nesting birds are vocal. The abundance of this species has increased significantly since 1980; only four reports precede this year. Most records are from Dunes State Park, often in the area near Wilson Shelter, but birds have been recorded at eight other Dunes area locations.

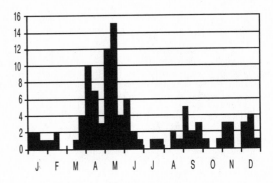

Peak counts

Spring:	2		Recorded on nine occasions
Fall:	2	4 Sep 1985	Dunes State Park

Status

Pileated Woodpeckers are now permanent residents of the Dunes area. In 1983 three occurrences involving four individuals were reported (IAQ 62:27) and a pair was present in Dunes State Park during spring of 1985. Pileateds have been recorded at the latter site every year since 1985, with nests found in 1987, 1989, and 1992.

FAMILY TYRANNIDAE: Flycatchers

OLIVE-SIDED FLYCATCHER (*Contopus borealis*)

Finding data

Finding Code = 6, during the fall migration; mid-August through the first half of September. This husky flycatcher is most frequently seen perched atop snags along Beverly Drive at Beverly Shores; the best area is east of Broadway. Olive-sided Flycatchers occasionally appear in the lakefront traps.

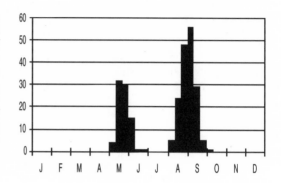

Peak counts

Spring:	3	19 May 1984	Dunes State Park
Fall:	6	4 Sep 1957	Baileytown
	6	14 Sep 1961	Baileytown

Status

The Olive-sided Flycatcher is a spring and fall transient through the Dunes. Occasionally June birds are heard singing. Migration data are:

	EARLIEST	ARRIVE	PEAK	DEPART	LATEST		N
Spring	4 May 85	13 May	22 May	6 Jun	22 Jun	59	80
Fall	5 Aug 61	17 Aug	1 Sep	14 Sep	1 Oct	89	122

EASTERN WOOD-PEWEE (*Contopus virens*)

Finding data

Finding Code = 2, from late May through mid-June when birds are actively calling. During this period the pewee is ubiquitous in woodlands of the High Dunes, and is especially numerous around Wilson Shelter in Dunes State Park. Pewees can usually be found in lakefront traps during fall migration.

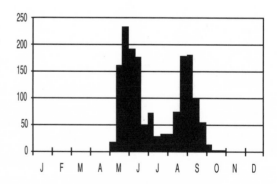

Peak counts

Spring:	16	26 May 1989	Dunes State Park
Summer:	41	13 June 1995	High Dunes
Fall:	20	20 Aug 1981	Dunes State Park

Status

This vociferous flycatcher is a summer resident and transient through the Dunes. Most nesting records are in June; a nest containing one egg was found 4 July 1917 in Dunes State Park (Stoddard notes). Smith (1936) reports a nest containing three young in Dunes State Park on 15 August 1934. Migration data from the lakefront traps (*) are:

	EARLIEST	ARRIVE	PEAK	DEPART	LATEST	N
Spring*	5 May 50	14 May	22 May	29 May	20 Jun 32	62
Fall *	9 Jul 88	28 Aug	14 Sep	29 Sep	24 Oct 51	86

GENUS EMPIDONAX

The five representatives of this genus that occur in the Dunes are notoriously difficult to identify in the field. Most birds are identified by song; consequently, fall migrations, when most are nonvocal, are poorly defined. Migration patterns of the Acadian, Alder, and Willow are also obscured by the presence of summering birds.

YELLOW-BELLIED FLYCATCHER (*Empidonax flaviventris*)

Finding data

Finding Code = 4, during the spring migration peak in late May. The Migrant Trap is an especially good location to find this species, which seems to prefer the scrubby second-growth areas. Spring birds often give the "chu-wee" call.

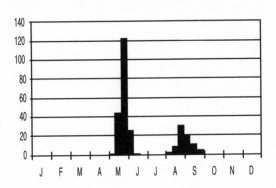

Peak counts

Spring:	10	29 May 1960	Baileytown
Fall:	2		Recorded on six occasions

Status

This Empid is a spring and fall transient through the Dunes. Migration data are:

	EARLIEST	ARRIVE	PEAK	DEPART	LATEST	N
Spring	8 May 83	18 May	23 May	1 Jun	17 Jun 58	131
Fall	7 Aug 61	20 Aug	31 Aug	19 Sep	25 Sep 94	69

ACADIAN FLYCATCHER (*Empidonax virescens*)

Finding data
Finding Code = 2, during the early nesting season, late May through mid-June. This species nests in damp forests with an understory, in generally shaded habitat. Trail 2 of Dunes State Park east of Wilson Shelter provides excellent nesting habitat. Nesting birds are also easily found in the Heron Rookery.

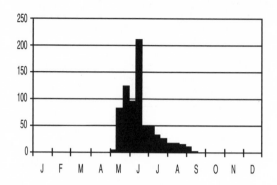

Peak counts
Spring:	12	30 May 1994	Furnessville
Summer:	48	13 Jun 1995	Beverly Shores and Heron Rookery
Fall:	10	5 Aug 1993	Heron Rookery

Status
The Acadian Flycatcher is a summer resident and undoubtedly a transient through the Dunes; however, migration limits are poorly defined as it is almost never identified away from breeding areas. Nesting records, most of which come from Dunes State Park, are in late June and July; however, an extremely late nest was found in the State Park 2 September 1990 in (Fields, 1990).

	EARLIEST	ARRIVE	PEAK	DEPART	LATEST	N
Spring	9 May 58	13 May	21 May	20 Jun	- - -	143
Fall	- - -	7 Aug	22 Aug	2 Sep	18 Sep 90	32

ALDER FLYCATCHER (*Empidonax alnorum*)

Finding data
Finding Code = 3, in spring migration: late May and early June. During this period calling birds are often heard in the interdunal marshes of Cowles Bog and Beverly Shores (especially on Beverly Drive near St. Claire Street). The fall migration begins in early July; southbound fall birds continue to sing into mid-August.

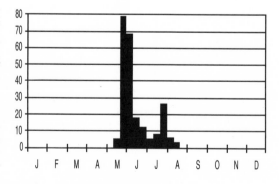

Peak counts
Spring:	11	29 May 1991	The High Dunes
Fall:	7	23 Jul 19988	Beverly Shores

Status

Although Graber et al. (1974) indicate that all nesting "Traill's" Flycatchers in Illinois have proven to be Willows, very strong evidence exists that the Alder Flycatcher in fact nests in the interdunal marshes of the National Lakeshore; however, nests have not been found. Territorial birds are recorded regularly at Beverly Shores.

	EARLIEST	ARRIVE	PEAK	DEPART	LATEST	N
Spring	14 May 79	22 May	31 May	13 Jun	- - -	74
Fall	- - -	- -	25 Jul	- -	17 Aug 96	28

WILLOW FLYCATCHER (*Empidonax traillii*)

Finding data

Finding Code = 3, during late May and early June. The distinctive "fitz-bew!" call of this flycatcher is heard from interdunal marshes throughout the High Dunes; Cowles Bog and Beverly Shores are especially good. The fall migration, which is extremely early, peaks in late July.

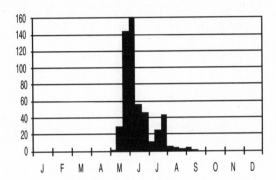

Peak counts

Spring:	18	1 Jun	1996	Beverly Shores
Fall:	9	22 Jul	1983	Beverly Shores

Status

The Willow Flycatcher is a summer resident of the Dunes. A nesting record of "Traill's" Flycatcher, which was almost certainly this species, comes from Smith (1936) who reported a nest at Lake George on 16 July 1935. A Willow Flycatcher nest was found near Chesterton 15 June 1985.

	EARLIEST	ARRIVE	PEAK	DEPART	LATEST	N
Spring	10 May 90	20 May	4 Jun	22 Jun	- - -	149
Fall	- - -	9 Jul	23 Jul	19 Aug	11 Sep 84	49

LEAST FLYCATCHER (*Empidonax minimus*)

Finding data
Finding Code = 3, during May. This small Empid is the most common member of this genus during migration, when it frequents most woodlands and lakeside parks. Summer birds are partial to stands of aspen saplings along margins of the interdunal marshes. Beverly Drive, west of Broadway, transects excellent habitat.

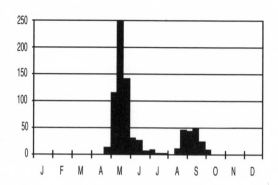

Peak counts
Spring:	14	12 May 1984	Dunes State Park
Fall:	7	21 Aug 1993	Lakefront traps

Status
The Least Flycatcher is primarily a spring and fall transient through the Dunes. Although many birds linger into July, no nest has been located. Migration data from the lakefront traps (*) are:

	EARLIEST	ARRIVE	PEAK	DEPART	LATEST	N
Spring*	25 Apr 89	5 May	18 May	28 May	8 Jun 90	83
Fall *	14 Aug 94	26 Aug	9 Sep	26 Sep	9 Oct 85	90

EASTERN PHOEBE (*Sayornis phoebe*)

Finding data
Finding Code = 4, in early April, when this harbinger of spring appears in lakefront parks. The Phoebe is the first flycatcher to arrive in spring and the last to depart in autumn. Early spring arrivals are often observed hawking insects above sheltered pools.

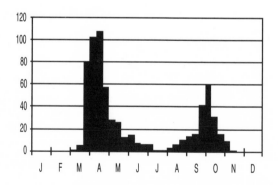

Peak counts
Spring:	25	5 Apr 1959	Baileytown
Fall:	5	10 Oct 1961	Baileytown

Status
Although the phoebe occasionally nests in the Dunes, it is primarily a spring and fall transient. Nests were reported by Smith (1936) 18 May 1935 at Dunes

144

State Park and Reuter-skiold (unpub. notes) 12 May 1946 near Baileytown. Migration data collected in the lakefront traps (*) are:

	EARLIEST	ARRIVE	PEAK	DEPART	LATEST	N
Spring	8 Mar 88	25 Mar	9 Apr	27 Apr	2 Jun 95	33
Fall	6 Sep 80	24 Sep	6 Oct	21 Oct	11 Nov 91	63

SAY'S PHOEBE (*Sayornis saya*)

Finding Code = 10; only one record. Members of a 4 April 1937 Chicago Ornithological Society field trip to the Indiana Dunes identified a Say's Phoebe near Wilson Shelter (Pitelka, 1938). During observation as close as 15 feet, the cinnamon-buff underparts, and gray-brown breast were noted. This sighting constitutes Indiana's only record of this western species.

GREAT-CRESTED FLYCATCHER (*Myiarchus crinitus*)

Finding data
Finding Code = 3, during May and early June when the birds actively call. This gravel-voiced flycatcher nests in Dunes State Park (east of Wilson Shelter) and along margins of the interdunal marshes at Cowles Bog and Beverly Shores. During migration Great-cresteds are often noted in the lakeside parks.

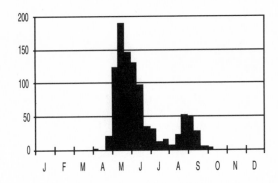

Peak counts
Spring:	15	8 May 1997	Lakefront traps
Summer:	18	14 Jun 1996	Dunes State Park and Beverly Shores
Fall:	5	13 Sep 1986	Lakefront traps

Status
This large, colorful flycatcher is a summer resident and transient through the Dunes. The only reported nest of the Great-crested Flycatcher consisted of three young and one egg on 21 June 1914 near Miller (Stoddard notes). The spring migration pulse, shown on the Occurrence Histogram, is inflated due to the presence of nesting birds. Migration data from lakefront traps (*) are:

	EARLIEST	ARRIVE	PEAK	DEPART	LATEST	N
Spring*	5 Apr 43	4 May	14 May	24 May	7 Jun 95	53
Fall *	21 Jul 57	28 Aug	7 Sep	18 Sep	2 Oct 82	37

WESTERN KINGBIRD (*Tyrannus verticalis*)

Finding Code = 8. The six records, all of single birds, are: 6 June 1939 in rural Porter County (Boyd notes); 12 September 1957 at Baileytown (AFN 12:36);

26 September 1960 in Baileytown (IAQ 39:30); 29 August 1982 at Long Lake and 11 September 1982 at Cowles Bog (AB 37:188); and 26 May 1984 at Michigan City Harbor (IAQ 63:36).

EASTERN KINGBIRD (*Tyrannus tyrannus*)

Finding data
Finding Code = 2, during spring migration in the first two-thirds of May when morning flights occur along the lakefront. Summer period Kingbirds occur throughout the Dunes in more open areas. The fall migration begins early and most birds are gone by September.

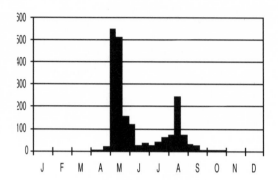

Peak counts

Spring:	150	10 May 1987	Lakefront flight at Beverly Shores
Fall:	150	16 Aug 1982	Long Lake (IAQ 61:124)

Status
The Eastern Kingbird is a summer resident and transient through the Dunes. Of the nine nesting records most are in June; the earliest was 2 June 1916. Young have been noted in early July. Migration data are:

	EARLIEST	ARRIVE	PEAK	DEPART	LATEST			N
Spring	4 Apr 33	4 May	15 May	5 Jun	-	-	-	244
Fall	- - -	15 Jul	12 Aug	5 Sep	28	Oct	43	221

SCISSOR-TAILED FLYCATCHER (*Tyrannus forficatus*)

Finding Code = 10; only two records. A single bird was identified (at close range) on two consecutive days, 3-4 May 1947, by many observers. The flycatcher was at Wolf Lake, about one-fourth mile from the Illinois state line (Bartel, 1948). A second bird was seen 28 October 1984 at Cowles Bog (IAQ 63:118).

FAMILY ALAUDIDAE: Larks

HORNED LARK (*Eremophila alpestris*)

Finding data
Finding Code = 4, during fall and winter; mid-October through February. Limited habitat restricts the occurrence of this species in the Dunes. It is most often observed along beaches or along roads at the Port of Indiana.

Peak counts

Spring:	25	26 Mar 1985	Dunes State Park
Fall:	1800	26 Oct 1957	Rural Porter County (H. West notes)

Status

The Horned Lark is a permanent resident and transient through the Dunes. Migration peaks are in mid-February and mid-November.

FAMILY HIRUNDINIDAE: Swallows

PURPLE MARTIN (*Progne subis*)

Finding data

Finding Code = 2, at martin nesting houses, for example along the lakefront at Beverly Shores (May through June). During the fall migration flocks are occasionally seen along the lakefront, especially where Lake Street crosses the Marquette Lagoons.

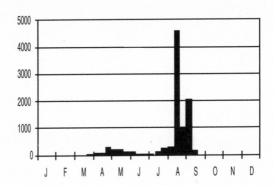

Peak counts

Spring:	108	25 Apr 1992	Long Lake
Fall:	3000	13 Aug 1979	Porter County lakefront

Status

The martin is a summer resident and transient through the Dunes. Migration data are:

	EARLIEST	ARRIVE	PEAK	DEPART	LATEST	N
Spring	25 Mar 56	8 Apr	1 May	20 May	- - -	204
Fall	- - -	16 Jul	14 Aug	8 Sep	27 Sep 88	229

TREE SWALLOW (*Tachycineta bicolor*)

Finding data

Finding Code = 2, during the spring migration in April. Migrants are most easily seen flying along the lakefront; hawk-watch sites provide excellent vantage points. This species is much harder to find in autumn.

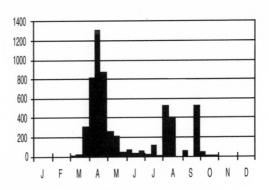

147

Peak counts

Spring:	214	27 Apr 1983	Dunes State Park
Fall:	500	1 Aug 1924	Lakefront
	500	28 Sep 1936	Lakefront

Status

This dapper swallow is a summer resident and transient through the Dunes. Nests containing eggs have been reported in June. Migration data are:

	EARLIEST	ARRIVE	PEAK	DEPART	LATEST	N
Spring	22 Feb 94	29 Mar	19 Apr	13 May	- - -	209
Fall	- - -	9 Jul	10 Sep	10 Oct	13 Nov 93	48

NORTHERN ROUGH-WINGED SWALLOW *(Stelgidopteryx serripennis)*

Finding data

Finding Code = 4, during spring migration; mid-April through May. Usually seen along the lakefront or hawking insects over inland ponds; it is difficult to find during the fall migration. The largest single party count of 300 on 28 July 1951 (Boyd notes) is extraordinary; daily counts of fewer than ten individuals are far more common.

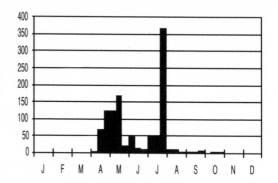

Peak counts

Spring:	26	30 Apr 1996	Oak Ridge Prairie County Park
Fall:	300	28 Jul 1951	Northern Porter County

Status

This brown-backed swallow is a summer resident and transient through the Dunes. Eifrig (1918) reports nesting in the Dunes on 10 June 1915. Migration data are:

	EARLIEST	ARRIVE	PEAK	DEPART	LATEST	N
Spring	6 Apr 92	20 Apr	8 May	5 Jun	- - -	172
Fall	- - -	7 Jul	24 Jul	15 Sep	24 Oct 94	34

BANK SWALLOW (*Riparia riparia*)

Finding data

Finding Code = 1, during the nesting season, mid-May until early July, when large colonies nest in the foredune sand banks carved by Lake Michigan. On most years colonies can be found along the Beverly Shores beach or at the Port of Indiana.

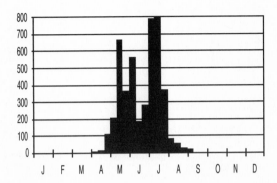

Peak counts

Spring:	100	12 May 1992	Migrant Trap
Fall:	350	14 Jul 1984	Port of Indiana

Status

The Bank Swallow is a summer resident and transient through the Dunes. Nesting records span the interval from late April through late June. Migration data are:

	EARLIEST	ARRIVE	PEAK	DEPART	LATEST	N
Spring	1 Apr 90	30 Apr	20 May	10 Jun	- - -	183
Fall	- - -	24 Jun	15 Jul	18 Aug	14 Oct 83	169

CLIFF SWALLOW (*Hirundo pyrrhonota*)

Finding data

Finding Code = 5, in May. This species, the rarest swallow in the Dunes, is usually seen among the migrating swallow flocks. When present the Cliff Swallow is easily detected by its stubby tail and buffy rump-patch. Distinct flights, consisting of more than a dozen individuals, are occasionally noted along the lakefront in late May.

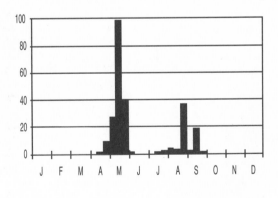

Peak counts

Spring:	32	18 May 1996	Michigan City Harbor
Fall:	24	22 Aug 1953	Lakefront

Status

The Cliff Swallow is a spring and fall transient through the Dunes. Migration data are:

149

	EARLIEST	ARRIVE	PEAK	DEPART	LATEST	N
Spring	17 Apr 82	1 May	14 May	23 May	1 Jun 95	63
Fall	18 Jul 92	- -	26 Aug	- -	29 Sep 84	16

BARN SWALLOW (*Hirundo rustica*)

Finding data
Finding Code = 2, from May through August. This is the most widely distributed swallow in the Dunes. It can usually be observed foraging above ponds, streams, and marshes.

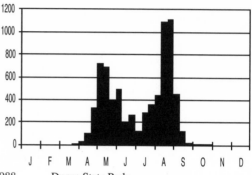

Peak counts

Spring:	200	7 May 1988	Dunes State Park
Fall:	200	18 Aug 1979	Lakefront

Status
This graceful aerialist is a summer resident and transient through the Dunes. The Barn Swallow nests, usually in small groups, at numerous locations throughout the lakeshore. Migration data are:

	EARLIEST	ARRIVE	PEAK	DEPART	LATEST	N
Spring	27 Mar 85	18 Apr	7 May	2 Jun	- - -	241
Fall	- - -	15 Jul	18 Aug	9 Sep	27 Oct 91	268

FAMILY CORVIDAE: Jays and Crows

BLUE JAY (*Cyanocitta cristata*)

Finding data
Finding Code = 1, during the spring migration peak in late April and Mid-May, when large flocks migrate along the lakefront. The Finding Code is 2 throughout the remainder of the year.   Blue Jays are widespread, occurring in almost every habitat in the Dunes area.

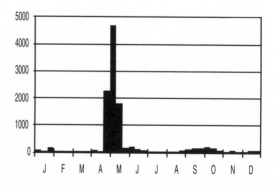

Peak counts

Spring:	2210	28 Apr 1981	West Beach (migrating along lakefront)
Fall:	50	12 Nov 1988	Beverly Shores

Status

Although the Blue Jay is a permanent resident of the Dunes, distinct migrations occur in both spring and fall. Impressive spring flights, comprised of loose flocks of eastbound birds, are frequently observed from the hawk-watch sites. Migration peaks are approximately 9 May in spring and 1 October in fall. Nests have been reported in June.

BLACK-BILLED MAGPIE (*Pica pica*)

Finding Code = 10; only one record. On 17 April 1980 a number of observers (including the author) saw one fly eastward past Mount Baldy.

AMERICAN CROW (*Corvus brachyrhynchos*)

Finding data

Finding Code = 1, during spring migration (March through early April); Code = 2, for balance of the year. Migrating Crows are ubiquitous at the spring hawk-watch sites. This large corvid is found throughout the Dunes.

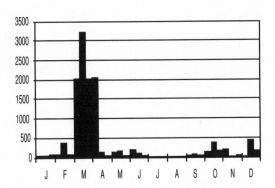

Peak counts

Spring:	2000	12 Mar 1958	Lakefront (migrating along lakefront)
	2000	6 Apr 1958	Lakefront (migrating along lakefront)
Fall:	175	5 Nov 1991	Purdue Univ. North Central

Status

The American Crow is a permanent resident and transient through the Dunes. Peak for the spring flight is March 15.

COMMON RAVEN (*Corvus corax*)

Finding Code = 10; only two old records. Mumford and Keller (1984) report that one was seen along Lake Michigan in 1919 and according to Reuter-skiold, another was observed at Miller on 17 October 1953.

FAMILY PARIDAE: CHICKADEES AND TITMICE

BLACK-CAPPED CHICKADEE (*Parus atricapillus*)

Finding data
Finding Code = 2, at winter bird feeders. Migrating birds are occasionally observed at the spring hawk-watch sites.

Peak counts
Spring:	230	31 Mar 1981	Mount Baldy (migrating along lakefront)
Fall:	25	25 Nov 1951	Northern Porter County

Status
The Black-capped Chickadee is a permanent resident, and as indicated above, is at least an occasional migrant though the Dunes. Nests have been observed in late April and May. Migration peaks are near 17 April and 15 September.

BOREAL CHICKADEE (*Parus hudsonicus*)

Finding Code = 9. Grow (1952) describes a mini-invasion of this northern species. Between 20 November 1951 and 13 March 1952, at least three birds were present; one each at a Jack Pine pinery in Porter County (one km south of Lake Michigan and about seven km east of Gary); at a feeding station in Gary; and in Dunes State Park. Subsequent to Grow's paper, two birds were observed 17 and 18 April 1952 in Jack Pines at Dunes State Park (Merrill Sweet, unpub. letter).

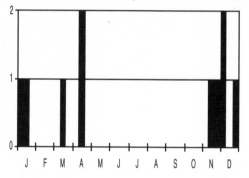

TUFTED TITMOUSE (*Parus bicolor*)

Finding data
Finding Code = 2, late April through June when birds are calling. This little bird with the big voice can usually be heard calling in woodlands throughout the High Dunes.

Peak counts
Spring:	15	8 May 1993	Dunes State Park
Summer:	26	14 Jun 1996	Dunes State Park and Beverly Shores
Fall:	15	24 Oct 1993	Furnessville

Status
The Tufted Titmouse is currently a permanent resident of the Dunes; however, it may be a new arrival. Eifrig (1918) refers to the titmouse as: "A rare resident. Has so far been found at Tremont only."

Observations

Lois Howes (pers. comm.) related the following example of this species' resourcefulness in appropriating nesting material. A raccoon that was behaving rather strangely was noted outside the Howes residence on a spring day. Closer observation revealed that a Tufted Titmouse would periodically fly down and tug at the long fur on the raccoon's posterior, which annoyed the latter no small amount.

FAMILY SITTIDAE: Nuthatches

RED-BREASTED NUTHATCH (*Sitta canadensis*)

Finding data

Finding Code = 4, during the fall migration, or at winter feeders (has a special taste for suet). Numbers of this irruptive species vary from year to year. It is usually observed near conifers, but migrants occur regularly in deciduous trees along the lakefront. One or two are often in the Migrant Trap during the fall flight.

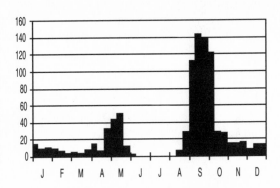

Peak counts

Spring:	12	11 May 1996	Dunes State Park
Fall:	40	5 Sep 1957	Near Baileytown (AFN 11:35)

Status

The Red-breasted Nuthatch is a winter resident and transient through the Dunes. The June record consisted of two birds observed between Miller and Cowles Bog (Stoddard notes). Migration data are:

	EARLIEST	ARRIVE	PEAK	DEPART	LATEST	N
Spring	- - -	31 Mar	3 May	18 May	2 Jun 17	130
Fall	14 Aug 85	3 Sep	24 Sep	29 Oct	- - -	317

WHITE-BREASTED NUTHATCH (*Sitta carolinensis*)

Finding data

Finding Code = 3, near feeding stations in the winter. Only nine birds have been recorded in the migration traps along the lakefront, suggesting that this species is relatively sedentary.

Peak counts

Spring:	10	31 Mar 1981	Mount Baldy
Fall:	14	3 Sep 1995	Furnessville

Status

The White-breasted Nuthatch is a permanent resident of the Dunes. Nest records are in May and June.

"brown-headed" NUTHATCH (*Sitta pusilla* or *pygmaea*)

A nuthatch, originally identified as a Brown-headed Nuthatch, was discovered by Archie F. Wilson in Whiting Park on 5 April 1932. The Indiana Rare Bird Committee deemed the documentation inadequate to eliminate the very similar Pygmy Nuthatch (*Sitta pygmaea*), though they agreed it was one of the two. The bird was studied at length, at close range; the identification was confirmed by a second observer on the following day. According to a letter written by Wilson 26 April 1932, the bird was about the size of a Red-breasted Nuthatch but lacked the white supercilium of that species. It possessed a "dirty grayish" cap with a "brownish tinge" and the tail showed a "narrow fringe of grayish white" on the outer rectrices. Underparts were tinged with buff, especially on under tail coverts. On several occasions the bird uttered a "warble, just a few liquid notes," which was markedly different from the nasal calls of the other two Eastern nuthatches.

FAMILY CERTHIIDAE: Creepers

BROWN CREEPER (*Certhia americana*)

Finding data

Finding Code = 3, during spring and fall migrations in April and late September through mid-October. The creeper can be found in almost any forested area, but shows some preference for wet woodlands. During migration it is regularly seen in the lakeside migration traps.

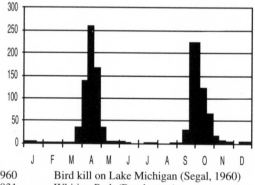

Peak counts

Spring:	47	16 Apr 1960	Bird kill on Lake Michigan (Segal, 1960)
Fall:	50	28 Sep 1931	Whiting Park (Boyd notes)

Status

The Brown Creeper is a spring and fall transient through the Dunes; however, it has been recorded every month. Most summer records are in early June, but two July reports, 20 July 1955 at Baileytown (IAQ 33:2) and 27 July 1969 in Dunes State Park (AFN 23:666), also exist. No nest has been located. Creepers are, of course, well known for their habit of creeping upward along the trunks of trees.

	EARLIEST		ARRIVE	PEAK	DEPART	LATEST		N
Spring*	1 Apr	31	8 Apr	19 Apr	1 May	22 May	82	47
Fall *	9 Sep	95	23 Sep	4 Oct	19 Oct	10 Nov	84	135

FAMILY TROGLODYTIDAE: Wrens

CAROLINA WREN (*Thryothorus ludovicianus*)

Finding data
Currently the Finding Code = 4, but the Dunes area population decreases substantially during bitter winters. There are no reliable locations at which to find this southern wren, but singing birds are regularly heard in Beverly Shores.

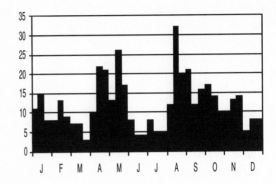

Peak counts
Spring:	14	16 Apr 1960	Bird kill on Lake Michigan (Segal, 1960)
Fall:	5	3 Oct 1975	Northern Porter County

Status
The hard winters of 1976-77 and 1977-78 decimated the Carolina Wren population. By 1990 numbers had rebounded, but decreased again following the winter 0f 1993-94.

BEWICK'S WREN (*Thryomanes bewickii*)

Finding data
Finding Code = 9; the last record was 11 April 1992 at the Migrant Trap (AB 46:432). The largest single party count was two on 23 April 1957 at Baileytown and at nest sites listed below.

Peak counts
Spring:	2	23 Apr 1957	Baileytown
Fall:	1	4 Aug 1924	Northern Porter County

Status
Currently the Bewick's Wren is a vagrant in the Dunes, but in former years it occurred much more regularly, and nested on several occasions. The earliest spring arrival was 4 April 1935. Nesting records are as follows: 1 May 1920 in Lake County (Boyd notes); 4 August 1924 in Porter County (Ford, 1956); and 1948 in the Dunes (Ford, 1956).

HOUSE WREN (*Troglodytes aedon*)

Finding data
Finding Code = 2, from early
May through June, when
territorial birds actively sing.
This ubiquitous wren is
perhaps most easily found in
the shrubs and bushes of
residential areas, but it is also
common along wood edges
and in second growth areas.

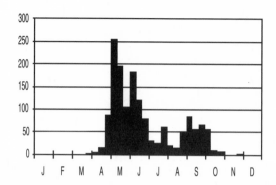

Peak counts

Spring:	18	8 May 1993	High Dunes
Fall:	10	10 Sep 1993	Migrant Trap

Status
The House Wren is a summer resident and transient through the Dunes. Nesting
dates range from early May through August. On 5 May 1926 Bretsch (banding
notes) observed a nest containing seven eggs in Gary. Migration data from
lakefront traps (*) are:

	EARLIEST	ARRIVE	PEAK	DEPART	LATEST	N
Spring*	27 Mar 33	27 Apr	8 May	20 May	7 Jun 91	56
Fall *	14 Aug 94	4 Sep	29 Sep	9 Oct	26 Nov 83	82

WINTER WREN (*Troglodytes troglodytes*)

Finding data
Finding Code = 4 during the autumn flight; late September through

October. This little wren is
most easily found in heavy
cover along the immediate
lakefront. The Migrant Trap
and Whiting Park are good
areas. The largest single party
count was 100 at Miller
Beach, 30 March 1919. The
latter report comes from a
comment, "(I) also saw
hundreds of Winter Wrens,"
taken from Stoddard's notes.

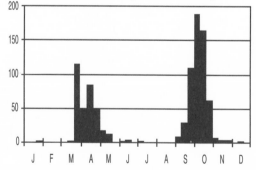

Peak counts

Spring:	100	30 Mar 1919	Miller Beach (Stoddard's notes)
Fall:	29	12 Oct 1985	Migrant Trap, Whiting Park, & George Lake

Status
Although several winter records and one summer report exist, the Winter Wren is mainly a spring and fall transient through the Dunes. A singing bird was present in the heavy cover of the wooded swamp along Trail 2, east of Wilson Shelter (Dunes State Park), from 9 June through 7 July 1974. No nest was located. Migration data, disregarding summer records, are:

	EARLIEST	ARRIVE	PEAK	DEPART	LATEST	N
Spring	20 Mar 48	31 Mar	16 Apr	5 May	29 May 97	123
Fall	1 Sep 52	22 Sep	7 Oct	22 Oct	- - -	247

SEDGE WREN (*Cistothorus platensis*)

Finding data
Finding Code = 4, from mid-May through June. This species nests in the sedges along the southern margin of Cowles Bog. Singing birds can sometimes be heard from the portion of Mineral Springs Road that crosses the sedge. Fall migrants appear regularly in the lakefront traps, especially at Whiting Park.

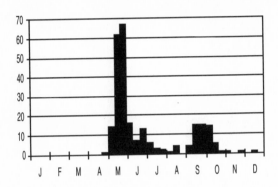

Peak counts
Spring:	50	20 May 1916	Near Cowles Bog (Eifrig, 1918)
Fall:	6	17 Sep 1994	Whiting Park

Status
The Sedge Wren in a summer resident and transient through the Dunes. Migration data are:

	EARLIEST	ARRIVE	PEAK	DEPART	LATEST	N
Spring	28 Apr 61	8 May	29 May	4 Jul	- - -	61
Fall	- - -	6 Sep	28 Sep	16 Oct	17 Dec 52	47

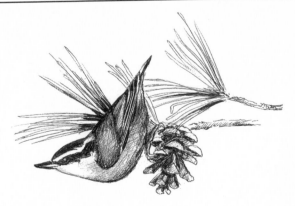

MARSH WREN (*Cistothorus palustris*)

Finding data
Finding Code = 2, from mid-May through June. This wren is found almost anywhere cattails grow in abundance. Good locations are fairly common on the Lacustrine Plain; singing birds can usually be heard at Roxana Pond. A few migrants occur annually in the lakefront traps.

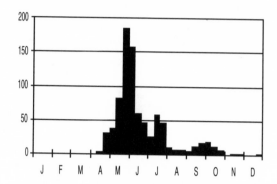

Peak counts
Spring:	75	30 May 1916	Long Lake (Eifrig, 1918)
Fall:	4	17 Sep 1994	Migrant Trap and Whiting Park

Status
The "Long-billed Marsh Wren," as this species was formerly known, is a summer resident and transient through the Dunes. A lingering bird was reported at Cowles Bog 21 December 1952 on the Michigan City Christmas Bird Count. Nesting has been reported from late May through late July. Migration data are:

	EARLIEST	ARRIVE	PEAK	DEPART	LATEST	N
Spring	16 Apr 60	5 May	29 May	16 Jun	- - -	154
Fall	- - -	14 Sep	2 Oct	21 Oct	26 Dec 52	57

FAMILY MUSCICAPIDAE: Old World Warblers, Thrushes, and Allies

GOLDEN-CROWNED KINGLET (*Regulus satrapa*)

Finding data
Finding Code = 2, during the height of fall migration in October. During migration both Kinglets are widespread across the region; birds noted in the lakefront traps are often quite tame and easily approached.

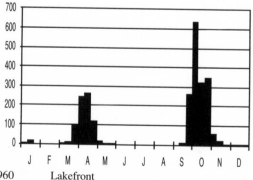

Peak counts
Spring:	25	16 Apr 1960	Lakefront
Fall:	100	4 Oct 1980	Lakefront

158

Status

The Golden-crowned Kinglet is primarily a transient; however, a few birds usually linger throughout the winter. Migration data are:

	EARLIEST	ARRIVE	PEAK	DEPART	LATEST	N
Spring	9 Mar 92	29 Mar	12 Apr	24 Apr	21 May 94	203
Fall	16 Sep 79	28 Sep	10 Oct	29 Oct	- - -	332

RUBY-CROWNED KINGLET (*Regulus calendula*)

Finding data

Finding Code = 2, from mid-April through early May and late September through mid-October. Distribution is similar to the previous species; it is ubiquitous during the migration periods. The largest single party count of 30 was recorded on at least five occasions.

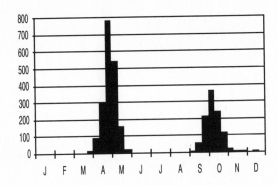

Peak counts

Spring:	48	23 Apr 1988	George Lake woodlot
Fall:	30	4 Oct 1980	Migrant Trap & Michigan City Harbor

Status

This highly active little kinglet is a spring and fall transient through the Dunes. Migration data are:

	EARLIEST	ARRIVE	PEAK	DEPART	LATEST	N
Spring	20 Mar 21	12 Apr	27 Apr	12 May	30 May 82	408
Fall	5 Sep 57	21 Sep	6 Oct	23 Oct	18 Dec 75	333

Observations

Both Kinglets are remarkably tame. On several occasions this species has flown within a meter of standing observers; once an especially curious bird even landed on a birder's telescope.

BLUE-GRAY GNATCATCHER (*Polioptila caerulea*)

Finding data

Finding Code = 3, from late April though May. The best locations for this tiny bird are in the breeding areas at the Heron Rookery and Indiana Dunes State Park (especially around Wilson Shelter). Spring migrants often join the wandering passerine flocks.

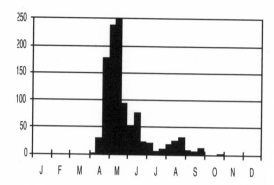

Peak counts

Spring:	32	15 May 1994	Dunes State Park
Fall:	4	2 Aug 1993	Chesterton

Status

The Gnatcatcher is a summer resident and spring transient through the Dunes. Nests have been observed in May, June, and on 18 July 1920 four birds "less than two days old" were observed near Cowles Bog. Migration data are:

	EARLIEST	ARRIVE	PEAK	DEPART	LATEST	N
Spring	6 Apr 86	23 Apr	9 May	2 Jun	- - -	319
Fall	- - -	31 Jul	21 Aug	21 Sep	21 Oct 85	76

EASTERN BLUEBIRD (*Sialia sialis*)

Finding data

On average the Finding Code = 3, at hawk-watch sites during the spring flight in March, but numbers vary from year to year. The best method for observing Bluebirds is to listen for calling birds as they pass over the hawk-watch sites.   These longshore migrants occasionally land in nearby trees.

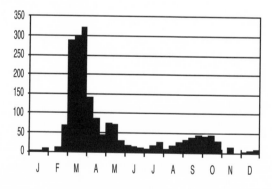

Peak counts

Spring:	83	5 Mar 1983	Mount Baldy (migrating along lakefront)
Fall:	18	28 Aug 1941	Northern Lake County

Status

The Bluebird occurs throughout the year, but is most common by far in early spring. In contrast to the distinct spring flight, the fall migration is poorly delineated. Winter birds occur most often in mild years. Fledged young have been noted as early as 6 June. Graber et al. (1971) point out that major bluebird population crashes occur periodically, and attribute them to cold weather in winter and spring. Present observations suggest that this species may be increasing. Migration data are:

	EARLIEST	ARRIVE	PEAK	DEPART	LATEST	N
Spring	- - -	3 Mar	23 Mar	17 Apr	- - -	265
Fall	- - -	21 Aug	29 Sep	24 Oct	- - -	89

TOWNSEND'S SOLITAIRE (*Myadestes townsendi*)

Finding Code = 10; only one acceptable record. A bird in juvenile plumage was seen regularly at West Beach between 24 November and 5 December 1995; a fine picture of this bird was also published in the *Audubon Field Notes* (50:64).

VEERY (*Catharus fuscescens*)

Finding data

Finding Code = 2, from late May through June when birds are singing. The Veery nests in Dunes State Park; the thin, downward spiraling songs of several birds can always be heard during an early morning walk along Trail 2, east of Wilson Shelter.

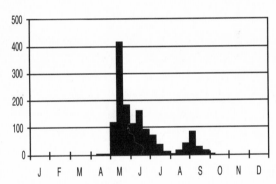

Peak counts

Spring:	57	11 May 1996	Dunes State Park
Fall:	16	3 Sep 1995	Furnessville

Status

This elusive thrush is a summer resident and transient through the Dunes. On 10 June 1979 a nest containing five eggs was found near Wilson Shelter in Dunes State Park; on 27 June the nest contained five featherless nestlings (IAQ 58:153). Migratory data from lakefront traps (*) are:

	EARLIEST	ARRIVE	PEAK	DEPART	LATEST	N
Spring*	11 Apr 31	7 May	16 May	25 May	2 Jun 92	50
Fall *	17 Aug 55	29 Aug	6 Sep	24 Sep	8 Oct 94	45

GRAY-CHEEKED THRUSH (*Catharus minimus*)

Finding data
Finding Code = 4, in mid-May. The Migrant Trap, Whiting Park, and Dunes State Park are excellent areas. It is far less common than the similar Swainson's Thrush; about nine Swainsons' are seen for every Gray-cheeked. Daily counts exceeding three birds are quite unusual.

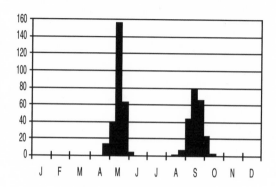

Peak counts
Spring:	50	13 May 1929	Whiting Park (Boyd Notes)
Fall:	10	17 Sep 1919	Lakefront (Stoddard Notes)

Status
The Gray-cheeked Thrush is a spring and fall transient through the Dunes. Migration data are:

	EARLIEST	ARRIVE	PEAK	DEPART	LATEST	N
Spring	23 Apr 43	5 May	14 May	23 May	3 Jun 94	141
Fall	11 Aug 60	4 Sep	18 Sep	2 Oct	14 Oct 77	158

SWAINSON'S THRUSH (*Catharus ustulatus*)

Finding data
Finding Code = 2, during the peak of fall migration; in early to mid-September. It occurs in habitat similar to that described for the Gray-cheeked Thrush. In some years large waves appear in September, when lakefront traps are awash with Swainson's Thrushes.

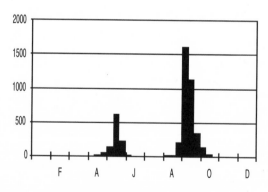

Peak counts
Spring:	65	11 May 1996	Beverly Shores
Fall:	200	9 Sep 1961	Baileytown (Reuter-skiold notes).

Status
This species, which is noticeably more common than the previous species, is a spring and fall transient through the Dunes. The June and July records probably represent stragglers; these is no evidence of breeding. On 31 January 1981 a

Swainson's Thrush was photographed in Dunes State Park (AB 35:306), providing the only winter record. Migration data are:

	EARLIEST	ARRIVE	PEAK	DEPART	LATEST	N
Spring	13 Apr 60	30 Apr	16 May	25 May	16 Jun 55	301
Fall	29 Jul 62	31 Aug	12 Sep	29 Sep	9 Nov 85	490

HERMIT THRUSH (*Catharus guttatus*)

Finding data
Finding Code = 2, during the migration peaks in mid-April and early October. Migrants are found throughout the area; the lakefront traps, Dunes State Park and the Beverly Shores interdunal marsh are excellent locations to find this thrush. On many years a few winter.

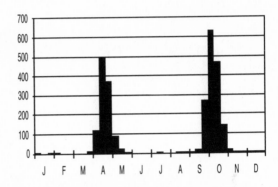

Peak counts
Spring:	147	16 Apr 1960	Kill on Lake Michigan (Segal, 1960)
Fall:	200	9 Sep 1961	Baileytown (Reuter-skiold notes).

Status
The Hermit Thrush is primarily a spring and fall transient; however, numerous winter records and one summer report, a singing bird 11 July 1993 near Dunes State Park (AB 47:1114), also exist. Migration data are:

	EARLIEST	ARRIVE	PEAK	DEPART	LATEST	N
Spring	- - -	8 Apr	21 Apr	4 May	25 May 13	296
Fall	12 Aug 89	26 Sep	8 Oct	22 Oct	- - -	361

WOOD THRUSH (*Hylocichla mustelina*)

Finding data
Finding Code = 2, during May when nesting birds actively sing. A fine area to locate this delightful songster is in the woods east of Wilson Shelter in Dunes State Park. Wood Thrushes also nest in the Heron Rookery and Beverly Shores. Migrants occasionally appear in the lakefront traps.

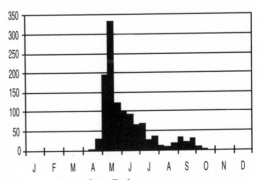

Peak counts
Spring:	27	11 May 1996	Dunes State Park
Fall:	5	8 Sep 1991	Furnessville

Status

The Wood Thrush is a summer resident and transient through the Dunes. Nests have been located from mid-May through mid-June. Migration data are:

	EARLIEST	ARRIVE	PEAK	DEPART	LATEST	N
Spring	12 Apr 88	4 May	16 May	10 Jun - - -		286
Fall	- - -	27 Aug	12 Sep	30 Sep	12 Oct 96	92

AMERICAN ROBIN (*Turdus migratorius*)

Finding data

Finding Code = 1, from mid-March through October. This common species prefers the lawns and shrubs of residential areas.

Peak counts

Spring:	5000	12 Mar 1990	Mount Baldy (lakefront migration)
Fall:	150	13 Sep 1941	Northern Lake County

Status

Although the Robin is present in the Dunes throughout the year, it is least common by far in winter. Migration peaks are near 6 April and 23 September. Robins begin nesting early; fully fledged young appear in late May.

VARIED THRUSH (*Ixoreus naevius*)

Finding Code = 8; six records in the study area. Mlodinow (1984) lists a 27 April 1968 record from Chesterton. Throughout January and February 1981 a Varied Thrush visited a feeding station in Beverly Shores (IAQ 60:81). On 13 February an excellent color photograph was taken by Nadine Schaeffer. A bird was seen 6 December 1987 in Dune Acres (IAQ 66:163) and another frequented the spring in west Beverly Shores in February and March 1988 (IAQ 67:34). Birds were seen near feeding stations at Ogden Dunes 23-25 Dec 1989 (IAQ 68:135) and in Michigan City 4-11 January 1995 (IAQ 73:196).

FAMILY MIMIDAE: Catbirds, Mockingbirds, and Thrashers

GRAY CATBIRD (*Dumetella carolinensis*)

Finding data

Finding Code = 2, from May through September. Distributed throughout virtually all habitats in the Dunes. The scrubby second growth of the Beverly Shores interdunal marsh is among the better locations to find this species. It is also common in lakefront traps during migration.

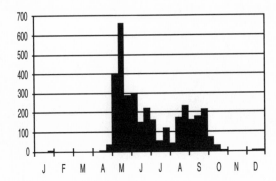

Peak counts

Spring:	90	8 May 1997	Lakefront traps
Fall:	30	15 Aug 1960	Baileytown

Status

The Catbird is a summer resident and transient through the Dunes, but birds rarely linger into early winter. Nest dates span the period from 1 June through 11 July. Migration data are:

	EARLIEST	ARRIVE	PEAK	DEPART	LATEST	N
Spring	19 Apr 92	4 May	18 May	9 Jun - - -	343
Fall	- - -	15 Aug	12 Sep	4 Oct	31 Dec 86	354

NORTHERN MOCKINGBIRD (*Mimus polyglottos*)

Finding data

Finding Code = 7; most reports occur in late April and May. There is no particular location at which this species can be found, but most are seen near the lakefront. Several have been recorded during spring hawk-watches.

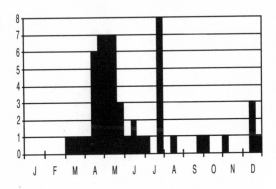

Peak counts

Spring:	2	10 May 1959	Northern Porter County
Summer:	6	21 Jul 1957	Near Chesterton (adults plus young in nest)
Fall:	1		All fall records are singletons

Status

The Mockingbird is a visitant to the Dunes that has nested on at least one occasion; six birds, two adults and four nestlings, were in rural Porter County 21 July 1957 (IAQ 36:51). Fall records fail to show any distinctive pattern. Spring migration data are:

	EARLIEST	ARRIVE	PEAK	DEPART	LATEST	N
Spring	5 Mar 96	4 Apr	1 May	23 May	- - -	34

BROWN THRASHER (*Toxostoma rufum*)

Finding data

Finding Code = 3, from mid-April until mid-May when the birds are actively singing. Perhaps this handsome species is most easily found at Cowles Bog and the interdunal marsh at Beverly Shores. It regularly occurs in lakefront traps during migration.

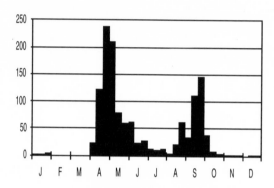

Peak counts

Spring:	31	16 Apr 1960	Kill on Lake Michigan (Segal, 1960)
Fall:	20	25 Aug 1961	Baileytown

Status

The Thrasher is a summer resident and transient through the Dunes; birds occasionally linger through the winter. Young birds of the year have been observed by 14 June. Migration data are:

	EARLIEST	ARRIVE	PEAK	DEPART	LATEST	N
Spring	28 Mar 97	16 Apr	2 May	2 Jun	- - -	386
Fall	- - -	25 Aug	21 Sep	4 Oct	26 Dec 88	221

FAMILY MOTACILLIDAE: Pipits

AMERICAN PIPIT (*Anthus rubescens*)

Finding data
Finding Code = 6, late March through May and mid-September through
October. Pipits are most often seen in moist agricultural fields and are
occasionally detected flying along the lakefront. The largest single party
count— 200 on 12 October 1958 in rural Porter County (IAQ 37:35) is atypical;
most reports consist of fewer than ten individuals.

Peak counts

Spring:	13	8 May 1953	Rural Porter County
Fall:	200	12 Oct 1958	Rural Porter County

Status
The "Water Pipit" is a regular transient through the Dunes; however, sparse
appropriate habitat limits its appearance. Migration data are:

	EARLIEST	ARRIVE	PEAK	DEPART	LATEST	N
Spring	26 Mar 88	- -	6 May	- -	28 May 86	26
Fall	10 Sep 88	- -	13 Oct	- -	26 Nov 61	25

FAMILY BOMBYCILLIDAE: Waxwings

BOHEMIAN WAXWING (*Bombycilla garrulus*)

Finding data
Finding Code = 8, from late
November through March. No
habitat preference is obvious,
but Stoddard (unpub. notes)
observed them feeding on
chokecherries in the interdunal
marshes. Most are seen within a
few kilometers of the lake.
Large numbers have not
appeared in recent decades;
recent sightings have come from
West Beach, Ogden Dunes, and
Chesterton, often accompanying
Cedar Waxwing flocks.

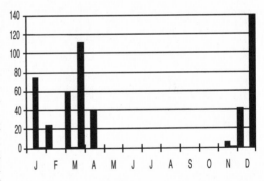

Peak counts

Spring:	100	30 Mar 1880	Whiting Park (Woodruff, 1907)
Fall:	6	12 Nov 1989	West Beach
Winter:	100	21 Dec 1919	Near Miller (Stoddard notes)

Status
Between 1880 and 1931 this northern species was reported 12 times, often in
large flocks. Bohemian Waxwings have been recorded only six times since
1931, and always in small numbers (maximum six). This pattern suggests a
change in the movements of this nomadic species.

CEDAR WAXWING (*Bombycilla cedrorum*)

Finding data

This Waxwing is extremely erratic, being common some years, and difficult to locate in others. On average the Finding Code = 4, during August and September. Flocks range throughout the Dunes; perhaps they are most commonly noted in the interdunal marshes of Beverly Shores. In spring large diurnal flights are occasionally noted along the lakefront.

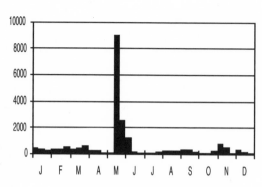

Peak counts

Spring:	5055	19 May 1996	Michigan City Harbor (longshore flight)
Fall:	174	4 Nov 1994	Purdue Univ. North Central

Status

Although the Cedar Waxwing is a permanent resident of the Dunes, the Occurrence Histogram is dominated by numbers recorded during sporadic late May longshore migrations. Nesting records are in June and July.

FAMILY LANIIDAE: Shrikes

Both North American shrikes occur in the Dunes; consequently, identification problems may well have introduced errors into the data. Generally the Loggerhead Shrike is the summer shrike and the Northern Shrike appears in the winter; however, Mumford (1967) cautions observers against assuming that all winter shrikes are the latter species.

NORTHERN SHRIKE (*Lanius excubitor*)

Finding data

Finding Code = 7 from mid-November through mid-January. Most Northern Shrikes are seen in the interdunal marshes of Cowles Bog and Beverly Shores. Other recent sightings have been made at West Beach and the Gary Airport. Northern Shrikes establish large winter territories and are remarkably difficult to find even when present.

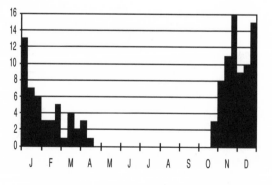

Peak counts

Spring:	1		All spring sightings consist of singletons
Fall:	2		Two were recorded on two occasions
Winter:	6	23 Dec 1956	Lakefront (IAQ 35:51)

Status

The Northern Shrike is a regular winter visitant in the Dunes. About a dozen young birds, in the brownish immature plumage, have been reported. Migration data are:

	EARLIEST	ARRIVE	PEAK	DEPART	LATEST	N
Winter	24 Oct 82	5 Nov	- -	26 Mar	13 Apr 57	111

Observations

Small birds apparently constitute a significant portion of the diet of wintering Northern Shrikes. On 24 January 1976 an individual of this species was observed capturing a Junco near Gary. The shrike flew some 30 meters carrying his prize. Subsequent investigation revealed the beheaded remains of the Junco suspended from the crotch of a thin branch, where it was apparently stored for future use.

LOGGERHEAD SHRIKE (*Lanius ludovicianus*)

Finding data

The current Finding Code = 8, in late March and April when wandering birds appear. This species was far more common in former years. Stoddard (unpub. notes), for example, observed this shrike regularly on his 1914-1920 summer trips into the Dunes.

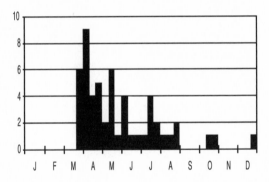

Peak counts

Spring:	3	24 Apr 1916	West Beach
Summer:	4	13 Jul 1915	Dunes State Park (nestlings)
Fall:	1		All fall records are singletons

Status

In earlier years the Migrant Shrike, as it was then named, was a summer resident and nesting species in the Dunes. Today, however, it must be considered a visitant. This near extirpation, which is observed throughout the Midwest, has been attributed to removal of fence-rows consisting of Osage Orange, but Graber et al. (1973) suggest that this explanation alone does not account for the sharp decline. The earliest spring record was 25 March 1982 and the spring peak is 24 April; there is little evidence of an autumn flight. The 27 December 1956 bird was collected in northern Lake County (Mumford, 1967). Nesting records, all from Stoddard's notes, include: 21 May 1916 (containing five eggs), Cowles Bog-Tremont area; 2 June 1916 (containing five eggs) at Cowles Bog; and 23 June 1917 near Baileytown.

FAMILY STURNIDAE: Starlings

EUROPEAN STARLING (*Sturnus vulgaris*)

Finding data
Finding Code = 1, throughout much of the year. This introduced bird, now widely detested, is found throughout the Calumet Region. The largest single party count was 20,000 seen migrating past Mount Baldy 12 March 1990.

Status
The first report of this European species in the Dunes was 27 July 1927, near Miller (Ford, 1956). Boyd (unpub. notes) reported nesting birds in northern Lake County the following year (8 March 1928), commenting, "Two Starlings at Bluebird boxes along grape arbor; also at Flicker hole in apple tree. Sparrows and Bluebirds were contesting the intrusion." The birds were observed carrying nesting materials into the Flicker box on 25 March and 9 April; two eggs were noted on 25 April. Today, querulous flocks of smoke-brown juveniles appear in early June.

FAMILY VIREONIDAE: Vireos

Seven representatives of this family have occurred in the Dunes. The White-eyed, Yellow-throated, Warbling, and Red-eyed Vireos are summer residents; the Solitary and Philadelphia Vireos are transients; and the Bell's Vireo is a visitant. Vireos are well known for their incessant singing. Not only do they vocalize throughout the midsummer day, but many also sing during the autumn migration, long after most other passerines are muted. Accordingly, many more vireos are heard than are seen.

WHITE-EYED VIREO (*Vireo griseus*)

Finding data
Finding Code = 3, in May and June when birds actively sing. This vireo is fairly well restricted to scrubby areas and wood edges along margins of the interdunal marsh. Beverly Shores is the most reliable site. Singing birds can often be heard from Beverly Drive.

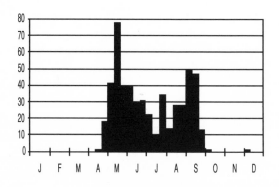

Peak counts

Spring:	5	17 May 1988	Beverly Shores & Cowles Bog
Summer:	8	31 Jul 1986	Beverly Shores
Fall:	5	1 Sep 1979	Beverly Shores

Status

This "southern species" is a summer resident and transient through the Dunes. Although the White-eyed Vireo undoubtedly breeds in the Dunes, no nests have been reported. Young birds, recognized by their dark eyes, have been observed in early September; one extremely late immature was found in Michigan City 5 December 1995 (Dancey, 1996a). Migration data are:

	EARLIEST	ARRIVE	PEAK	DEPART	LATEST	N
Spring	16 Apr 60	2 May	17 May	9 Jun	- - -	166
Fall	- - -	25 Jul	31 Aug	17 Sep	5 Dec 95	135

BELL'S VIREO (*Vireo bellii*)

Finding data

Finding Code = 8; the most recent reports consist of singletons at Gibson Woods Preserve 11 May 1993 and in the Migrant Trap 25 May 1997. Summer birds occurred in scrubby habitat south of Mt. Baldy during the summers of 1989, 90, and 91.

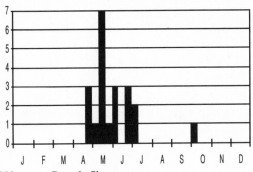

Peak counts

Spring:	2	14 May 1983	Beverly Shores
Summer:	2	3 Jul 1954	Seven Dolors Shrine
Fall:	1	9 Oct 1950	Northern Lake County (Mumford notes)

Status

Bell's Vireo is an erratic summer resident and occasional migrant. It was reported several times between 1943 and 1962, and nests were located on the grounds of Seven Dolors Shrine (Porter County) in 1954 and 1955. According to Mumford (unpub. notes) the 1954 nest contained two eggs and the 1955 nest, which was located one meter up in a hawthorn, fledged two young. Territorial birds were found near Mount Baldy in 1989, 1990, and 1991.

SOLITARY VIREO (*Vireo solitarius*)

Finding data

Finding Code = 5, during the height of migration; mid-May and late September - early October. This striking vireo is usually found among the mixed warbler-vireo flocks that wander the Dunes during migration; lakeside traps are especially good sites for this species. Spring birds occasionally sing.

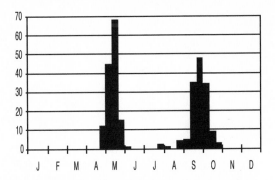

Peak counts

Spring:	7	11 May 1996	Beverly Shores
Fall:	6	20 Sep 1989	High Dunes

Status

The Solitary Vireo is a spring and fall transient through the Dunes. Migration data are:

	EARLIEST	ARRIVE	PEAK	DEPART	LATEST	N
Spring	22 Apr 53	1 May	11 May	21 May	2 Jun 74	111
Fall	23 Jul 82	11 Sep	26 Sep	10 Oct	24 Oct 92	116

YELLOW-THROATED VIREO (*Vireo flavifrons*)

Finding data

Finding Code = 2, from mid-May through June when the birds are singing. The raspy notes of this species can invariably be heard on Trails 2 and 10 east of Wilson Shelter in Dunes State Park and in the Heron Rookery. This species is rarely seen in the lakefront traps.

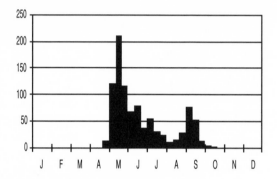

Peak counts

Spring:	14	14 May 1994	Dunes State Park
Fall:	5	16 Sep 1979	Beverly Shores

Status

The Yellow-throated Vireo is a summer resident and transient through the Dunes. Active nests have been observed in Dunes State Park from mid-May through mid-June. Migration data are as follows:

	EARLIEST	ARRIVE	PEAK	DEPART	LATEST	N
Spring	24 Apr 94	4 May	18 May	10 Jun	- - -	264
Fall	- - -	14 Aug	7 Sep	22 Sep	19 Oct 86	145

172

WARBLING VIREO (*Vireo gilvus*)

Finding data
Finding Code = 3, during the intense singing in May. This species seems to display a distinct preference for cottonwood or poplar trees. Singing birds can often be heard in the poplars along Beverly Drive (west of Broadway) in Beverly Shores. It is detected far more often in spring than fall.

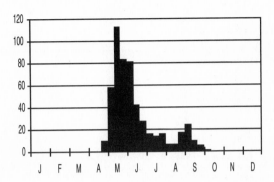

Peak counts
Spring:	8	18 May 1924	Northern Porter County
Summer:	9	13 Jun 1982	Breeding Bird Survey
Fall:	3	22 Sep 1954	Baileytown

Status
This drab vireo is a summer resident and transient through the Dunes. Smith (1936) gives a nesting record on 22 June 1935 in Hammond; the nest contained four eggs. Another nest, containing three featherless young, was observed 25 June 1983 along Squirrel Creek in rural Porter County. Migration data are:

	EARLIEST	ARRIVE	PEAK	DEPART	LATEST	N
Spring	24 Apr 76	6 May	20 May	9 Jun	- - -	215
Fall	- - -	22 Aug	4 Sep	17 Sep	1 Oct 42	55

PHILADELPHIA VIREO (*Vireo philadelphicus*)

Finding data
Finding Code = 5, during the fall migration in mid-September (less common in spring). This species usually joins the loose flocks of migrating warblers and vireos that pass through the Dunes in autumn. It is often seen in the lakeside parks.

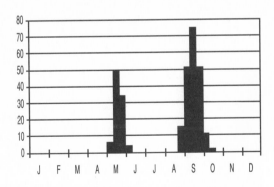

Peak counts
Spring:	4	19 May 1984	Dunes State Park
Fall:	5	14 Sep 1996	Lakefront

This vireo is a spring and fall transient through the Dunes. Migration data are:

	EARLIEST	ARRIVE	PEAK	DEPART	LATEST	N
Spring	1 May 53	11 May	19 May	27 May	4 Jun 84	70
Fall	26 Aug 62	2 Sep	14 Sep	28 Sep	13 Oct 85	162

RED-EYED VIREO (*Vireo olivaceus*)

Finding data
Finding Code = 1, from mid-May through June when territorial birds are singing. Nesting Red-eyed Vireos are easily found in Dunes State Park. This species is also frequently observed among the migrant passerine flocks in lakefront traps.

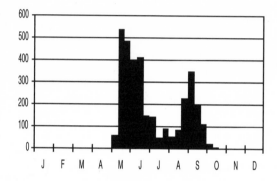

Peak counts
Spring:	120	15 May 1994	Dunes State Park
Fall:	45	14 Sep 1974	Northern Porter County

Status
This perpetual singer is a summer resident and transient through the Dunes. Nests containing eggs have been observed in late June, and young birds by 11 July. Migration data from the lakefront traps (*) are:

	EARLIEST	ARRIVE	PEAK	DEPART	LATEST	N
Spring*	30 Apr 85	17 May	22 May	29 May	3 Jun 83	49
Fall *	22 Aug 88	30 Aug	11 Sep	24 Sep	12 Nov 87	98

SUBFAMILY PARULINAE: Warblers

Perhaps no group of birds generates more excitement among birders than the wood warblers. Singing males are in crisp breeding plumage as they arrive fresh from tropical wintering grounds; in cool years many appear prior to extensive foliage development, adding splashes of brilliance to the somber landscape. Autumn woods are often awash with the olive and yellow tints of the ambiguous appearing fall warblers, which provide an entirely different, but equally fascinating, attraction. These darting birds, in cryptic plumages, test the mettle of even the most experienced observers. Accordingly, for many birders the term "migration" is virtually synonymous with "warbler migration," and warblers constitute the very quintessence of birding.

An understanding of migratory behavior aids in finding warblers in the Dunes. By nature these relatively weak flyers are subject to the capricious temperament of the weather. Accordingly, atmospheric perturbations often generate "migratory waves," which advance under favorable meteorological conditions and are grounded during adverse weather. The net result is wide daily variations in the number of warblers present. One day the woods can be alive with warblers and the following day it might be difficult to find any birds whatsoever.

Foraging migrants frequently band together in loose flocks (often accompanied by other small passerines such as vireos, kinglets, creepers, or chickadees), which move slowly through the foliage more or less as a unit. Birds within a flock apparently communicate by uttering thin call notes; these subtle sounds often betray the flock's presence.

Warbler flocks usually frequent the trees of woodlands, parks, or orchards; however, on cold days with biting winds they seek sheltered areas, often quite near the ground. Virtually any location affording trees can serve as suitable sites to find warblers. Established areas that have proved productive over the years are woodlands of Dunes State Park, the Heron Rookery, west Beverly Drive, Whiting Park, Gibson Woods Preserve, and the Migrant Trap. Lakeside traps apparently have the added benefit of accumulating birds seeking refuge from Lake Michigan.

The upper Midwest is arguably North America's finest location for finding migrant warblers. In this geographical region the three primary spring migration paths (the Caribbean-Florida, trans-Gulf, and Central American routes) converge. Accordingly, the diversity of migrant spring warblers near the Great Lakes in unparalleled elsewhere on the Continent.

The Dunes area is nestled within this region of migratory warbler convergence. Each spring 36 warbler species occur regularly in the Dunes area, though two, Worm-eating and Kentucky, are quite rare. Spring migration begins in early April with the arrival of Yellow-rumpeds and the appearance of Louisiana Waterthrush on nesting territories. The primary warbler migration period is between 3 May and 28 May. The average peak of the spring flight, calculated from the peak dates in the migration envelopes, is approximately 14 May. Near this date it is possible to find more than 30 species of warblers during a day's birding in the Dunes area.

Warbler diversity is lower in fall, with about 30 species occurring regularly. Several of these, however, (e.g., Blue-winged, Prairie, Cerulean, Louisiana Waterthrush, and Hooded) are birds that linger on the breeding grounds, rather than migrants. The primary autumn migration period falls between 25 August and 5 October. Based on peak dates in the migration envelopes, the average fall migration peak is near 12 September. A good mid-September day can yield 25 warbler species.

The relative abundances in the Dunes Area of the 36 regular warblers are summarized in the table below. In this listing the total number of each species recorded through December 1996 is tabulated along with seasonal abundance rankings. Rankings are based on numbers reported during the spring and fall seasons.

MIGRATION DATA FOR 36 WARBLER SPECIES

	Total Nos.	Spring Rank	Fall Rank		Total Nos.	Spring Rank	Fall Rank
Blue-winged	568	19	24	Bay-breasted	877	17	13
Golden-winged	355	24	22	Blackpoll	1448	21	5
Tennessee	1584	8	11	Cerulean	797	14	32
Orange-crowned	266	28	20	Black & White	1279	11	8
Nashville	930	15	14	Am. Redstart	5412	3	2
N. Parula	174	30	27	Prothonotary	179	29	33
Yellow	2704	4	23	Worm-eating	39	36	34
Chestnut-sided	1185	9	15	Ovenbird	2091	7	7
Magnolia	2829	6	4	N. Waterthrush	900	10	17
Cape May	829	23	10	L. Waterthrush	390	22	29
Black-th. Blue	433	27	16	Kentucky	70	35	36
Yellow-rumped	10842	1	1	Connecticut	236	26	26
Black-th. Green	1156	12	9	Mourning	502	20	21
Blackburnian	570	18	19	C. Yellowthroat	3697	5	6
Yellow-throated	111	33	35	Hooded	359	25	28
Pine	173	34	25	Wilson's	995	16	12
Prairie	196	32	31	Canada	857	13	18
Palm	4681	2	3	Yellow-br. Chat	221	31	30

Spring and Fall rankings are similar for most species, however, there are a few exceptions. Most notable are the Yellow and Cerulean Warblers, which are far more common in spring than in fall, reflecting the departure of these nesting Warblers in July. An opposite pattern is shown by the Blackpoll, Cape May, and Black-throated Blue; these three are considerably more common in fall than in spring.

BLUE-WINGED WARBLER (*Vermivora pinus*)

Finding data

Finding Code = 3, during the active nesting period: May through early June. Singing Blue-wingeds are easily found in Dunes State Park along Trail 2 east of the Wilson Shelter where they inhabit the wood edge adjacent to the interdunal marsh. Blue-wingeds are almost never seen in the lakefront traps.

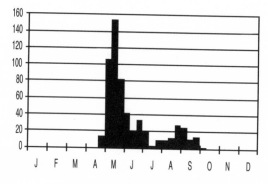

Peak counts

Spring:	10	14 May 1988	Dunes State Park
Fall:	5	1 Sep 1925	Northern Porter County

Status

This warbler is a summer resident and transient through the Dunes. Migration data are:

	EARLIEST	ARRIVE	PEAK	DEPART	LATEST	N
Spring	22 Apr 82	4 May	13 May	26 May	- - -	199
Fall	- - -	1 Aug	30 Aug	23 Sep	5 Oct 96	85

GOLDEN-WINGED WARBLER (*Vermivora chrysoptera*)

Finding data

Finding Code = 5, during the migration peaks: mid-May and early September.   Territorial birds occur in scrubby second growth of the interdunal marsh or in recent burns; however, summer Golden-winged Warblers are far less common than Blue-wings. Most are observed among the mixed flocks of migrant warblers.

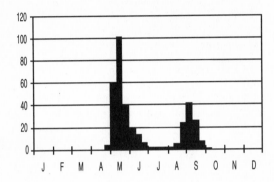

Peak counts

Spring:	6	19 May 1984	Dunes State Park
Fall:	6	14 Sep 1961	Baileytown

Status

The Golden-winged Warbler is a transient and summer resident in the Dunes. Pitcher (1974-79) reported up to four nesting territories in a burn along Furnessville Road. Interestingly, Golden-wings occupied the burn only during the first three years of regrowth. Migration data are:

	EARLIEST	ARRIVE	PEAK	DEPART	LATEST	N
Spring	25 Apr 86	7 May	17 May	10 Jun	- - -	191
Fall	- - -	22 Aug	4 Sep	16 Sep	1 Oct 82	86

Observations

Blue-wing x Golden-wing hybrids are noted regularly in the Dunes. More than two dozen "Brewster's" and several "Lawrence's" have been reported, mostly at Baileytown and Dunes State Park. In late June 1952, a Blue-wing brooding five young, with an apparent Golden-wing territorial male, were observed in the High Dunes (AFN 6:285).

TENNESSEE WARBLER (*Vermivora peregrina*)

Finding data
Finding Code = 2, during the spring migration peak in mid-May. Tennessee Warblers, the most numerous representative of this genus, are usually found among the mixed flocks of migrating warblers. Large numbers are often present during the spring flight; their songs emanate from virtually every tree top.

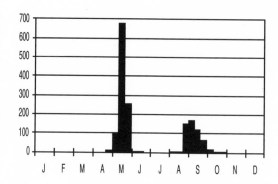

Peak counts
Spring:	63	19 May 1984	Dunes State Park (IAQ 63:48)
Fall:	20	27 Aug 1961	Baileytown

Status
The Tennessee Warbler is a transient through the Dunes. Migration data are:

	EARLIEST	ARRIVE	PEAK	DEPART	LATEST	N
Spring	25 Apr 85	7 May	16 May	24 May	14 Jun 74	281
Fall	7 Aug 93	26 Aug	9 Sep	26 Sep	24 Oct 90	300

ORANGE-CROWNED WARBLER (*Vermivora celata*)

Finding data
Finding Code = 5, during the migration peaks: late April - early May and the first half of October. This species occurs in the lakefront traps. Fall birds are extremely rare before the third week of September; many early reports may be misidentified. In autumn it occasionally forages in open areas especially on goldenrod.

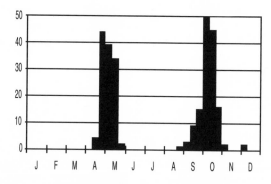

Peak counts
Spring:	4	29 Apr 1962	Baileytown
Fall:	7	16 Oct 1983	Cowles Bog

Status
This drab warbler is a spring and fall transient through the Dunes. A winter record, two birds at Whiting Park 2 December 1936, is given by Smith (1936). Migration data are:

	EARLIEST	ARRIVE	PEAK	DEPART	LATEST	N
Spring	17 Apr 80	23 Apr	4 May	16 May	27 May 19	94
Fall	26 Aug 62	20 Sep	9 Oct	21 Oct	2 Nov 91	111

NASHVILLE WARBLER (*Vermivora ruficapilla*)

Finding data
Finding Code = 3, during the migration peaks: early May and the last half of September. Nashville Warblers usually occur among the loose flocks of migrating passerines. Accordingly the lakeside parks and woodlands often yield this species during migration.

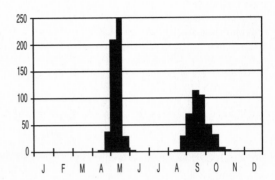

Peak counts
Spring:	24	8 May 1997	Lakefront traps
Fall:	10	11 Sep 1959	Baileytown

Status
The Nashville Warbler is a transient through the Dunes. Migration data are as follows:

	EARLIEST	ARRIVE	PEAK	DEPART	LATEST		N
Spring	19 Apr 92	30 Apr	10 May	20 May	5 Jun	50	255
Fall	16 Aug 55	2 Sep	18 Sep	7 Oct	3 Nov	90	272

NORTHERN PARULA (*Parula americana*)

Finding data
Finding Code = 5, during the height of spring migration in mid-May. A majority of the recent records come from Dunes State Park and the Heron Rookery. Parulas are most often detected among the spring warbler flocks; they are difficult to find in fall. Most autumn birds are seen in the lakefront parks.

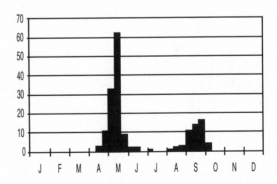

Peak counts
Spring:	6	14 May 1988	Heron Rookery
Fall:	2	5 Oct 1985	Migrant Trap and George Lake woodlot

Status
The Parula is a transient through the Dunes; several summer record exists. Migration data are:

	EARLIEST	ARRIVE	PEAK	DEPART	LATEST		N
Spring	16 Apr 91	29 Apr	11 May	20 May	14 Jun	94	80
Fall	6 Aug 88	30 Aug	13 Sep	30 Sep	7 Oct	54	51

YELLOW WARBLER (*Dendroica petechia*)

Finding data

Finding Code = 1, during initial stages of nesting in May. The Yellow Warbler is widespread throughout the Dunes, and is especially common in the Beverly Shores interdunal marsh. After nesting activities have concluded in July, this species departs quickly and becomes quite difficult to find.

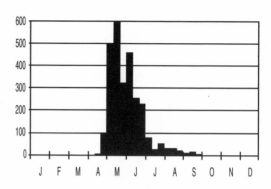

Peak counts

Spring:	83	6 May 1987	High Dunes
Summer:	95	14 Jun 1996	Beverly Shores (along Beverly Drive)
Fall:	8	3 Aug 1984	Beverly Shores

Status

The Yellow Warbler is a summer resident and transient through the Dunes. Nests have been found in June and young birds observed in July and August. Migration data from the lakefront traps (*) are:

	EARLIEST		ARRIVE	PEAK	DEPART	LATEST		N
Spring*	11 Apr	31	5 May	17 May	1 Jun	9 Jul	88	49
Fall *	29 Jul	90	10 Aug	28 Aug	16 Sep	30 Sep	28	32

CHESTNUT-SIDED WARBLER (*Dendroica pensylvanica*)

Finding data

Finding Code = 3, in the last half of May when migrants and territorial males actively sing. Summering birds are reported annually in the State Park; they can usually be found along the north edge of the interdunal marsh toward the eastern end of Trail 10. Summer birds also occur regularly in the Beverly Shores marsh.

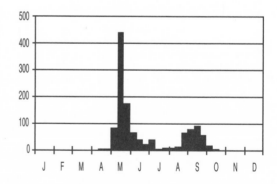

Peak counts

Spring:	25	20 May 1987	Whiting Park
Fall:	6	27 Aug 1961	Baileytown

Status

Although this species is primarily a transient, a few pairs linger each summer to breed in the High Dunes. Nests have been located in June and early July. Migration data based solely on reports from lakefront traps (*) are:

	EARLIEST	ARRIVE	PEAK	DEPART	LATEST	N
Spring*	20 Apr 86	9 May	18 May	23 May	29 May 93	53
Fall *	25 Aug 89	28 Aug	13 Sep	26 Sep	11 Oct 79	108

Observations

On 6 July 1977 a singing male Chestnut-sided Warbler was noted along the Calumet Bike Trail immediately south of the State Park. Patient observation revealed that a pair was present, and that they were carrying food. Both parents would enter the upper north side of a 3m maple sapling, work their way diagonally down the tree, and exit into shrubs south of the maple. The nest was ultimately found in a low blackberry bramble some 3m south of the maple. The parents' movements through the maple were apparently intended for deception. The nest, which was about .5m above the ground, contained a very young nestling and one egg.

MAGNOLIA WARBLER (*Dendroica magnolia*)

Finding data

Finding Code = 2, during the migration peaks: mid-May and mid-September. This striking warbler is one of the most common species among the migrant passerine flocks. It is easily found in the lakefront traps during migration.

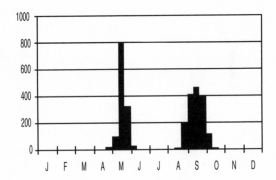

Peak counts

Spring:	42	11 May 1996	Dunes State Park
Fall:	30	12 Sep 1961	Baileytown

Status

The Magnolia Warbler is a fall and spring transient through the Dunes. Mumford and Keller (1984) list two midsummer records for the lakefront (29 July 1961 and 11 July 1978). Migration data are:

	EARLIEST	ARRIVE	PEAK	DEPART	LATEST	N
Spring	8 Apr 49	10 May	18 May	27 May	15 Jun 46	365
Fall	11 Jul 78	30 Aug	14 Sep	30 Sep	19 Oct 55	638

Observations

The hazard Lake Michigan poses to migrant passerines was graphically demonstrated 14 September 1977. On that morning a Magnolia Warbler, apparently completing a nocturnal crossing, was observed flying in off the lake. It narrowly cleared the surf and almost landed on the wave-swashed sand, then fluttered weakly up the beach, settling on the dry foredune sand several meters from the nearest vegetation. When the bird was approached it remained motionless; close inspection revealed that it was asleep. Not until the observer was within a few centimeters of the warbler did the bird opened an eye; it surveyed the intruder, then immediately fell asleep again, too exhausted to even be frightened.

CAPE MAY WARBLER (*Dendroica tigrina*)

Finding data
Finding Code = 4, during the migration peaks in mid-May and early September. Numbers vary considerably from year to year. Cape Mays are usually seen among the flocks of migrant warblers, but this species also shows a penchant for conifers. A few are usually present in the lakefront traps during migration.

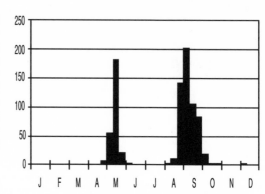

Peak counts
Spring:	14	13 May 1995	Gibson Woods Preserve
Fall:	31	28 Aug 1986	Lakefront

Status
The Cape May Warbler is a spring and fall transient through the Dunes; however, a winter bird was observed at a suet feeder in Chesterton 3 and 4 December 1983. Migration data are:

	EARLIEST	ARRIVE	PEAK	DEPART	LATEST	N
Spring	30 Apr 57	5 May	14 May	20 May	3 Jun 92	143
Fall	10 Aug 52	26 Aug	7 Sep	25 Sep	4 Dec 83	294

BLACK-THROATED BLUE WARBLER (*Dendroica caerulescens*)

Finding data
Finding Code = 5, during the fall migration in September. Black-throated Blues are reported about twice as often in fall as in spring. This species is usually seen among the mixed flocks of migrating warblers, although they occasionally travel in small family (?) groups. Among the sexed birds, males outnumber females by 1.6 to one.

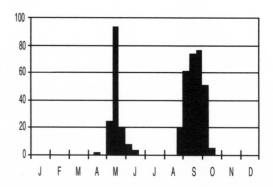

Peak counts
Spring:	7	11 May 1991	George Lake woodlot & Gibson Woods
Fall:	5		Recorded on three occasions

	EARLIEST	ARRIVE	PEAK	DEPART	LATEST	N
Spring	13 Apr 88	7 May	16 May	23 May	17 Jun 89	108
Fall	22 Aug 92	4 Sep	17 Sep	7 Oct	20 Oct 58	214

YELLOW-RUMPED WARBLER (*Dendroica coronata*)

Finding data

Finding Code = 2, during the migration peaks in late April and in early October. Yellow-rumps are the earliest spring and latest fall warblers. Large migrant flocks, consisting almost exclusively of Yellow-rumpeds, are found throughout the Dunes.   Flocks exceeding 50 birds are fairly common during the migration peaks.

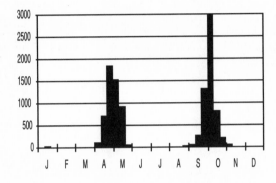

Peak counts

Spring:	150	26 Apr 1960	Baileytown
Fall:	1000	7 Oct 1949	N. Lake County (Mumford & Keller, 1984)

Status
The "Myrtle Warbler," as it was formerly known, is a spring and fall transient
through the Dunes. A few lingering birds have been reported on Christmas
Bird Counts. Migration data are:

	EARLIEST	ARRIVE	PEAK	DEPART	LATEST	N
Spring	18 Mar 79	13 Apr	29 Apr	14 May	5 Jun 83	502
Fall	22 Aug 80	17 Sep	3 Oct	20 Oct	23 Dec 56	562

BLACK-THROATED GRAY WARBLER (*Dendroica nigrescens*)

Finding Code = 10, only one record. A female was seen at close range 27
September 1983 at Dunes State Park. The bird, seen by only one observer, was
compared with a nearby Black-and-White Warbler. Yellow loral areas were
clearly noted (Brock 1984).

TOWNSEND'S WARBLER (*Dendroica townsendi*)

Finding Code = 10, only one record. On 1 May 1983 a male was discovered
along Trail 10 of Dunes State Park. The bird was seen again briefly the
following morning (perhaps attracted by a recording of its song) by a second
observer (Brock, 1984).

BLACK-THROATED GREEN WARBLER (*Dendroica virens*)

Finding data
Finding Code = 3, during the migration peaks in mid-May and the last two-thirds of September. This species is frequently observed among the migrating passerine flocks in lakefront parks.

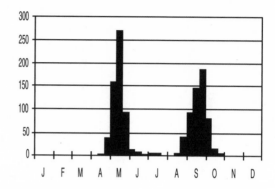

Peak counts

Spring:	25	17 May 1974	High Dunes
Fall:	10	21 Sep 1954	Baileytown

Status
The Black-throated Green is primarily a transient through the Dunes, but several mid-summer reports and one breeding record exist (see below). Migration data, excluding the breeding birds, are:

	EARLIEST	ARRIVE	PEAK	DEPART	LATEST	N
Spring	16 Apr 91	2 May	13 May	26 May	29 Jun 94	284
Fall	13 Aug 86	2 Sep	19 Sep	4 Oct	25 Oct 75	366

Observations
During summer 1983 Black-throated Green Warblers successfully nested in mature deciduous woods 200m east of Dunes State Park. On 15 June the female was observed carrying nesting materials. The male was heard singing regularly throughout June and early July. On 11 July a single fledgling was observed being fed by both adults.

BLACKBURNIAN WARBLER (*Dendroica fusca*)

Finding data
Finding Code = 3, during the spring migration peak in mid-May. Considerably fewer birds are recorded in autumn. Fall birds are among the early migrants; the peak flight occurs in late August and early September. The Black-burnian is a regular member of the loose flocks that frequent the lakefront traps.

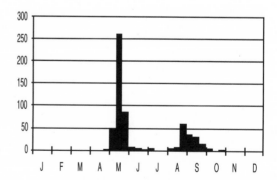

184

Peak counts

Spring:	31	14 May 1983	Dunes State Park
Fall:	5	30 Aug 1955	Michigan City Harbor

Status

This brilliantly plumed warbler is a spring and fall transient through the Dunes. Although nests have not been found, Blackburnians may breed in Dunes State Park. Territorial pairs were found in the park 4 July 1995 (IAQ 74:155) and 22 June 1996. Migration data are:

	EARLIEST	ARRIVE	PEAK	DEPART	LATEST	N
Spring	30 Apr 95	9 May	17 May	28 May	14 Jun 74	221
Fall	5 Aug 93	24 Aug	3 Sep	24 Sep	25 Oct 83	128

YELLOW-THROATED WARBLER (*Dendroica dominica*)

Finding data

Finding Code = 5, in late April and early May when singing males occupy territories in the Heron Rookery. The status of Yellow-throated Warblers changed significantly after the 1984 discovery of breeding birds along the Little Calumet River in the Heron Rookery. Only four records occurred prior to 1984.

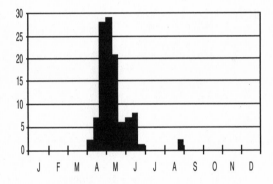

Peak counts

Spring:	5	26 Apr 1991	Heron Rookery
Fall:	1	21 Aug 1960	Baileytown
	1	25 Aug 1989	Heron Rookery

Status

Yellow-throated Warblers are now local summer residents and vagrants. Migration data are:

	EARLIEST	ARRIVE	PEAK	DEPART	LATEST	N
Spring	8 Apr 88	21 Apr	4 May	6 Jun	29 Jun 86	62
Fall	21 Aug 60	-	-	-	-	-	25 Aug 89	2

PINE WARBLER (*Dendroica pinus*)

Finding data

Finding Code = 6, although this species may have been more common in past years. A majority of recent sightings have been in the Migrant Trap and George Lake woodlot during late April. Pine Warblers usually occur among the mixed flocks of migrating warblers.

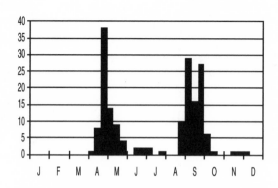

Peak counts

Spring:	3		Recorded on three occasions
Fall:	10	27 Sep 1949	Northern Porter County

Status

Today the Pine Warbler is a transient through the Dunes; however, Ford (1956) refers to young found in a Lake County pinery in July 1874, and Butler (1906) lists June observations near Michigan City in 1904. These records suggest that the Pine Warbler formerly nested in the Dunes. Migration data, excluding the summer records, are:

	EARLIEST	ARRIVE	PEAK	DEPART	LATEST	N
Spring	5 Apr 84	19 Apr	28 Apr	14 May	30 May 94	57
Fall	23 Jul 91	31 Aug	12 Sep	2 Oct	1 Dec 95	68

KIRTLAND'S WARBLER (*Dendroica kirtlandii*)

Finding Code = 9, five records exist. Four records are in May and one in September. The May reports include two old sightings listed in Ford *et al.* (1934): 25 May 1918 and 9 May 1924. There are two modern spring records: a female was photographed 17 May 1981 in Chesterton (Brock, 1982) and a singing male was photographed 22-23 May 1983 at Michigan City Harbor (AB 37:877). The fall Kirtland's was seen 24 September 1994 in Whiting Park. Based on colored leg-bands, it was determined that the bird had been banded on the breeding grounds July 16, 1992 in Ogemaw County, Michigan. Banders described the warbler as an adult female with brood patch; she was recaptured nearby July 22, 1992, but never seen again— until she reappeared at Whiting Park (Brock, 1995).

Peak counts

All observations consist of single birds.

	EARLIEST	ARRIVE	PEAK	DEPART	LATEST	N
Spring	9 May 24	-	-	-	-	-	-	22 May 83	4

PRAIRIE WARBLER (*Dendroica discolor*)

Finding data
Finding Code = 4, during the nesting season. A small colony of Prairie Warblers nests in the blowouts of Dunes State Park. Singing birds can usually be located there during late May and June. Migrants are almost never reported. A few birds linger in the breeding areas well into September.

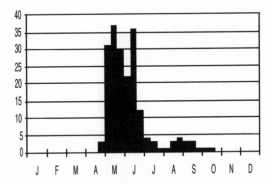

Peak counts
Spring:	8	30 May 1920	Dunes State Park
Summer:	19	11 Jun 1988	Dunes State Park
Fall:	2	22 Aug 1995	Dunes State Park

Status
Although established nesting areas north of Indiana dictate that a few Prairie Warblers undoubtedly migrate through the Dunes, virtually all records consist of the summer residents in the blowouts. Nests have been recorded in June and July.

	EARLIEST	ARRIVE	PEAK	DEPART	LATEST	N
Spring	24 Apr 85	6 May	19 May	11 Jun	- - -	83
Fall	- - -		1 Sep		12 Oct 90	16

Observations
The Dunes Park Prairie Warbler colony, which constitutes a unique isolated breeding outpost for this species, maintains a precarious existence in the blowouts. Observers should avoid the use of tape recorders or other forms of harassment when seeking these birds.

PALM WARBLER (*Dendroica palmarum*)

Finding data
Finding Code = 2, in the first week of May and during the last week of September. This ground-loving species prefers more open habitat than most other warblers; migrants are easily seen at the Migrant Trap and along the shore of Long Lake at West Beach.

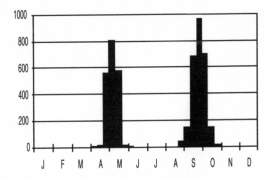

Peak counts

Spring:	150	12 May 1984	West Beach
Fall:	64	16 Sep 1995	Michigan City Harbor & Port of Indiana

Status

This tail-wagger is a transient through the Dunes. Migration data are:

	EARLIEST	ARRIVE	PEAK	DEPART	LATEST	N
Spring	31 Mar 90	24 Apr	6 May	17 May	3 Jun 79	384
Fall	25 Aug 65	9 Sep	26 Sep	9 Oct	28 Oct 16	477

BAY-BREASTED WARBLER (*Dendroica castanea*)

Finding data

Finding Code = 3, during the migration peaks: mid-May and mid-September. This warbler is usually found among the mixed flocks of small passerines that move through the lakefront parks and woodlands during migration. Interestingly, in fall about 2.4 Blackpolls are seen for every Bay-breasted.

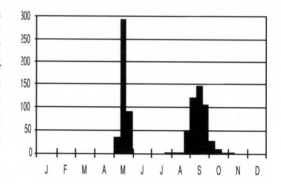

Peak counts

Spring:	30	14 May 1983	Dunes State Park
Fall:	19	21 Sep 1996	Lakefront traps

Status

The Bay-breasted Warbler is a spring and fall transient through the Dunes. Migration data are:

	EARLIEST	ARRIVE	PEAK	DEPART	LATEST	N
Spring	3 May 88	10 May	17 May	25 May	30 May 55	191
Fall	23 Jul 95	31 Aug	13 Sep	30 Sep	1 Nov 80	284

BLACKPOLL WARBLER (*Dendroica striata*)

Finding data
Finding Code = 3, during the height of fall migration in mid-September. Both the migration habitats and timing are similar to those of the former species. Blackpolls are one of the more common members of the autumn warbler flocks.

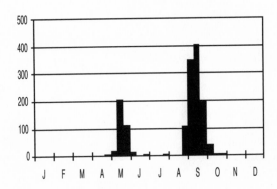

Peak counts
Spring:	17	14 May 1983	Dunes State Park
Fall:	29	9 Sep 1995	Lakefront traps

Status
The Blackpoll is a spring and fall transient through the Dunes. Migration data are:

	EARLIEST	ARRIVE	PEAK	DEPART	LATEST	N
Spring	27 Apr 85	11 May	19 May	28 May	26 Jun 74	174
Fall	31 Jul 88	1 Sep	13 Sep	26 Sep	26 Oct 96	474

CERULEAN WARBLER (*Dendroica cerulea*)

Finding data
Finding Code = 3, during the last half of May and June, when territorial males are singing. Ceruleans nest in the tall trees along Trail 2 east of Wilson Shelter in Dunes State Park and along the river in the Heron Rookery. Nesting birds dwell in the treetops; if the song is not recognized summer birds are almost impossible to find in the dense foliage.

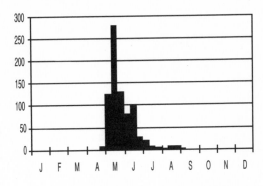

Peak counts
Spring:	27	9 May 1987	Dunes State Park
Fall:	3	18 Aug 1989	Heron Rookery

Status
The Cerulean Warbler is a summer resident and certainly a common breeder in the Dunes, but the only observed nest consists of one, only 4.5 meters above the ground, noted in Dunes State Park 29 May 1971 (AB 25:753). In addition to the latter site, this species probably nests in woodlands of the Heron Rookery

unit and Moraine State Nature Preserve. Migrants are almost never seen in either spring or fall. With the termination of nesting activities this species quietly vanishes from the Dunes.

	EARLIEST	ARRIVE	PEAK	DEPART	LATEST	N
Spring	26 Apr 60	6 May	19 May	11 Jun	- - -	220
Fall	- - -	- - -	21 Aug	- -	3 Sep 92	14

BLACK-AND-WHITE WARBLER (*Mniotilta varia*)

Finding data
Finding Code = 3, in mid-May and mid-September. Black-and-Whites usually associate with the woodland flocks of migrating warblers. They are regularly seen in the lakefront traps. A few birds often summer in Dunes State Park and Beverly Shores.

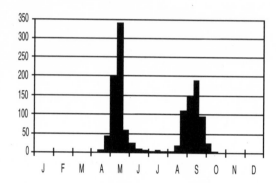

Peak counts
Spring:	41	11 May 1996	Dunes State Park
Fall:	25	12 Sep 1961	Baileytown

Status
Although this dapper warbler is primarily a migrant through the Dunes, a few nesting records exist. Stoddard (unpub. notes) found a nest containing four young 15 July 1917, and Ford (1956) reported a nest 19 June 1921. Additionally, numerous June and July records exist. Migration data from the lakefront traps (*) are:

	EARLIEST	ARRIVE	PEAK	DEPART	LATEST	N
Spring*	8 Apr 91	2 May	11 May	22 May	28 May 64	60
Fall*	12 Aug 89	27 Aug	11 Sep	28 Sep	13 Oct 79	136

Observations
An unexpected peril for small migrating passerines was discovered 10 May 1979 at the Migrant Trap. A female Black-and-White was working each of the small trees in the "creeper" fashion typical of this species, flying to the base and making her way up the trunk. About half way up one sapling she encountered an American Robin nest with the owner in attendance. The occupant exploded from the nest, seizing the surprised warbler by the wing, and both birds fell to the ground. Dust and feathers flew. Ultimately the warbler broke free and stood her ground valiantly with wings spread and bill open, facing the Robin. For a few moments the two birds remained motionless, only a short distance apart. Then the avian David-and-Goliath encounter ended; the Robin returned to the nest and the Black-and-White managed to flutter away. But the outer primaries of one wing were broken and pointing outward at an awkward angle. Nine days later the same warbler, identified by the broken wing feathers, was

again noted in the Migrant Trap. Although able to fly sufficiently well to forage in the trees, her spring migration was apparently over.

AMERICAN REDSTART (*Setophaga ruticilla*)

Finding data
Finding Code = 2, during the migration peaks: mid-May and the first half of September. This colorful species is one of the most common warblers in the migrant flocks. Redstarts nest in Dunes State Park and along the Little Calumet River in the Heron Rookery. Numerous singing males can be heard at the latter site in late May and early June.

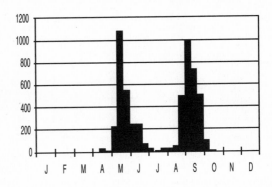

Peak counts
Spring:	50	17 May 1924	Whiting Park
Fall:	60	11 Sep 1993	Lakefront traps

Status
The Redstart is a summer resident and transient through the Dunes. A nest, with both parents feeding young, was observed 15 June 1984 in the Heron Rookery unit of the National Lakeshore. Migration data from the lakefront traps (*) are:

	EARLIEST	ARRIVE	PEAK	DEPART	LATEST	N
Spring*	26 Apr 91	9 May	19 May	29 May	2 Jun 82	94
Fall *	15 Aug 87	29 Aug	12 Sep	29 Sep	25 Oct 95	316

PROTHONOTARY WARBLER (*Protonotaria citrea*)

Finding data
Finding Code = 5, in May at nest sites in Dunes State Park. In recent years Prothonotarys have nested in the interdunal marsh in the State Park. The most commonly used site is near the footbridge just north of Wilson Shelter. This species is almost never recorded in the lakefront traps.

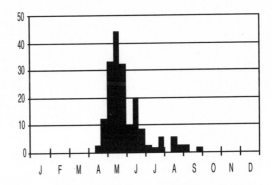

Peak counts
Spring:	6	31 May 1987	Dunes State Park
Fall:	3	12 Aug 1983	Dunes State Park

Status

The Prothonotary Warbler is a local summer resident. For several years birds were observed entering nest holes in a dead stump near the footbridge in Dunes State Park. Migration data are:

	EARLIEST	ARRIVE	PEAK	DEPART	LATEST	N
Spring	19 Apr 95	30 Apr	14 May	13 Jun	- - -	110
Fall	12 Aug 83	- -	24 Aug	- -	24 Sep 85	8

WORM-EATING WARBLER (*Helmitheros vermivorus*)

Finding data

Finding Code = 7, in mid-May. A majority of the records come from the wooded dunes of the State Park, especially along Trail 10. A few have been recorded at the Moraine State Nature Preserve and in lakefront traps. Most birds are detected by song. This species is rarely seen in fall.

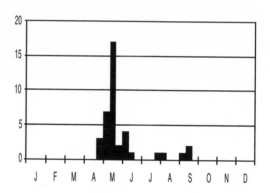

Peak counts

All observations consist of single birds.

Status

The Worm-eating Warbler is primarily a spring visitor to the Dunes. Migration data are:

	EARLIEST	ARRIVE	PEAK	DEPART	LATEST	N
Spring	23 Apr 85	3 May	13 May	2 Jun	12 Jun 76	34
Fall	23 Jul 95	- -	6 Sep	- -	19 Sep 92	5

OVENBIRD (*Seiurus aurocapillus*)

Finding data

Finding Code = 2, during late May and June when nesting birds are quite vocal. In Dunes State Park an early morning walk along Trail 2 will invariably yield singing birds on territory. Ovenbirds are also regularly found in dense cover of the lakefront traps during migration.

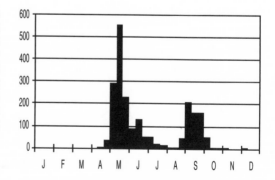

Peak counts

Spring:	68	11 May 1996	Dunes State Park
Fall:	24	8 Sep 1994	George Lake

Status

The Ovenbird is a summer resident and transient. A winter bird was seen in Tremont 4 December 1989. Migration data from the lakefront traps (*) are:

	EARLIEST	ARRIVE	PEAK	DEPART	LATEST		N
Spring*	12 Apr 12	2 May	10 May	23 May	28 May	83	75
Fall *	17 Aug 96	31 Aug	15 Sep	2 Oct	9 Nov	68	168

NORTHERN WATERTHRUSH (*Seiurus noveboracensis*)

Finding data

Finding Code = 3, during the second week of May when spring migrants actively sing; silent fall birds are more difficult to locate. This species prefers heavy cover and is rarely found far from water. Good locations include damp woodlands of Beverly Shores, Indiana Dunes State Park, and Cowles Bog.

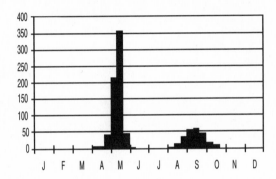

Peak counts

Spring:	62	11 May 1996	Dunes State Park
Fall:	6	14 Sep 1993	Gibson Woods

Status

This remarkable songster is a spring and fall transient through the Dunes. Migration data are:

	EARLIEST	ARRIVE	PEAK	DEPART	LATEST		N
Spring	6 Apr 58	28 Apr	10 May	21 May	7 Jun	74	247
Fall	5 Aug 55	23 Aug	12 Sep	4 Oct	20 Oct	61	175

LOUISIANA WATERTHRUSH (*Seiurus motacilla*)

Finding data
Finding Code = 3, in May when territorial birds are singing. Each year a few pairs nest in the moist woods south and east of Wilson Shelter (Dunes State Park). Summer birds are also present in similar habitat in the Heron Rookery. Migrants are rarely observed in the lakefront traps.

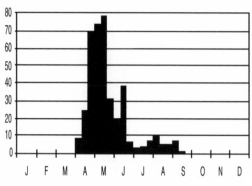

Peak counts
Spring:	7	26 Apr 1989	Heron Rookery
Fall:	4	31 Jul 1986	High Dunes

Status
The Louisiana Waterthrush is a local summer resident of the Dunes, occurring in the cool, damp cover of mature woods. After the birds cease singing in mid-June, they are rarely observed. Migration data are:

	EARLIEST	ARRIVE	PEAK	DEPART	LATEST	N
Spring	5 Apr 87	21 Apr	9 May	6 Jun	- - -	201
Fall	- - -	13 Jul	7 Aug	7 Sep	14 Sep 46	32

KENTUCKY WARBLER (*Oporornis formosus*)

Finding data
Finding Code = 7, in mid-May. Most records come from Dunes State Park in May and June, where singing males are detected; Trail 10 is especially good. A few birds have been found in July. Only two fall records exist; both were in September.

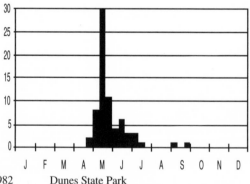

Peak counts
Spring:	2	9 May 1982	Dunes State Park
Fall:	1		All fall records are singletons

Status
This southern warbler is a late spring and summer visitant to the Dunes. Migration and summer data are:

	EARLIEST	ARRIVE	PEAK	DEPART	LATEST	N
Spring	29 Apr 84	6 May	17 May	10 Jun	- - -	67
Fall	1 Sep 85	- -	- -	- -	21 Sep 96	2

CONNECTICUT WARBLER (*Oporornis agilis*)

Finding data
Finding Code = 6, during spring migration in late May and the fall flight in early September. Spring birds occasionally sing, rendering them more easily found. In recent years most records of this furtive species have come from the Migrant Trap. It is sometimes found in heavy cover along Trails 2 and 10 of the State Park.

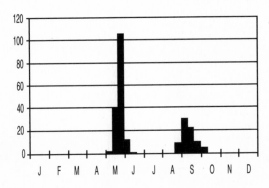

Peak counts
Spring:	30	21 May 1915	Wolf Lake (Stoddard, 1969)
Fall:	2		Recorded on six occasions

Status
The Connecticut Warbler is a transient through the Dunes. Migration data are:

	EARLIEST	ARRIVE	PEAK	DEPART	LATEST	N
Spring	8 May 85	15 May	22 May	31 May	14 Jun 85	109
Fall	21 Aug 50	31 Aug	10 Sep	28 Sep	3 Oct 83	73

MOURNING WARBLER (*Oporornis philadelphia*)

Finding data
Finding Code = 4 during the spring flight in late May when the presence of skulking males is betrayed by their distinctive song. The Mourning Warbler is fond of heavy cover, especially along wood edges. Good sites include the trails near Wilson Shelter in Dunes State Park, and the Migrant Trap. Most fall records come from the lakefront traps.

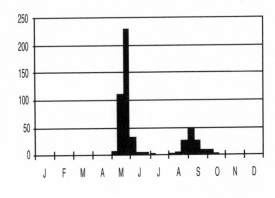

Peak counts
Spring:	12	20 May 1961	Baileytown
Fall:	12	7 Sep 1996	Lakefront traps.

Status
The Mourning Warbler is primarily a spring and fall transient through the Dunes, but several summer records exist. The summer status of this species is difficult to assess. Many summer birds are probably just late migrants;

however, records in late June and July suggest possible nesting. Graber et al. (1983) provide definite nesting records in nearby Cook County, Illinois. Migration data are:

	EARLIEST	ARRIVE	PEAK	DEPART	LATEST	N
Spring	8 May 93	16 May	24 May	1 Jun	4 Jul 81	241
Fall	6 Aug 88	24 Aug	7 Sep	25 Sep	13 Oct 79	97

COMMON YELLOWTHROAT (*Geothlypis trichas*)

Finding data
Finding Code = 1, in May when territorial birds are singing. This colorful species is widely distributed throughout the Dunes and is an especially common nesting species in the interdunal marshes of Beverly Shores and Cowles Bog. Fall migrants appear regularly in the lakefront traps.

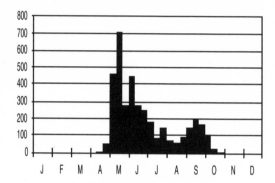

Peak counts
Spring:	49	13 May 1987	High Dunes
Fall:	30	17 Sep 1994	Whiting Park & Migrant Trap

Status
The Yellowthroat is a summer resident and transient through the Dunes. The winter record was 6 December 1952 at Baileytown (Reuter-skiold notes). Nests have been located in late May and June. Migration data from lakefront traps (*) are:

	EARLIEST	ARRIVE	PEAK	DEPART	LATEST	N
Spring*	19 Apr 92	1 May	12 May	28 May	18 Jun 86	70
Fall *	16 Aug 89	4 Sep	23 Sep	8 Oct	26 Oct 57	155

HOODED WARBLER (*Wilsonia citrina*)

Finding data
Finding Code = 4, during the nesting season in late May and June when males are singing. The most reliable site is Furnessville, where singing males can be heard from Ly-co-ki-we Trail. Territorial birds are also regular in mature woods of the State Park. On rare occasions migrants appear in the lakefront traps.

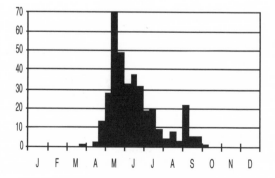

Peak counts

Spring:	6	17 May 1993	Furnessville
Fall:	3	15 Aug 1993	Furnessville

Status

This handsome songster is a local summer resident and transient through the Dunes. The remarkably early March record consisted of a male seen in Whiting (Mumford and Keller, 1984). R. Tweit (pers. comm.) found a nest 28 June 1975 near the artesian well in the Beverly Shores interdunal marsh. Migration data are:

	EARLIEST	ARRIVE	PEAK	DEPART	LATEST	N
Spring	25 Mar 54	5 May	17 May	9 Jun	- - -	135
Fall	- - -	12 Aug	4 Sep	22 Sep	3 Oct 95	37

WILSON'S WARBLER (*Wilsonia pusilla*)

Finding data

Finding Code = 3, during the migration peaks: last half of May and early September. This warbler is usually found among the large flocks of migrating warblers, although it does show a preference for scrubby habitat. During migration they are plentiful in the lakefront traps.

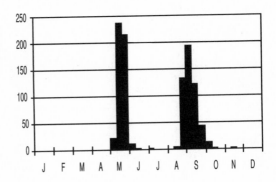

Peak counts

Spring:	18	21 May 1988	Lakefront traps
Fall:	12	1 Sep 1979	Beverly Shores

Status

Wilson's Warbler is a spring and fall transient through the Dunes. One summer record exists: 3 July 1953 at Baileytown. Migration data are as follows:

	EARLIEST	ARRIVE	PEAK	DEPART	LATEST	N
Spring	5 May 92	12 May	20 May	28 May	19 Jun 85	250
Fall	16 Aug 92	27 Aug	7 Sep	23 Sep	17 Nov 90	326

CANADA WARBLER (*Wilsonia canadensis*)

Finding data
Finding Code = 3, during the peak of spring migration in late May. In migration the Canada Warbler associates with the mixed warbler flocks. Summer birds can usually be heard singing along the eastern ends of Trails 2 and 10 in the State Park. Canada Warblers depart quite early in fall.

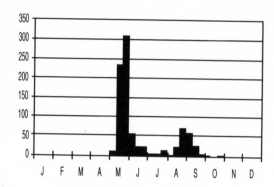

Peak counts

Spring:	19	22 May 1988	High Dunes
Fall:	7	19 Aug 1988	Lakefront traps

Status
This warbler of the northern forests is a transient and local summer resident in the Dunes. Migration data from the lakefront traps (*) are:

	EARLIEST	ARRIVE	PEAK	DEPART	LATEST	N
Spring*	7 May 88	14 May	22 May	29 May	31 May 85	63
Fall *	12 Aug 88	21 Aug	31 Aug	18 Sep	21 Oct 90	57

Observations
Although no nest has been found, the Canada Warbler is present throughout the summer and almost certainly nests in the High Dunes. It is recorded regularly throughout the summer, especially in Dunes State Park adjacent to the interdunal marsh. Ray Grow (pers. comm.) observed adults feeding a young cowbird 21 June 1958, and an adult with a young bird was noted just outside the eastern end of the State Park 23 July 1979.

YELLOW-BREASTED CHAT (*Icteria virens*)

Finding data
Finding Code = 4, during the nesting period when territorial birds sing and display; mid-May through June. Chats are most often found along margins of the interdunal marsh at Beverly Shores and Cowles Bog. An especially productive site is near the intersection of Beverly Drive and St. Clair Street. Only rarely, do Chats appear in the lakefront traps.

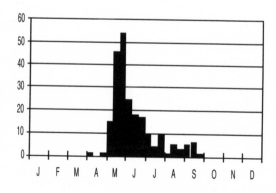

Peak counts

Spring:	5	24 May 1958	High Dunes
Summer:	7	6 Jun 1987	Beverly Shores
Fall:	1		All records are singletons

Status

The Yellow-breasted Chat is a summer resident and transient through the Dunes. Migration data are:

	EARLIEST	ARRIVE	PEAK	DEPART	LATEST	N
Spring	6 Apr 28	10 May	21 May	8 Jun	- - -	116
Fall	- - -	- -	3 Sep	- -	28 Sep 91	21

SUBFAMILY THRAUPINAE: Tanagers

SUMMER TANAGER (*Piranga rubra*)

Finding data

Finding Code = 7, in May. Prior to 1984 only five records existed for the Dunes; however, a mini-invasion that year initiated the current era in which Summer Tanagers are reported annually. Most records come from Dunes State Park; birds have been observed taking suet from the Nature Center's feeders.

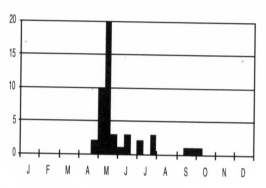

Peak counts

Spring:	2	Two were recorded on six different occasions
Fall:	1	All observations are singletons

Status

The Summer Tanager is now a rare transient and summer resident.

	EARLIEST	ARRIVE	PEAK	DEPART	LATEST	N
Spring	27 Apr 92	6 May	12 May	- -	- - -	31
Fall	17 Sep 86	- -	- -	- -	8 Oct 93	3

SCARLET TANAGER (*Piranga olivacea*)

Finding data

Finding Code = 3, during the nesting season between mid-May and the end of June. This brilliantly plumed species nests in Dunes State Park; it can invariably be heard in the woods east of Wilson Shelter in early summer. Migrants are seen only infrequently in the lakefront parks.

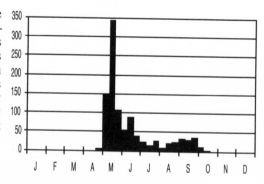

Peak counts

Spring:	20	19 May 1988	Dunes State Park
Fall:	6	22 Aug 1981	Dunes State Park

Status

The Scarlet Tanager is a transient and summer resident in the Dunes. Nests have been observed in Dunes State Park in July. Migration data are:

	EARLIEST	ARRIVE	PEAK	DEPART	LATEST	N
Spring	26 Apr 90	7 May	14 May	- -	- - -	193
Fall	- - -	12 Aug	10 Sep	27 Sep	12 Oct 74	124

WESTERN TANAGER (*Piranga ludoviciana*)

Finding data
Finding Code = 10, only one record. An adult male, first seen briefly 5 May 1996 near Waverly Road (north of Chesterton) reappeared at a Furnessville feeding station 9 May. It was seen regularly at that location through 16 May; a photo was published in the Audubon Field Notes (50:289).

SUBFAMILY CARDINALINAE: Cardinals and Buntings

NORTHERN CARDINAL (*Cardinalis cardinalis*)

Finding data
Finding Code = 2, throughout the year. The Cardinal can be found at virtually any location with trees; it is also a regular visitor to winter feeding stations. The largest single party count of 25 on 8 May 1993 undoubtedly underestimates this widespread species. Most birders simply do not bother keeping track of all Cardinals seen on a given day.

Status
This southerly species is apparently a relatively recent immigrant into the Dunes. Butler (1898) indicates, "It has not been reported from Lake County;....Porter County scarce;....(and in) LaPorte County, Michigan City, one record." Just prior to the 1920s, Eifrig (1918) referred to the Cardinal "as a permanent resident, but seen only in a few chosen places." By mid-century, Ford (1956) considered the species a common resident. Nests have been noted in mid-June and young birds have been reported by mid-July.

Observations
On calm sunny days in early February Cardinals terminate their winter silence with the first song of spring, a certain indication that warmer days lie ahead.

ROSE-BREASTED GROSBEAK (*Pheucticus ludovicianus*)

Finding data
Finding Code = 3, during the first half of May, when the liquid songs of this species permeate the spring woods. This species is often observed in Dunes State Park, Cowles Bog, and the Beverly Shores area. Occasional lakefront flights are recorded in spring. Grosbeaks occur sparingly in the lakefront traps.

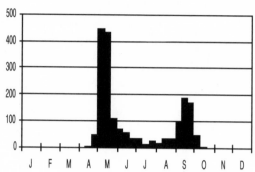

Peak Counts

Spring	38	7 May 1993	Gibson Woods Preserve
Fall	16	22 Sep 1984	Beverly Shores

Status
The Rose-breasted Grosbeak is a transient and summer resident in the Dunes. Young birds have been noted by mid-July. The November record consisted of a singing adult male at a feeding station. Migration data are (fall data based on records from lakefront traps(*):

	EARLIEST	ARRIVE	PEAK	DEPART	LATEST	N
Spring	17 Apr 55	3 May	13 May	5 Jun	- - -	292
Fall *	27 Aug 94	10 Sep	19 Sep	28 Sep	8 Nov 96	44

Observations
In autumn Grosbeaks often congregate in the Beverly Shores interdunal marsh near St. Clair Street. In mid-September it is not unusual to observe a dozen individuals, many of which are young birds, in this area.

BLUE GROSBEAK (*Guiraca caerulea*)

Finding Code = 9. The five records of this species are: 10 May 1943 in Dunes State Park (Ford, 1956); 1-5 May 1954 at Baileytown (Reuter-skiold notes); 15 May 1960 at the former site (AFN 14:392); 11 May 1985 at Beverly Shores (IAQ 64:83); and two males in rural Porter County 13 May 1990 (Don & Peg Mohar pers. comm.).

INDIGO BUNTING (*Passerina cyanea*)

Finding data
Finding Code = 2, from early May through June when territorial males sing incessantly. This widely dispersed species requires open areas with dense cover and singing perches; it is found at virtually every location possessing these characteristics. An especially good area is the interdunal marsh near Beverly Shores.

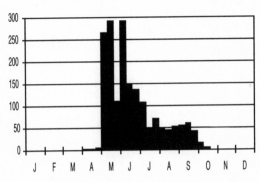

Peak Counts
Spring	104	5 May 1985	Michigan City Harbor (longshore migration)
Fall	15	11 Sep 1984	Northern Porter County

Status
The Indigo Bunting is a summer resident and transient through the Dunes. Although it is certainly a widespread breeding species, the only specific nesting record is 20 June 1934 in Hammond (Smith, 1936). Migration data from the lakefront traps (*) are:

	EARLIEST	ARRIVE	PEAK	DEPART	LATEST	N
Spring*	9 Apr 83	5 May	17 May	25 May	17 Jun 95	39
Fall *	5 Jul 79	25 Aug	13 Sep	7 Oct	19 Oct 53	46

DICKCISSEL (*Spiza americana*)

Finding data
Finding Code = 6, on average, but somewhat variable. Dickcissels are virtually restricted to agricultural regions of the Lacustrine Plain, especially in Porter County. Within this area they occur irregularly and show a distinct preference for alfalfa fields.

Peak Counts
Spring	3	18 May 1924	Northern Porter County
Summer	6	25 Jun 1988	Wolf Lake
Fall	1	16 Aug 1959	Northern Porter County

Status
This species is primarily a summer resident of the open fields south of the High Dunes. The earliest spring report was 7 May 1979 and the single fall record was 16 August 1959 (Landing notes).

SUBFAMILY EMBERIZINAE: Sparrows

Twenty-five species in this family have been recorded in the Dunes area. Of these, seven are regular breeders, six are regular migrants, two are winter residents, six are rare migrants, and four are visitants. Numbers of individuals recorded in the Dunes Area through December 1996, along with abundance rankings during the migrations are tabulated below.

MIGRATION DATA FOR 25 SPARROWS

	Total Nos.	Spring Rank	Fall Rank		Total Nos.	Spring Rank	Fall Rank
Eastern Towhee	1856	7	13	Nelson's Sharp-tail	33	21	18
Bachman's	2	24	25	Fox	2047	6	7
Am. Tree	7484	5	4	Song	3674	3	9
Chipping	2306	9	6	Lincoln's	801	12	11
Clay-colored	28	18	19	Swamp	3326	4	5
Field	1596	8	12	White-throated	13133	2	3
Vesper	495	13	16	White-crowned	1699	10	10
Lark Sparrow	11	22	23	Harris'	110	19	14
Lark Bunting	2	25	24	Dark-eyed Junco	20380	1	1
Savannah	605	11	15	Lapland Longspur	1190	16	8
Grasshopper	28	20	20	Smith's Longspur	11	23	22
Henslow's	84	15	21	Snow Bunting	13768	14	2
LeConte's	58	17	17				

EASTERN TOWHEE (*Pipilo erythrophthalmus*)

Finding data
Finding Code = 2, during the migration peak in April when birds actively call. This species occurs in dryer scrubby vegetation throughout much of the Dunes area. It is especially common along margins of the Beverly Shores interdunal marsh.

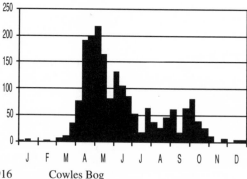

Peak Counts

Spring	30	20 May 1916	Cowles Bog
Fall	15	26 Sep 1951	Baileytown

Status
The towhee is primarily a summer resident and transient; however, a few winter in most years. Nests have been found in late June and young birds noted by mid-July. Migration data, collected from the lakefront traps (*), are:

	EARLIEST	ARRIVE	PEAK	DEPART	LATEST	N
Spring*	4 Apr 94	18 Apr	30 Apr	16 May	2 Jun 88	58
Fall *	22 Aug 88	1 Oct	9 Oct	24 Oct	24 Nov 77	42

BACHMAN'S SPARROW (*Aimophila aestivalis*)

Finding data
Finding Code = 10, only two records. Mumford and Keller (1984) list a sighting in the High Dunes on 4 April 1939. On 15 May 1955, V. Reuter-skiold (unpub. notes) reported observing a "Pine Woods Sparrow" at the Scoffield residence on Old Porter Road west of Chesterton.

AMERICAN TREE SPARROW (*Spizella arborea*)

Finding data
Finding Code = 4: November through March. Flocks of this species, occasionally mixed with Dark-eyed Juncos, are found throughout the more open areas of the Dunes. This is the most common sparrow during the winter months. It shows a strong flocking tendency.

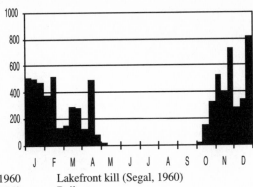

Peak Counts
Spring	331	16 Apr 1960	Lakefront kill (Segal, 1960)
Fall	200	9 Nov 1952	Baileytown

Status
The Tree Sparrow is a winter resident of the Dunes. Arrival and departure data are as follows:

	EARLIEST	ARRIVE	PEAK	DEPART	LATEST	N
Winter	20 Sep 49	19 Oct	- -	13 Apr	13 May 96	630

Observations
The similarity between this and the following species may have contributed to identification errors, especially during the migration periods (April and October) when both species are present.

CHIPPING SPARROW (*Spizella passerina*)

Finding data
Finding Code = 2, during May
and June when territorial birds
actively sing. This small
sparrow shows a preference
for the lawns and plantings of
residential areas. Accordingly
it can usually be found in
residential areas and parks.
Migrants are regular in the
lakefront traps.

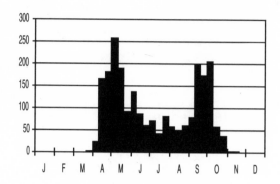

Peak Counts

Spring	30	16 Apr 1995	Long Lake
Fall	60	21 Sep 1995	Purdue Univ. North Central

Status
The Chipping Sparrow is a summer resident and transient through the Dunes.
Nests have been recorded in early June and streaked juvenile birds have been
observed by late June. Migration data based on records from the lakefront
traps (*) are:

	EARLIEST	ARRIVE	PEAK	DEPART	LATEST	N
Spring*	29 Mar 94	16 Apr	1 May	16 May	23 May 84	35
Fall *	21 Aug 93	9 Sep	26 Sep	15 Oct	18 Nov 93	49

CLAY-COLORED SPARROW (*Spizella pallida*)

Finding data
Finding Code = 7 during the
migration peaks in mid-May
and early October. The status
of this species has been
clarified in recent years. It is a
regular migrant that occurs
sparingly with migrant
sparrows in the lakefront
parks. Recent reports are
from Whiting Park, Whihala
Beach, Migrant Trap and
Dunes State Park.

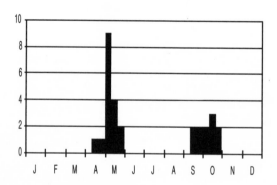

Peak Counts

Spring	2	10 May 1995	Migrant Trap & Whiting Park
	2	8 May 1997	Migrant Trap & Hammond
Fall	1		All fall records are singletons

206

Status

The first Clay-Colored ever recorded in the Dunes was a female collected by Stoddard (1921) on 25 May 1919 near West Beach. Spring migration data are:

	EARLIEST	ARRIVE	PEAK	DEPART	LATEST	N
Spring	19 Apr 85	- -	10 May	- -	26 May 89	17
Fall	14 Sep 95	- -	9 Oct	- -	26 Oct 58	11

Observations

A report by Bretsch (1927) is highly atypical and has been excluded from the above data. Bretsch, who banded birds in his Gary yard, commented, "There must have been hundreds, if not thousands, of them in Lake County alone....I caught and banded nineteen Clay-colored Sparrows (during the interval 4-14 October 1926) in our yard."

FIELD SPARROW (*Spizella pusilla*)

Finding data

Finding Code = 3, during the last half of April and May when territorial birds actively sing. This sparrow prefers open areas with scrubby growth or wood edges; it can usually be found at West Beach and in the blowouts of Dunes State Park. It is also a regular member of the migrant sparrow flocks in the lakefront traps.

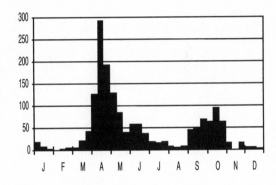

Peak Counts

Spring	55	19 Apr 1992	Migrant Trap
Fall	11	26 Nov 1983	Cowles Bog

Status

The Field Sparrow is a permanent resident and transient through the Dunes, but numbers are greatly reduced during the winter. Stoddard (unpub. notes) reported a nest at West Beach 20 June 1920, and juveniles have been seen by late June. Migration data from the lakefront traps (*) are:

	EARLIEST	ARRIVE	PEAK	DEPART	LATEST	N
Spring*	23 Mar 91	9 Apr	20 Apr	5 May	19 May 94	51
Fall *	18 Sep 82	28 Sep	15 Oct	27 Oct	9 Nov 91	56

VESPER SPARROW (*Pooecetes gramineus*)

Finding data

Finding Code = 4, in April, May, and early June when territorial birds are singing. The species is most easily found in agricultural areas (it can usually be detected in fields near the Heron Rookery unit); however, a few also summer in the blowouts of the State Park. It is rarely found in the lakefront traps.

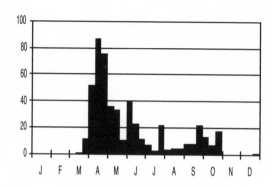

Peak Counts

Spring	25	25 Apr 1917	Near West Beach
Fall	8	24 Oct 1995	Purdue Univ. North Central

Status

The Vesper Sparrow is a summer resident and transient through the Dunes. Nesting has been observed as early as 1 June (Stoddard notes). Migration data are:

	EARLIEST	ARRIVE	PEAK	DEPART	LATEST	N
Spring	15 Mar 95	6 Apr	27 Apr	5 May	- - -	152
Fall	- - -	22 Aug	28 Sep	24 Oct	28 Dec 91	55

LARK SPARROW (*Chondestes grammacus*)

Finding Code = 8. Smith (1936) reported this sparrow 27 April in the 1930s (exact year not given) in Whiting. According to Ford (1956) two pairs nested in Dunes State Park in June 1949. In 1950, Boyd (unpub. notes) saw two in rural Porter County, and Grow (pers. comm.) observed nesting in northern Porter County on 15 June of the same year. One was seen 24 April 1955 at Baileytown (Reuter-skiold notes). This species was recorded twice during spring migration 1996: 9 May at Whiting Park and 15 May at the Migrant Trap, and once in 1997: 7 May at the Migrant Trap.

LARK BUNTING (*Calamospiza melanocorys*)

Finding Code = 10, only two positive records. Landing (1962) reported a Lark Bunting 18 April 1956, perched upon the railing surrounding the duck pens at Washington Park Zoo (Michigan City) and a breeding-plumed male was seen in the blowouts of Dunes State Park on 2 June 1985 (AB 39:920).

Observations

On 30 January 1952, Reuter-skiold (unpub. notes) described a bird seen at her Baileytown feeder on 8 January that may have been this species. She initially believed that the bird was a Purple Finch; however, unlike the latter, this bird had white wing patches.

SAVANNAH SPARROW (*Passerculus sandwichensis*)

Finding data
Finding Code = 4, during the nesting season in May and June. Breeding areas are apparently confined to the open or cultivated fields. One or two migrants are usually seen along the lakefront each year. This species is surprisingly difficult to find in the lakefront traps.

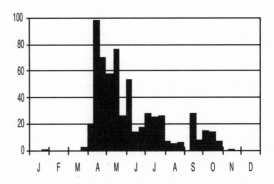

Peak Count

Spring	50	16 Apr 1960	Kill on Lake Michigan (Segal, 1960)
Fall	25	18 Sep 1996	East Chicago lakefront

Status
This small sparrow is a transient and summer resident of agricultural areas. A few winter records exist. Nests were reported in late May and early June (Smith, 1936) near George Lake. A winter bird was seen at the Migrant Trap 25 January 1995. Migration data from the lakefront traps (*) are:

	EARLIEST	ARRIVE	PEAK	DEPART	LATEST		N
Spring*	25 Mar 91	13 Apr	30 Apr	21 May	6 Jun	35	37
Fall *	31 Aug 79	- -	4 Oct	- -	14 Nov	87	23

Observations
On 24 April 1916, Eifrig (1918) reported "quite a number" of Savannah Sparrows on the large swale at Mineral Springs. This site, which provided a prairie habitat, no longer exists.

GRASSHOPPER SPARROW (*Ammodramus savannarum*)

Finding data
Finding Code = 8. Most records consist of migrants observed along the lakefront (usually in May); however, it is possible that nesting birds may have been overlooked in rural areas where birds have been noted in June and July.

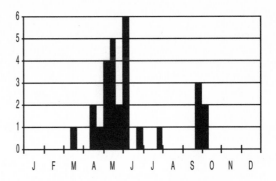

Peak Counts

Spring	2	16 Apr 1960	Kill on Lake Michigan (Segal, 1960)
	2	8 May 1997	Whiting Park & Michigan City Harbor
Summer	4	10 Jun 1984	Rural N. Lake & Porter Counties
Fall	1		All records are singletons

Status

This small sparrow is a transient through the Dunes. Migration data are:

	EARLIEST	ARRIVE	PEAK	DEPART	LATEST	N
Spring	17 Mar 53	- -	11 May	- -	- - -	18
Fall	24 Sep 88	- -	- -	- -	8 Oct 94	5

HENSLOW'S SPARROW (*Ammodramus henslowii*)

Finding data

Finding Code = 8, during the migration peak in late April. The largest single party count was the incredible 32 dead birds found on the beaches on 16 April 1960, following a storm over the lake (Segal, 1960). Sporadic nesting has occurred in the Dunes area (see below); the most recent was at Oak Ridge Prairie Park.

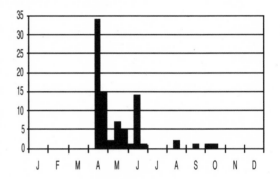

Peak Counts

Spring	32	16 Apr 1960	Kill on Lake Michigan (Segal, 1960)
Summer	10	17 Jun 1917	Nesting colony near Tremont
Fall	1		All records are singletons

Status

The status of this species has changed dramatically over the decades. Evidence of nesting earlier this century is extensive. Eifrig (1918) reported a breeding colony in 1915 and 1916 located in a swale at Mineral Springs. According to Ford (1956) a nest containing five eggs was found in Dunes State Park on 22 June 1919. Henslow's Sparrows have not been detected at these sites in recent years; however, the count of dead birds on 16 April 1960 suggests that this furtive species continues to migrate through the Dunes. Migration data are:

	EARLIEST	ARRIVE	PEAK	DEPART	LATEST	N
Spring	16 Apr 60	- -	19 Apr	- -	- - -	19
Fall	12 Sep 23	- -	- -	- -	15 Oct 60	5

LE CONTE'S SPARROW (*Ammodramus leconteii*)

Finding data
Finding Code = 7, during fall migration in early October. Most birds are found in tall grassy cover adjacent to the lakefront; they display a penchant for little bluestem. Recent observations have been made at Whihala Beach, Whiting Park, and the Migrant Trap.

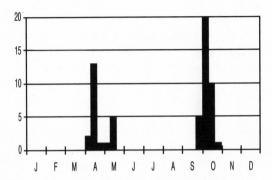

Peak Counts
Spring	10	16 Apr 1960	Kill on Lake Michigan (Segal, 1960)
Fall	6	3 Oct 1956	Gary Harbor

Status
LeConte's Sparrow is a transient through the Dunes; most records are in October.

	EARLIEST	ARRIVE	PEAK	DEPART	LATEST	N
Spring	3 Apr 59	- -	20 Apr	- -	12 May 84	13
Fall	28 Sep 53	- -	7 Oct	- -	28 Oct 73	25

Observations
The first report of this species in the Dunes consists of a specimen collected near Mineral Springs 10 October 1916 (Stoddard notes).

NELSON'S SHARP-TAILED SPARROW (*Ammodramus nelsoni*)

Finding data
Finding Code = 8, during the fall migration in late September. Almost all records come from the lakefront traps, often very near the lake. The largest single party count of 12 is described below; all other records consist of singletons.

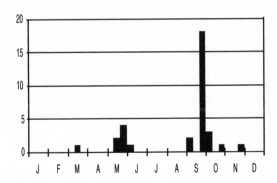

Peak Counts
Spring	1	16 Apr 1960	All spring records are singletons
Fall	12	25 Sep 1875	Berry Lake (Woodruff, 1907)

211

Status
The Sharp-tailed Sparrow is a transient through the Dunes. Migration data are:

	EARLIEST	ARRIVE	PEAK	DEPART	LATEST	N
Spring	12 Mar 52	- -	- -	- -	1 Jun 84	8
Fall	7 Sep 87	- -	25 Sep	- -	30 Nov 52	14

Observations
Regarding this species, Woodruff (1907) commented: "Mr. H. K. Coale informs me that he saw a dozen Sharp-tailed Finches in grass along Berry Lake, Lake County, Indiana, 25 September 1875."

FOX SPARROW (*Passerella iliaca*)

Finding data
Finding Code = 3, during the migration peaks in early April and mid-October. This shy sparrow is often found near heavy cover in lakeside parks, especially at the Migrant Trap. It is also fairly easily found in dense cover and under-growth of the interdunal marshes at Cowles Bog and Beverly Shores.

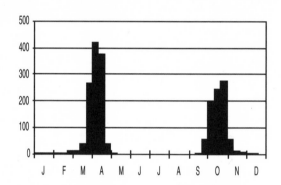

Peak Counts

Spring	54	16 Apr 1960	Bird kill on Lake Michigan (Segal 1960)
Fall	42	23 Oct 1986	Migrant Trap

Status
This large sparrow is primarily a spring and fall transient through the Dunes. A few occasionally winter at local feeding stations. Migration data are:

	EARLIEST	ARRIVE	PEAK	DEPART	LATEST	N
Spring	- - -	20 Mar	6 Apr	18 Apr	7 May 26	287
Fall	16 Sep 95	30 Sep	13 Oct	4 Nov	- - -	266

SONG SPARROW (*Melospiza melodia*)

Finding data
Finding Code = 2, throughout most of the year. Slightly more common during the migration periods in April and October. This is perhaps the most widespread sparrow of the Dunes, occurring in brushy sites, especially near water, throughout the area.

Peak Counts

Spring	50	19 Mar 1980	Cowles Bog
Fall	45	28 Oct 1996	Whiting Park

Status
The Song Sparrow is a permanent resident and transient through the Dunes. Nesting has been reported in early May. Migration data are:

	EARLIEST	ARRIVE	PEAK	DEPART	LATEST	N
Spring	- - -	19 Mar	17 Apr	17 May	- - -	282
Fall	- - -	8 Aug	8 Oct	28 Oct	- - -	262

LINCOLN'S SPARROW (*Melospiza lincolnii*)

Finding data
Finding Code = 4, during the migration peaks in mid-May and late September. This secretive sparrow is most easily found in the dense cover of lakeside parks, but also occurs regularly in Dunes State Park and along the dike at Cowles Bog.

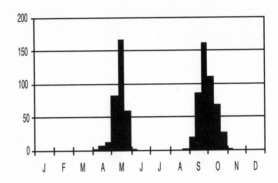

Peak Counts
Spring	28	8 May 1997	Lakefront traps
Fall	25	28 Sep 1995	Migrant Trap and Whiting Park

Status
This natty sparrow is a spring and fall transient through the Dunes. Migration data are:

	EARLIEST	ARRIVE	PEAK	DEPART	LATEST	N
Spring	4 Apr 28	2 May	15 May	23 May	10 Jun 27	187
Fall	26 Aug 27	14 Sep	28 Sep	14 Oct	6 Nov 26	232

Observations
A remarkable example of avian navigation was documented by Bretsch, who on 23 October 1926 banded a Lincoln's Sparrow (band no. 89015) in his Gary yard. This migrant was apparently bound for southerly wintering grounds. The following spring, on 14 April at exactly the same location, Bretsch again netted 89015, capturing the migrant enroute to its Canadian breeding grounds.

SWAMP SPARROW (*Melospiza georgiana*)

Finding data

Finding Code = 2 in late April and May when territorial birds actively sing. During this period the protracted trills of numerous birds can invariably be heard in cattails of the interdunal marshes at Cowles Bog and Beverly Shores. Migrants, especially in fall, abound in the lakeside parks.

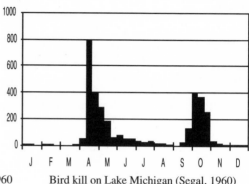

Peak Counts

Spring	633	16 Apr 1960	Bird kill on Lake Michigan (Segal, 1960)
Fall	50	15 Oct 1995	Michigan City Harbor

Status

The Swamp Sparrow is a permanent resident, though winter numbers are considerably reduced, and transient through the Dunes. Nests have been found in late May through early July. Migration data from the lakefront traps (*) are:

	EARLIEST	ARRIVE	PEAK	DEPART	LATEST	N
Spring*	26 Mar 88	13 Apr	29 Apr	14 May	23 May 81	72
Fall*	4 Aug 84	25 Sep	10 Oct	24 Oct	17 Nov 90	126

Observations

Bretsch (banding notes, 1926-1929) reported banding this species in Gary during every month except January.

WHITE-THROATED SPARROW (*Zonotrichia albicollis*)

Finding data

Finding Code = 1, in lakefront traps during the fall migration peak in late September-early October. This species, without doubt the most numerous sparrow during migration, is widespread throughout the Dunes. Flocks exceeding 100 birds appear in the lakefront parks during the fall flight.

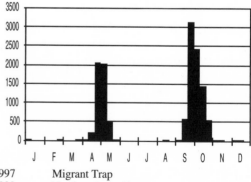

Peak Counts

Spring	300	8 May 1997	Migrant Trap
Fall	800	28 Sep 1928	Northern Lake County

Status

Although it has been recorded in every month, this sparrow is primarily a transient. Despite the presence of a few June and July records, nesting evidence is lacking. Migration data collected from the lakefront traps (*) are:

	EARLIEST	ARRIVE	PEAK	DEPART	LATEST	N
Spring*	1 Apr 31	21 Apr	2 May	16 May	7 Jun 97	76
Fall*	10 Jul 48	17 Sep	1 Oct	19 Oct	3 Nov 57	177

WHITE-CROWNED SPARROW (*Zonotrichia leucophrys*)

Finding data

Finding Code = 3, during migration peaks in mid-May and October. Migrant flocks can usually be found in the lakeside parks where they forage in the open areas. The Migrant Trap and Whiting Park are especially good locations.

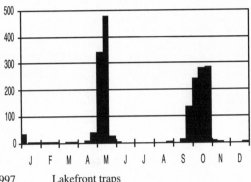

Peak Counts

Spring	48	8 May 1997	Lakefront traps
Fall	75	15 Oct 1976	Cowles Bog

Status

This handsome sparrow is primarily a spring and fall transient; however, a few individuals generally winter. Individuals of the Gambel's race are occasionally noted. Many of the autumn birds are in the rusty-crowned immature plumage. Migration data are:

	EARLIEST	ARRIVE	PEAK	DEPART	LATEST	N
Spring	- - -	30 Apr	10 May	19 May	6 Jun 75	215
Fall	30 Aug 86	26 Sep	8 Oct	24 Oct	- - -	222

HARRIS' SPARROW (*Zonotrichia querula*)

Finding data

Finding Code = 7. This species is most often recorded in the fall, especially in October, when individuals are detected among the migrant sparrow flocks. Many recent sightings have come from Beverly Shores and the Migrant Trap. It occasionally appears at feeding stations.

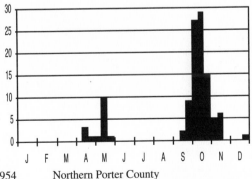

Peak Counts

Spring	3	15 Apr 1954	Northern Porter County
	3	11 May 1996	Beverly Shores
Fall	8	20 Oct 1957	near Michigan City Harbor

Status

This large sparrow is primarily a fall visitant to the Dunes, but several spring and a few winter records also exist. Migration data are:

	EARLIEST	ARRIVE	PEAK	DEPART	LATEST	N
Spring	15 Apr 54	- -	1 May	- -	22 May 90	11
Fall	13 Sep 88	29 Sep	11 Oct	28 Oct	24 Dec 61	50

Observations

A majority of the Harris' Sparrows appearing in the Dunes are young birds; of those aged, 12 were adults and 26 were immatures.

DARK-EYED JUNCO (*Junco hyemalis*)

Finding data

Finding Code = 1, during the fall migration peak in mid-October. This northern species is found in virtually every habitat. October storms often sweep flocks containing hundreds of birds into the Dunes. During migration peaks many can be found at West Beach and in the lakefront traps.

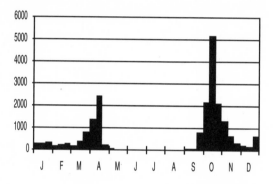

Peak Counts

Spring	1000	16 Apr 1960	Bird kill on Lake Michigan (Segal, 1960)
Fall	1000	13 Oct 1941	Indiana Dunes
	1000	20 Oct 1941	Lakefront

Status

The Junco is a transient and winter resident of the Dunes. Migration data are:

	EARLIEST	ARRIVE	PEAK	DEPART	LATEST	N
Spring	- - -	14 Mar	7 Apr	24 Apr	8 Jun 91	299
Fall	5 Sep 57	27 Sep	16 Oct	12 Nov	- - -	473

LAPLAND LONGSPUR (*Calcarius lapponicus*)

Finding data
Finding Code = 5, in late October when flocks of Snow Buntings migrate along the lakefront. A few sometimes accompany the Snow Bunting flocks; when present they are detected by their smaller size and darker plumage. When winter snows cover the ground one or two are occasionally seen along the main road at the Port of Indiana

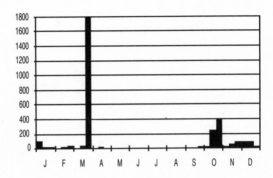

Peak Counts
Spring	1779	20 Mar 1997	Johnson Beach hawk-watch site
Fall	200	20 Oct 1957	Northern Porter County

Status
The Lapland Longspur is primarily a fall transient through the Dunes; it is rarely seen in winter or spring. Data for the spring and fall flights are:

	EARLIEST		ARRIVE		PEAK	DEPART		LATEST		N
Spring	-	-	-	-	-	18 Mar	-	-	14 Jun 89*	21
Fall	19 Sep 81		4 Oct		9 Nov	15 Dec		-	- -	56

*The June record consisted of a specimen collected in 1889 (Woodruff, 1907).

SMITH'S LONGSPUR (*Calcarius pictus*)

Finding data
Finding Code = 8, only seven records, involving eleven birds exist. Five have been reported in the past 15 years. Most records come from agricultural areas in Porter County, but a few birds have appeared along the lakefront; usually in foredune marram grass.

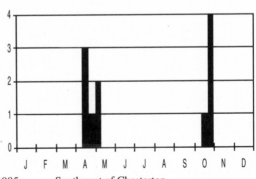

Peak Counts
Spring	2	19 Apr 1985	Southwest of Chesterton
Fall	4	26 Oct 1957	Northern Porter County

Status
Migration data are:

	EARLIEST		ARRIVE	PEAK	DEPART		LATEST		N
Spring	16 Apr 60		-	-	30 Apr	-	-	9 May 93		5
Fall	15 Oct 83		-	-	-	-	-	26 Oct 57		2

SNOW BUNTING (*Plectrophenax nivalis*)

Finding data
Finding Code = 4 during the fall flight in November. Most Snow Buntings are observed in flocks migrating along the beaches or over the lake. On heavy flight days several hundred may be seen. Following a fresh snowfall, a few Snow Buntings often occur along the main road at the Port of Indiana.

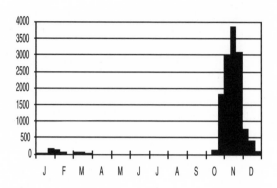

Peak Counts
Spring	50	2 Mar 1919	West Beach
Fall	1000	24 Nov 1957	Michigan City Harbor

Status
"Snowflake," as it is commonly called, is primarily a fall transient through the Dunes; however, some often winter and a few are detected in the spring. Migration data are:

	EARLIEST	ARRIVE	PEAK	DEPART	LATEST		N
Spring	- - -	8 Feb	2 Mar	24 Mar	10 Apr	82	23
Fall	7 Oct 77	26 Oct	11 Nov	4 Dec	- -	-	300

BOBOLINK (*Dolichonyx oryzivorus*)

Finding data
Finding Code = 4, in late May and June when breeding birds actively display. This colorful species is most reliably found in cultivated fields and pastures in Porter County. Spring migrants are occasionally noted along the lakefront. It is extremely rare in fall.

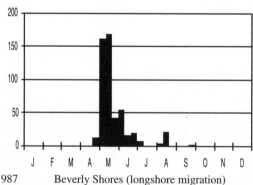

Peak Counts
Spring	38	9 May 1987	Beverly Shores (longshore migration)
Fall	20	14 Aug 1920	Cowles Bog

Status
The Bobolink is a summer resident and transient through the Dunes. Smith (1936) reported that a nest containing four young was found in Hammond on 12 June 1935. Spring migration data, which are somewhat obscured by summering birds, are:

	EARLIEST	ARRIVE	PEAK	DEPART	LATEST	N
Spring	24 Apr 77	5 May	15 May	9 Jun	- - -	116
Fall	3 Aug 19	- -	- -	- -	28 Sep 95	4

SUBFAMILY ICTERINAE: Blackbirds and Orioles

RED-WINGED BLACKBIRD (*Agelaius phoeniceus*)

Finding data
Finding Code = 1, between April and May when territorial birds occupy the cattail marshes. Red-winged Blackbirds are widely distributed in marshes throughout the Dunes. In fall enormous blackbird flocks, often consisting dominantly of this species, are frequently observed in September and October.

Peak Counts
Spring	1,000,000	24 Apr 1961	Gary (AFN 15:415)
Fall	200,000	1 Nov 1960	Gary

Status
The Red-winged Blackbird is both a transient and a permanent resident of the Dunes, but numbers are reduced considerably in winter. Migration peaks are 21 March in spring and 14 October in fall.

EASTERN MEADOWLARK (*Sturnella magna*)

Finding data
Finding Code = 2, from mid-March through June when nesting birds actively call. This species is most easily observed in agricultural areas and cultivated fields, but is also noted as a migrant along the lakefront. Migrants are seen regularly at the hawk-watches in March and April.

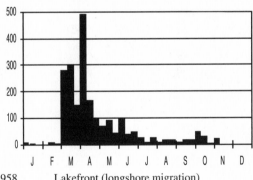

Peak Counts
Spring	400	6 Apr 1958	Lakefront (longshore migration)
Fall	11	14 Oct 1983	Northern Porter County

Status
This colorful Icterid is a transient and summer resident of the Dunes. A few winter records also exist. Migration data from the lakefront traps (*) are:

	EARLIEST	ARRIVE	PEAK	DEPART	LATEST	N
Spring*	19 Feb 94	- -	26 Mar	- -	9 May 96	28
Fall *	13 Sep 23	- -	- -	- -	26 Oct 85	8

Nests containing eggs have been observed at Wolf Lake 5 July 1924 and at Seven Dolors Shrine 1 July 1978.

WESTERN MEADOWLARK (*Sturnella neglecta*)

Finding data
Finding Code = 6, during the nesting period (April-June) when territorial birds sing. Virtually all records come from the cultivated fields of rural Porter County, where at least one pair is present most years. Nesting locations vary from year to year. This species is extremely rare in fall.

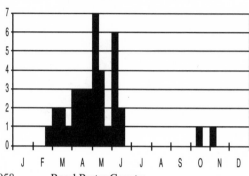

Peak Counts

Spring	4	4 May 1958	Rural Porter County
Fall	1	12 Oct 1953	Wolf Lake
	1	4 Nov 1961	Rural Porter County

Status
This skillful songster is a summer resident of the agricultural areas. Interestingly, Eifrig (1918) fails to mention this species in his bird list for the Sand Dunes. Migration data are:

	EARLIEST	ARRIVE	PEAK	DEPART	LATEST	N
Spring	26 Feb 55	- -	4 May	- -	- - -	27
Fall	12 Oct 53	- -	- -	- -	4 Nov 61	2

YELLOW-HEADED BLACKBIRD (*Xanthocephalus xanthocephalus*)

Finding data
Finding Code = 7 due to a colony of nesting birds at Eggers Marsh, Illinois. During the nesting season foraging birds from this site sporadically fly across I-90 to Wolf Lake, Indiana. From 1980 through 1984 a large colony nested at Gleason Park, however, this habitat was destroyed.

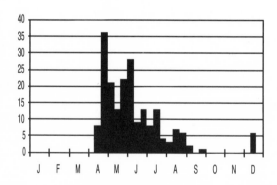

Peak Counts

Spring	11	30 Apr 1981	Gleason Park
Fall	5	15 Aug 1981	Gleason Park

Status
Today this colorful blackbird is a transient and local summer resident just outside the Dunes area.   In former years the Yellow-headed Blackbird may

have been a more widespread nester in marshes of the Lacustrine Plain. Bognar (1951) reported nesting at Lake George in 1936 and 1940. Between Bognar's report and 1980 no evidence of nesting was forthcoming, though this species nested in nearby Illinois marshes. On 26 April 1980 birds showing territorial behavior were noted at Gleason Park where Arvin (1981) located two nests on 21 May. Evidence of nesting was also obtained in 1981, 1982, 1983, and 1984. The sprinkling of winter records have been associated with the large nomadic Icterid flocks that linger in the Dunes in mild winters. Migration data are:

	EARLIEST	ARRIVE	PEAK	DEPART	LATEST	N
Spring	14 Mar 80	22 Apr	13 May	6 Jun	- - -	68
Fall	- - -	- -	29 Aug	- -	18 Dec 75	14

RUSTY BLACKBIRD (*Euphagus carolinus*)

Finding data
Finding Code = 4, during the spring migration peak, mid-March through early April. Rustys often join the large mixed blackbird flocks during migration. This species also shows a distinct preference for wooded swamps. In recent years, large numbers have not been encountered during the fall flight.

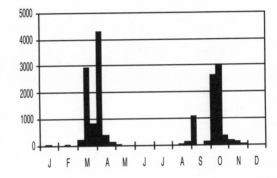

Peak Counts
Spring	3000	5 Apr 1963	Gary
Fall	1000	2 Oct 1943	Northern Porter County

Status
The Rusty Blackbird is primarily a transient through the Dunes, but a few winter records also exist. Migration data are:

	EARLIEST	ARRIVE	PEAK	DEPART	LATEST	N
Spring	- - -	11 Mar	31 Mar	22 Apr	16 May 81	119
Fall	13 Aug 48	24 Sep	13 Oct	9 Nov	- - -	116

BREWER'S BLACKBIRD (*Euphagus cyanocephalus*)

Finding data

Finding Code = 8, but this species was more easily observed in former years when nesting occurred. No reliable sites are currently known. Today Brewer's Blackbird is most commonly observed among the large blackbird flocks during spring migration in April.

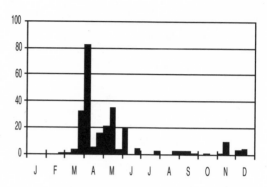

Peak Counts

Spring	75	5 Apr 1959	Northern Porter County (IAQ 38:50)
Fall	9	16 Nov 1953	Northern Porter County

Status

Currently this species must be considered a transient; however, at least two distinct nesting colonies were present during the 1950s. One was in Lake County near Schererville (Mumford, 1954) and the other was in Porter County near the Heron Rookery. Eggs and young birds were reported in May. A few winter records exist.

	EARLIEST	ARRIVE	PEAK	DEPART	LATEST	N
Spring	26 Feb 55	- -	27 Apr	- -	- - -	23
Fall	21 Aug 77	- -	16 Nov	- -	17 Dec 77	12

COMMON GRACKLE (*Quiscalus quiscula*)

Finding data

Finding Code = 1, from early March through October. This species is ubiquitous in residential, suburban, industrial, and agricultural areas throughout the region. Enormous flock build up in autumn before migration. The largest single party count, of 10,000 has been recorded on several occasions.

Status

The "Bronzed Grackle" is a transient and permanent resident, but numbers are much lower in winter. Migration peaks are 24 April in spring and 4 October in fall. It often nests in evergreens of residential areas. Young birds out of the nest are usually observed in early June.

BROWN-HEADED COWBIRD (*Molothrus ater*)

Finding data
Finding Code = 2, during the nesting season, from mid-March through June. It becomes more difficult to locate after the post-breeding dispersal. This nest parasite is widespread in the more open areas of the region.

Peak Counts
Spring	230	19 Apr 1990	Gleason Park
Fall	1000	14 Oct 1931	Whiting Park
	1000	11 Sep 1942	High Dunes

Status
The Cowbird is a transient and permanent resident; it is far more common in summer than in winter. Migration peaks are approximately 27 April in spring and 26 October in fall.

Observations
Eifrig (1918) refers to this species as a nuisance, and after observing several hundred during a hike from Tremont to Mineral Springs on 15 April 1915, suggested that Cowbirds were detrimental to indigenous nesting passerines and should be "thinned out."

ORCHARD ORIOLE (*Icterus spurius*)

Finding data
Finding Code = 6, in May. Most May birds are probably spring over-migrants. Several recent observations come from the lakeside parks. This species nested at Oak Ridge Prairie County Park in 1994, 1995, and 1996. If this becomes a permanent nesting site the Finding Code will decrease to 3.

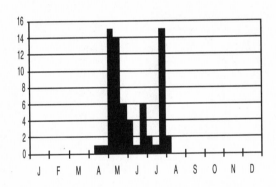

Peak Counts
Spring	2		Recorded three times in May
Fall	15	22 Jul 1995	Michigan City Harbor

Status
This oriole is primarily a spring transient and at least an occasional summer resident. The large July count is anomalous; it consisted of a group of migrating birds (IAQ 74:159). Spring migration data are:

	EARLIEST	ARRIVE	PEAK	DEPART	LATEST	N
Spring	20 Apr 96	2 May	11 May	28 May	- - -	36
Fall	22 Jul 95	- -	- -	- -	10 Aug 94	3

BALTIMORE ORIOLE (*Icterus galbula*)

Finding data
Finding Code = 2, during the first half of May when territorial birds are singing. This colorful species occurs in virtually any location offering the combination of mature trees and wood edges; singing birds can usually be heard at the Beverly Shores interdunal marsh.

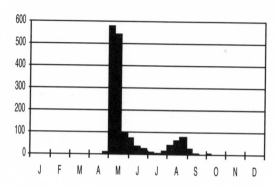

Peak Counts

Spring	124	6 May 1986	Michigan City Harbor (longshore migration)
Fall	12	10 Aug 1960	Baileytown

Status
The Baltimore Oriole is a summer resident and transient through the Dunes. Migration data from the lakefront traps (*) are:

	EARLIEST	ARRIVE	PEAK	DEPART	LATEST	N
Spring*	26 Apr 90	5 May	11 May	22 May	21 May 85	46
Fall *	12 Aug 90	14 Aug	25 Aug	7 Sep	10 Oct 24	30

Observations
The Baltimore Oriole is one of the earlier fall migrants through the Dunes; most individuals have already departed before the other transient passerines begin their southbound flight.

FAMILY FRINGILLIDAE: Finches

PINE GROSBEAK (*Pinicola enucleator*)

Finding data
Finding Code = 8, on average, but this species is more easily found in invasion years. A majority of the records are from Dunes State Park; many records come from State Park Boundary Road, along the southern margin of the park. This species has not been recorded in the Dunes Area since 9 November 1985.

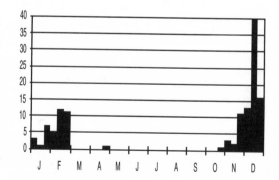

Peak Counts

Spring	1	28 Apr 1962	Baileytown
Fall	5	22 Nov 1951	Gary
Winter	25	18 Dec 1977	Near Pines (Mumford & Keller, 1984)

Status
The Pine Grosbeak is an irregular winter visitant. Records suggest that major invasions occurred during the winters of 1951-52, 1957-58, 1977-78 and 1980-81. The late April record consisted of a singing male at Baileytown (Reuterskiold notes). Migration data are:

	EARLIEST	ARRIVE	PEAK	DEPART	LATEST	N
Winter	30 Oct 51	16 Nov	- -	21 Feb	28 Apr 62	38

PURPLE FINCH (*Carpodacus purpureus*)

Finding data
Finding Code = 4, during spring migration in late April and at winter feeding stations. This species is most reliably found at feeders during the winter months. Fall migrants sometimes congregate in shrubs of the Beverly Shores interdunal marsh near the intersection of Beverly Drive and St. Clair Street.

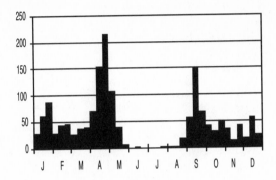

Peak Counts
Spring	32	22 Apr 1982	Chesterton
Fall	50	16 Sep 1980	Beverly Shores

Status
This species is a transient and winter resident of the Dunes. A few summer records exist. Migration data are:

	EARLIEST	ARRIVE	PEAK	DEPART	LATEST	N
Spring	- - -	19 Mar	21 Apr	9 May	14 Jun 84	178
Fall	28 Jul 82	3 Sep	30 Sep	24 Nov	- - -	158

HOUSE FINCH (*Carpodacus mexicanus*)

Finding data
Finding Code = 2. The status of this species has changed drastically over the past decade. Prior to 1982 the Finding Code was 10. By 1985 several territorial pairs were established at locations in Michigan City and Chesterton, rendering this species much easier to find.

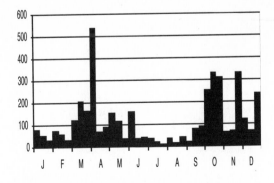

Spring	200	2 Apr 1993	Johnson Beach hawk-watch site (migrating)
Fall	300	21 Nov 1992	Roxana Pond

Status

This westward-moving species is now well established as a transient and permanent resident in the Dunes. The House Finch was first recorded in Indiana by James E. Landing in Michigan City on 16 November 1958, an anomalous date among the early records for the Midwest. The expansion into the Midwest occurred in 1970 and 1980. The next Indiana report did not come until 28 March 1976 (Keller et al., 1976). The 1958 individual clearly violates the western expansion pattern. Migration peaks occur in late March and mid-October.

RED CROSSBILL (*Loxia curvirostra*)

Finding data

Finding Code = 6, during the first half of November when migrants occasionally land in the jack pine grove at West Beach. Other than the above, little pattern seems to exist for the movements of this erratic species. It has been recorded in every month except January and August.

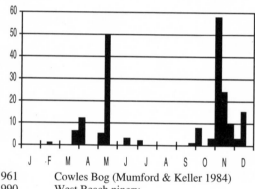

Peak Counts

Spring	50	15 May 1961	Cowles Bog (Mumford & Keller 1984)
Fall	21	3 Nov 1990	West Beach pinery

Status

The Red Crossbill is an erratic visitant to the Dunes. Although most reports are in November and December, several spring and summer records also exist.

WHITE-WINGED CROSSBILL (*Loxia leucoptera*)

Finding data

Finding Code = 8. This species is attracted to feeders more often than the former. In the 1980s several sightings were made along State Park Boundary Road (southern margin of Dunes State Park) where birds were attracted to winter feeding stations.

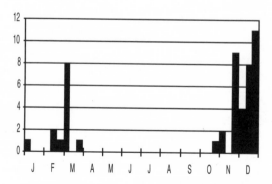

226

Peak Counts

Spring	6	6 Mar 1990	Gary feeding station
Fall	4	27 Nov 1977	Dunes State Park (Boundary Road)
Winter	7	11 Dec 1954	High Dunes

Status

In contrast to the Red Crossbill, all records of this species are in winter. The migration envelope is:

	EARLIEST	ARRIVE	PEAK		DEPART		LATEST	N
Winter	30 Oct 21	9 Nov	-	-	-	-	28 Mar 83	20

COMMON REDPOLL (*Carduelis flammea*)

Finding data

Finding Code = 6, on average, but may drop to 1 or 2 in heavy invasion years. Flocks are usually seen in weedy fields. This species also frequents winter feeding stations where it may become numerous during invasion years. Migrant flocks have been seen flying past the Migrant Trap.

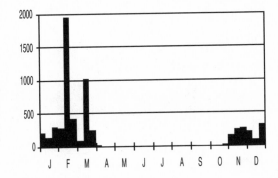

Peak Counts

Spring	500	11 Mar 1917	Miller Beach
Fall	115	16 Nov 1991	Migrant Trap (migration flocks)
Winter	1000	19 Feb 1978	A field near Burns Harbor

Status

The Redpoll is an irregular winter visitor and transient through the Dunes. Eifrig (1918) reported that flocks of several hundred were present in the swamp at Mineral Spring (Cowles Bog) during the winters of 1915-16 and 1916-17, where they fed on seeds of birch and alder. The last major invasion occurred in February 1978. Migration data are:

	EARLIEST	ARRIVE	PEAK		DEPART	LATEST	N
Winter	26 Oct 57	6 Nov	-	-	20 Mar	24 Apr 95	366

HOARY REDPOLL (*Carduelis hornemanni*)

Finding data
Finding Code = 9, seven records. Accompanies the Common Redpoll flocks during invasion years. Birds visiting feeders often provide the requisite close viewing necessary for identification. Most appear paler than the extremely similar Common Redpolls.

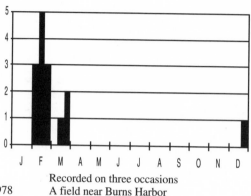

Peak Counts

Spring	1		Recorded on three occasions	
Winter	3	19 Feb 1978	A field near Burns Harbor	

Status
Indiana's first record of this boreal species was gleaned 23 December 1916 when Stoddard collected a specimen near Mineral Springs. Subsequently, records have occurred erratically, apparently correlated with major invasions of the Common Redpoll. Four records occurred in 1953 and four more in 1978. One of the latter was a pink-rumped individual that visited a Chesterton feeding station from 14 February until 23 March.

PINE SISKIN (*Carduelis pinus*)

Finding data
Finding Code = 4, on average, but is much lower when birds frequent winter feeding stations during invasion years. In some years Siskins are entirely absent. Occasionally southbound flocks are observed along the lakefront in October and November, otherwise most birds are seen at feeders.

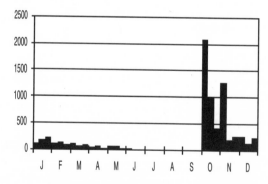

Peak Counts

Spring	30	26 Mar 1950	Northern Porter County	
Fall	2000	9 Oct 1919	Cowles Bog (Stoddard notes)	

Status
The Siskin must be regarded as an irregular transient and winter visitor to the Dunes. The spring flight is not well delineated. The migration envelope is:

	EARLIEST	ARRIVE	PEAK	DEPART	LATEST	N
Winter	20 Aug 92	13 Oct	- -	11 May	13 Jun 87	340

AMERICAN GOLDFINCH (*Carduelis tristis*)

Finding data

Finding Code = 2, during the migration peaks in May and October. The Finding Code = 3, for balance of the year. This widely dispersed species can be found in virtually every habitat except mature woodland, and it is often heard flying over this habitat. It flocks to winter feeders.

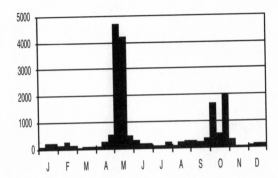

Peak Counts

Spring	1715	19 May 1996	Michigan City Harbor (longshore migration)
Fall	1200	27 Oct 1995	Port of Indiana

Status

Although the Goldfinch is a permanent resident, distinct spring and fall migrations are evident. Migration peaks are about 9 May in spring and 1 October in autumn. Nests containing eggs have been reported in late July and August.

EVENING GROSBEAK (*Coccothraustes vespertinus*)

Finding data

Finding Code = 6, on average, but varies with the invasionary character of this species. Grosbeaks have appeared less frequently in the 1990s. Many records come from State Park Boundary Road (southern margin of Dunes State Park), but airborne flocks are detected throughout the High Dunes. This species is also attracted to feeders.

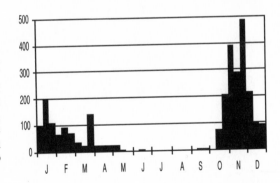

Peak Counts

Spring	60	30 Mar 1916	Miller Beach
Fall	200	24 Nov 1951	High Dunes

Status

The Evening Grosbeak is an erratic transient and winter visitor to the Dunes; one summer record exists. Migration data are:

	EARLIEST	ARRIVE	PEAK	DEPART	LATEST	N
Winter	15 Sep 88	29 Oct	- -	27 Apr	15 Jun 84	222

FAMILY PASSERIDAE: Weaver Finches

HOUSE SPARROW (*Passer domesticus*)

Finding data
Finding Code = 1. This introduced species is virtually impossible to miss in urban and suburban areas. The largest single party count of 361 fails to accurately reflect the abundance of this species; most birders simply ignore House Sparrows.

Status
This species, which is generally considered a nuisance, is a permanent resident.

INDEX

APPENDIX A

BAR GRAPHS

Bar graphs for all birds, except those species that are extinct or extirpated, are shown on the following pages. Graphical data display the finding codes for each species throughout the year (months are divided into thirds). For convenience the graphical representation of each finding code tabulated at the bottom of each page. The finding code definitions are repeated below.

FINDING CODE DEFINITIONS

Code	EFFORT REQUIRED	
	For single observer	For all observers in area
1	25 birds per hour	-
2	1 bird per hour	-
3	1 bird per half day	-
4	1 bird per day	-
5	1 bird per week	-
6	1-2 birds per season	4-20 birds per year
7	-	1-3 birds per year
8	-	1 bird every 2 years
9	-	1 bird every 20 years
10	-	1 bird per century

	Jan	Feb	Mar	Apr	May	Jun	Jul	Aug	Sep	Oct	Nov	Dec
Red-throated Loon												
Pacific Loon												
Common Loon												
Pied-billed Grebe												
Horned Grebe												
Red-necked Grebe												
Eared Grebe												
Western Grebe												
Northern Gannet												
White Pelican												
Brown Pelican												
Double-Cr. Cormorant												
Magnificent Frigatebird												
American Bittern												
Least Bittern												
Great Blue Heron												
Great Egret												
Snowy Egret												
Little Blue Heron												
Cattle Egret												
Green Heron												
Black-crn Night Heron												
Yellow-crn Night Heron												
Tundra Swan												
Mute Swan												
White-fronted Goose												
Snow Goose												
Brant												

FC=1 FC=2 FC=3 FC=4 FC=5 FC=6 FC=7 FC=8 FC=9 FC=10

232

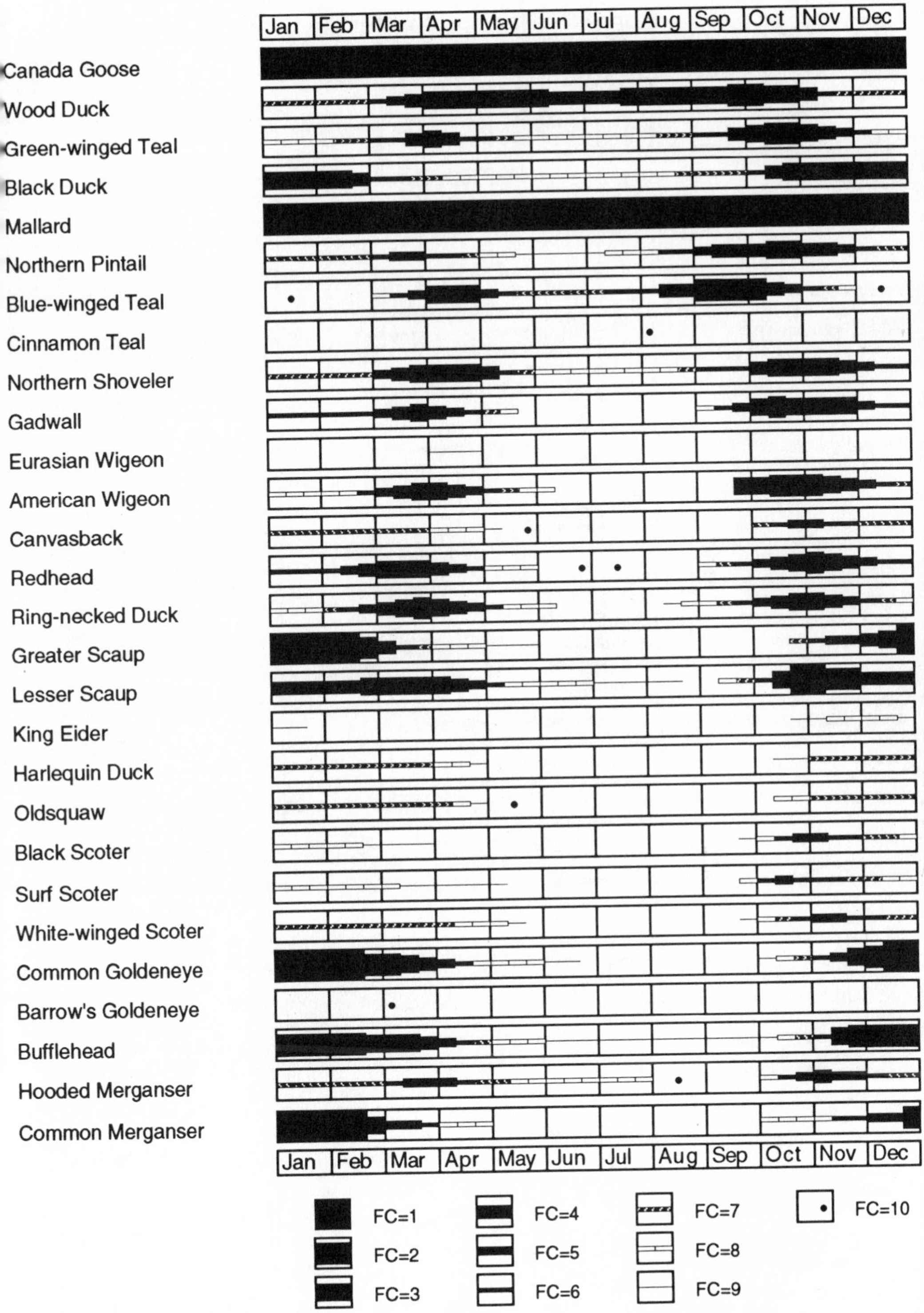

	Jan	Feb	Mar	Apr	May	Jun	Jul	Aug	Sep	Oct	Nov	Dec

Canada Goose
Wood Duck
Green-winged Teal
Black Duck
Mallard
Northern Pintail
Blue-winged Teal
Cinnamon Teal
Northern Shoveler
Gadwall
Eurasian Wigeon
American Wigeon
Canvasback
Redhead
Ring-necked Duck
Greater Scaup
Lesser Scaup
King Eider
Harlequin Duck
Oldsquaw
Black Scoter
Surf Scoter
White-winged Scoter
Common Goldeneye
Barrow's Goldeneye
Bufflehead
Hooded Merganser
Common Merganser

FC=1	FC=4	FC=7	FC=10
FC=2	FC=5	FC=8	
FC=3	FC=6	FC=9	

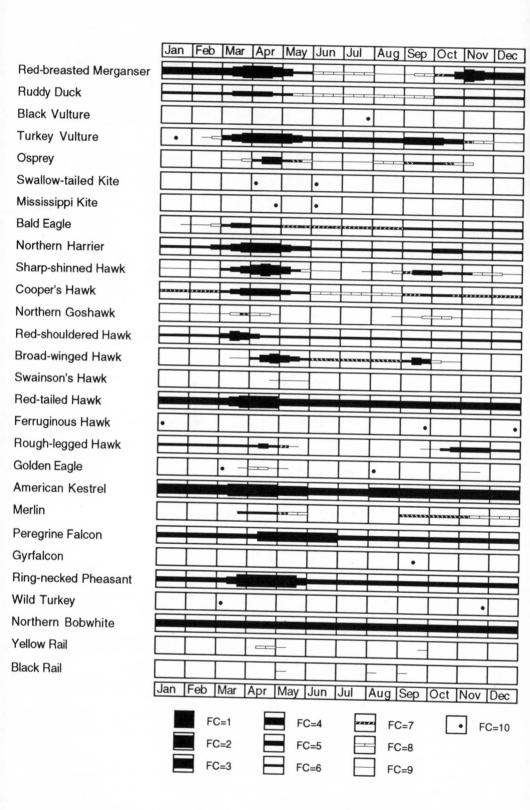

	Jan	Feb	Mar	Apr	May	Jun	Jul	Aug	Sep	Oct	Nov	Dec
Red-breasted Merganser												
Ruddy Duck												
Black Vulture												
Turkey Vulture												
Osprey												
Swallow-tailed Kite												
Mississippi Kite												
Bald Eagle												
Northern Harrier												
Sharp-shinned Hawk												
Cooper's Hawk												
Northern Goshawk												
Red-shouldered Hawk												
Broad-winged Hawk												
Swainson's Hawk												
Red-tailed Hawk												
Ferruginous Hawk												
Rough-legged Hawk												
Golden Eagle												
American Kestrel												
Merlin												
Peregrine Falcon												
Gyrfalcon												
Ring-necked Pheasant												
Wild Turkey												
Northern Bobwhite												
Yellow Rail												
Black Rail												

FC=1   FC=4   FC=7   FC=10

FC=2   FC=5   FC=8

FC=3   FC=6   FC=9

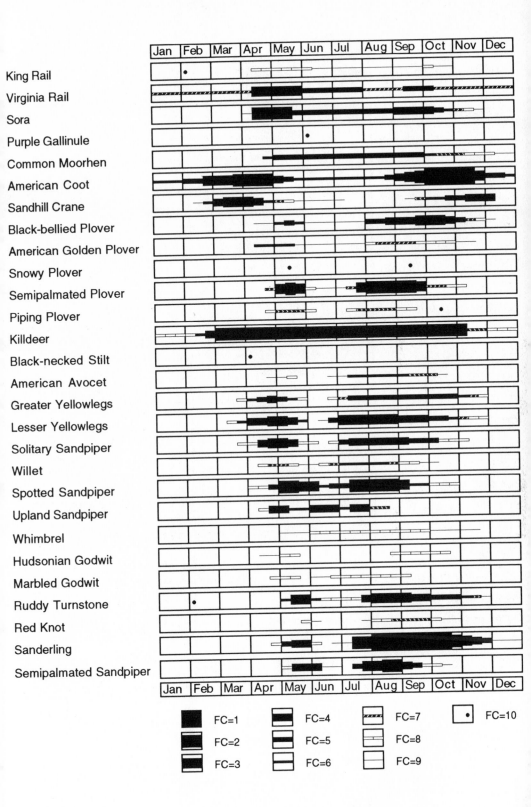

	Jan	Feb	Mar	Apr	May	Jun	Jul	Aug	Sep	Oct	Nov	Dec
King Rail												
Virginia Rail												
Sora												
Purple Gallinule												
Common Moorhen												
American Coot												
Sandhill Crane												
Black-bellied Plover												
American Golden Plover												
Snowy Plover												
Semipalmated Plover												
Piping Plover												
Killdeer												
Black-necked Stilt												
American Avocet												
Greater Yellowlegs												
Lesser Yellowlegs												
Solitary Sandpiper												
Willet												
Spotted Sandpiper												
Upland Sandpiper												
Whimbrel												
Hudsonian Godwit												
Marbled Godwit												
Ruddy Turnstone												
Red Knot												
Sanderling												
Semipalmated Sandpiper												

FC=1 FC=4 FC=7 FC=10

FC=2 FC=5 FC=8

FC=3 FC=6 FC=9

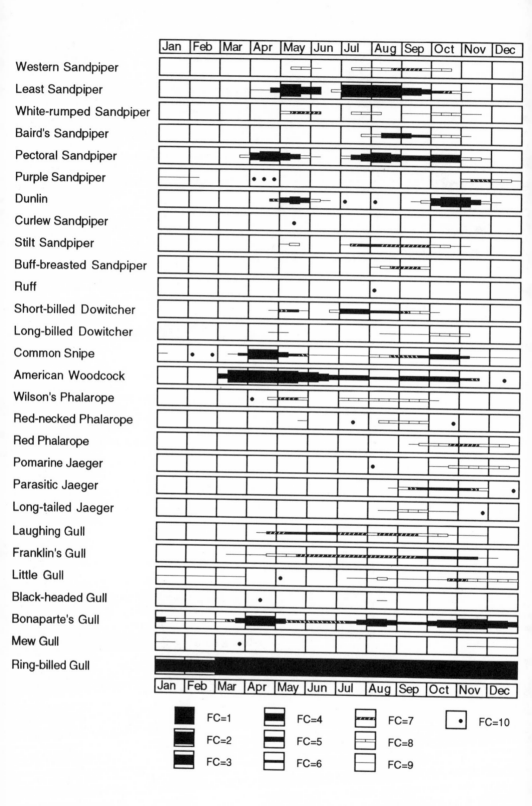

	Jan	Feb	Mar	Apr	May	Jun	Jul	Aug	Sep	Oct	Nov	Dec
Western Sandpiper												
Least Sandpiper												
White-rumped Sandpiper												
Baird's Sandpiper												
Pectoral Sandpiper												
Purple Sandpiper												
Dunlin												
Curlew Sandpiper												
Stilt Sandpiper												
Buff-breasted Sandpiper												
Ruff												
Short-billed Dowitcher												
Long-billed Dowitcher												
Common Snipe												
American Woodcock												
Wilson's Phalarope												
Red-necked Phalarope												
Red Phalarope												
Pomarine Jaeger												
Parasitic Jaeger												
Long-tailed Jaeger												
Laughing Gull												
Franklin's Gull												
Little Gull												
Black-headed Gull												
Bonaparte's Gull												
Mew Gull												
Ring-billed Gull												

FC=1   FC=4   FC=7   FC=10
FC=2   FC=5   FC=8
FC=3   FC=6   FC=9

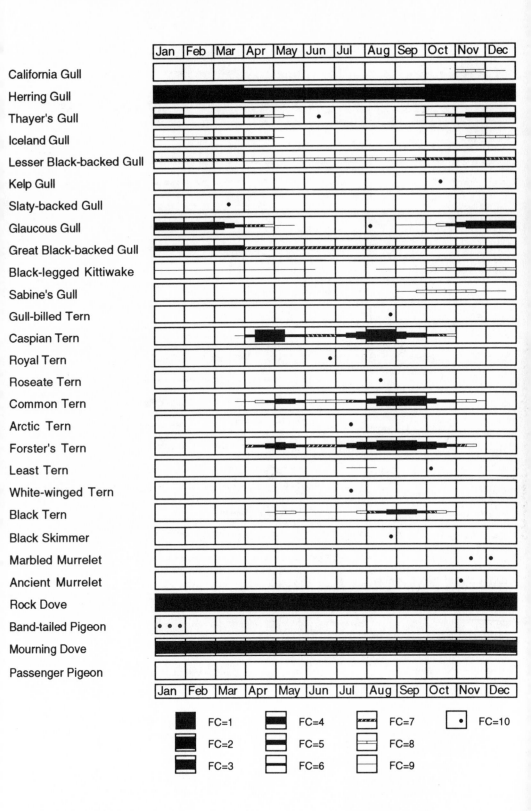

	Jan	Feb	Mar	Apr	May	Jun	Jul	Aug	Sep	Oct	Nov	Dec
California Gull												
Herring Gull												
Thayer's Gull												
Iceland Gull												
Lesser Black-backed Gull												
Kelp Gull												
Slaty-backed Gull												
Glaucous Gull												
Great Black-backed Gull												
Black-legged Kittiwake												
Sabine's Gull												
Gull-billed Tern												
Caspian Tern												
Royal Tern												
Roseate Tern												
Common Tern												
Arctic Tern												
Forster's Tern												
Least Tern												
White-winged Tern												
Black Tern												
Black Skimmer												
Marbled Murrelet												
Ancient Murrelet												
Rock Dove												
Band-tailed Pigeon												
Mourning Dove												
Passenger Pigeon												

FC=1 FC=4 FC=7 FC=10
FC=2 FC=5 FC=8
FC=3 FC=6 FC=9

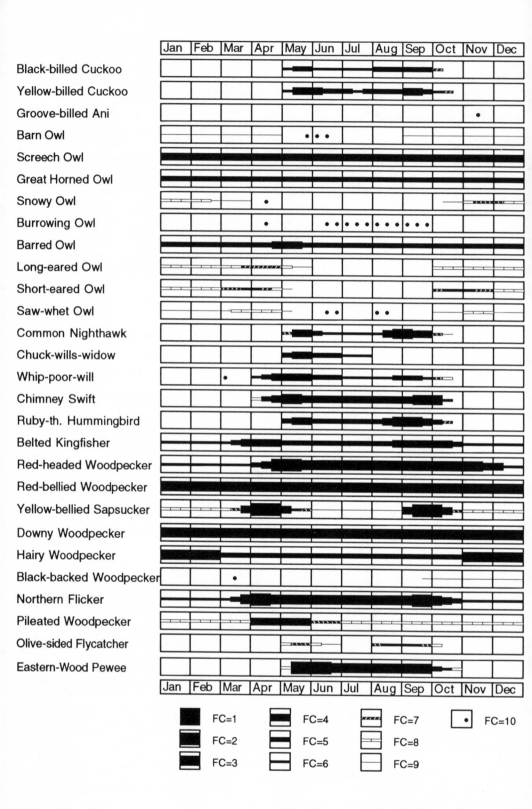

	Jan	Feb	Mar	Apr	May	Jun	Jul	Aug	Sep	Oct	Nov	Dec
Black-billed Cuckoo												
Yellow-billed Cuckoo												
Groove-billed Ani												
Barn Owl												
Screech Owl												
Great Horned Owl												
Snowy Owl												
Burrowing Owl												
Barred Owl												
Long-eared Owl												
Short-eared Owl												
Saw-whet Owl												
Common Nighthawk												
Chuck-wills-widow												
Whip-poor-will												
Chimney Swift												
Ruby-th. Hummingbird												
Belted Kingfisher												
Red-headed Woodpecker												
Red-bellied Woodpecker												
Yellow-bellied Sapsucker												
Downy Woodpecker												
Hairy Woodpecker												
Black-backed Woodpecker												
Northern Flicker												
Pileated Woodpecker												
Olive-sided Flycatcher												
Eastern-Wood Pewee												

| | Jan | Feb | Mar | Apr | May | Jun | Jul | Aug | Sep | Oct | Nov | Dec |

FC=1 FC=4 FC=7 FC=10
FC=2 FC=5 FC=8
FC=3 FC=6 FC=9

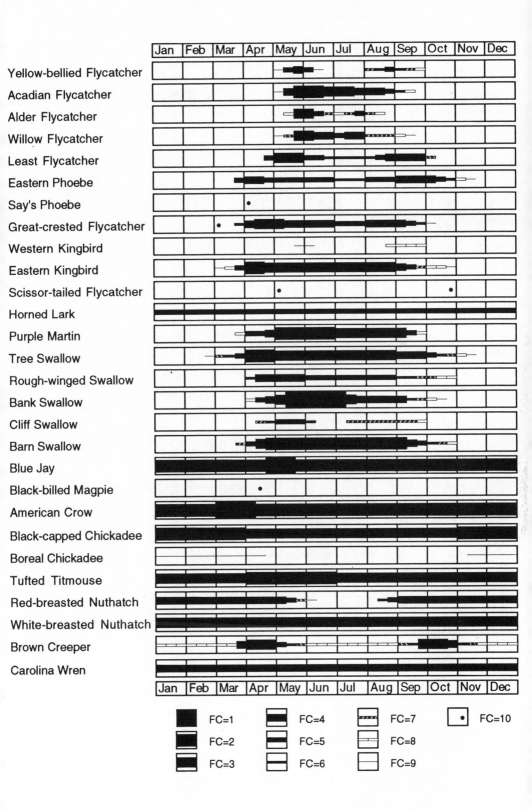

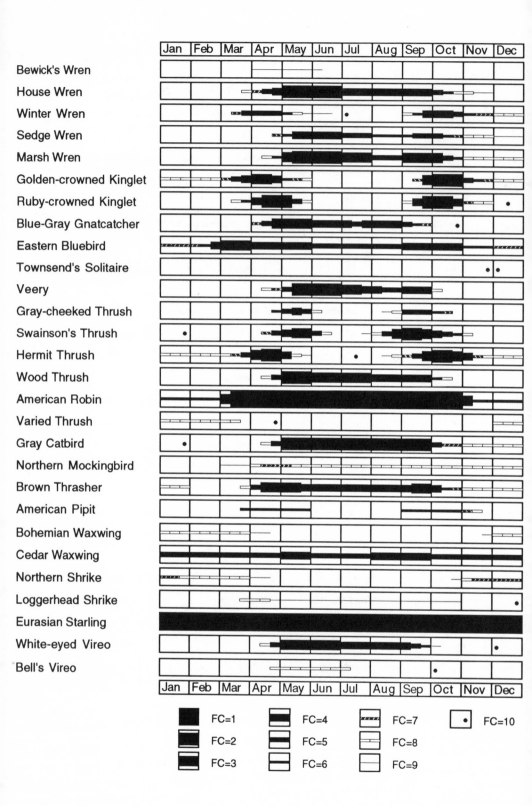

	Jan	Feb	Mar	Apr	May	Jun	Jul	Aug	Sep	Oct	Nov	Dec
Bewick's Wren												
House Wren												
Winter Wren												
Sedge Wren												
Marsh Wren												
Golden-crowned Kinglet												
Ruby-crowned Kinglet												
Blue-Gray Gnatcatcher												
Eastern Bluebird												
Townsend's Solitaire												
Veery												
Gray-cheeked Thrush												
Swainson's Thrush												
Hermit Thrush												
Wood Thrush												
American Robin												
Varied Thrush												
Gray Catbird												
Northern Mockingbird												
Brown Thrasher												
American Pipit												
Bohemian Waxwing												
Cedar Waxwing												
Northern Shrike												
Loggerhead Shrike												
Eurasian Starling												
White-eyed Vireo												
Bell's Vireo												

FC=1 FC=2 FC=3 FC=4 FC=5 FC=6 FC=7 FC=8 FC=9 FC=10

240

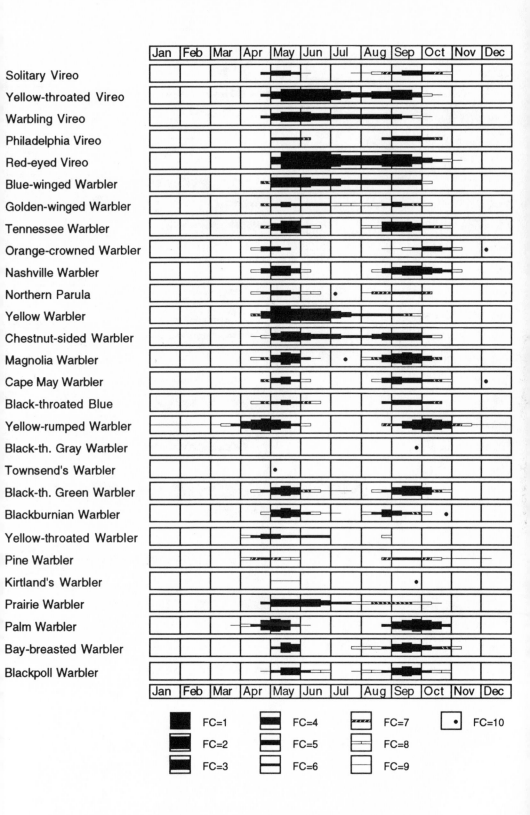

	Jan	Feb	Mar	Apr	May	Jun	Jul	Aug	Sep	Oct	Nov	Dec
Solitary Vireo												
Yellow-throated Vireo												
Warbling Vireo												
Philadelphia Vireo												
Red-eyed Vireo												
Blue-winged Warbler												
Golden-winged Warbler												
Tennessee Warbler												
Orange-crowned Warbler												
Nashville Warbler												
Northern Parula												
Yellow Warbler												
Chestnut-sided Warbler												
Magnolia Warbler												
Cape May Warbler												
Black-throated Blue												
Yellow-rumped Warbler												
Black-th. Gray Warbler												
Townsend's Warbler												
Black-th. Green Warbler												
Blackburnian Warbler												
Yellow-throated Warbler												
Pine Warbler												
Kirtland's Warbler												
Prairie Warbler												
Palm Warbler												
Bay-breasted Warbler												
Blackpoll Warbler												
	Jan	Feb	Mar	Apr	May	Jun	Jul	Aug	Sep	Oct	Nov	Dec

FC=1 FC=4 FC=7 FC=10
FC=2 FC=5 FC=8
FC=3 FC=6 FC=9

241

	Jan	Feb	Mar	Apr	May	Jun	Jul	Aug	Sep	Oct	Nov	Dec
Cerulean Warbler												
Black & White Warbler												
American Redstart												
Prothonotary Warbler												
Worm-eating Warbler												
Ovenbird												
Northern Waterthrush												
Louisiana Waterthrush												
Kentucky Warbler												
Connecticut Warbler												
Mourning Warbler												
Common Yellowthroat												
Hooded Warbler												
Wilson's Warbler												
Canada Warbler												
Yellow-breasted Chat												
Summer Tanager												
Scarlet Tanager												
Western Tanager												
Northern Cardinal												
Rose-breasted Grosbeak												
Blue Grosbeak												
Indigo Bunting												
Dickcissel												
Rufous-sided Towhee												
Bachman's Sparrow												
Tree Sparrow												
Chipping Sparrow												

| | Jan | Feb | Mar | Apr | May | Jun | Jul | Aug | Sep | Oct | Nov | Dec |

FC=1   FC=4   FC=7   FC=10

FC=2   FC=5   FC=8

FC=3   FC=6   FC=9

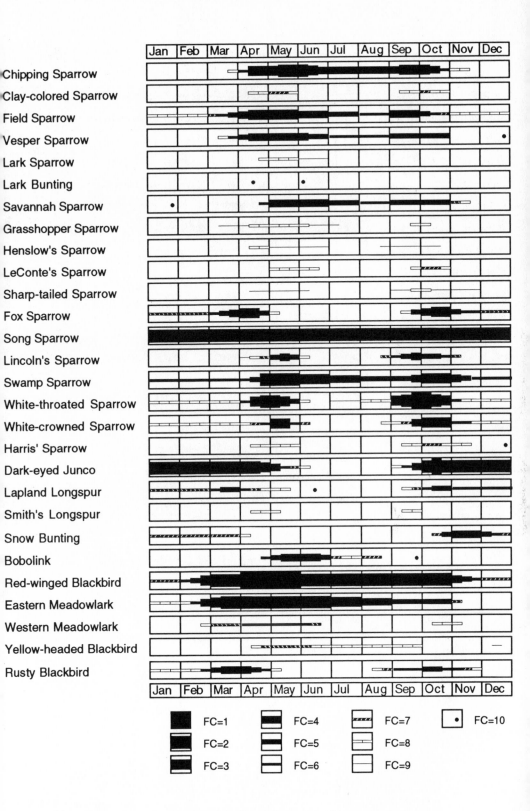

	Jan	Feb	Mar	Apr	May	Jun	Jul	Aug	Sep	Oct	Nov	Dec
Chipping Sparrow												
Clay-colored Sparrow												
Field Sparrow												
Vesper Sparrow												
Lark Sparrow												
Lark Bunting												
Savannah Sparrow												
Grasshopper Sparrow												
Henslow's Sparrow												
LeConte's Sparrow												
Sharp-tailed Sparrow												
Fox Sparrow												
Song Sparrow												
Lincoln's Sparrow												
Swamp Sparrow												
White-throated Sparrow												
White-crowned Sparrow												
Harris' Sparrow												
Dark-eyed Junco												
Lapland Longspur												
Smith's Longspur												
Snow Bunting												
Bobolink												
Red-winged Blackbird												
Eastern Meadowlark												
Western Meadowlark												
Yellow-headed Blackbird												
Rusty Blackbird												

FC=1 FC=2 FC=3 FC=4 FC=5 FC=6 FC=7 FC=8 FC=9 FC=10

	Jan	Feb	Mar	Apr	May	Jun	Jul	Aug	Sep	Oct	Nov	Dec
Brewer's Blackbird												
Common Grackle												
Brown-headed Cowbird												
Orchard Oriole												
Baltimore Oriole												
Pine Grosbeak												
Purple Finch												
House Finch												
Red Crossbill												
White-winged Crossbill												
Common Redpoll												
Hoary Redpoll												
Pine Siskin												
American Goldfinch												
Evening Grosbeak												
House Sparrow												

	Jan	Feb	Mar	Apr	May	Jun	Jul	Aug	Sep	Oct	Nov	Dec

FC=1 FC=4 FC=7 FC=10

FC=2 FC=5 FC=8

FC=3 FC=6 FC=9

REFERENCES CITED

Several frequently cited journals are abbreviated in the text as follows:

AB *American Birds*
AFN *Audubon Field Notes*
IAQ *Indiana Audubon Quarterly*

Arvin, D. Z. (1981). Xanthocephalus (the Yellow-headed Blackbird) returns to Indiana. *Ind. Aud. Quart.*, 59:56-58.

Bartel, K. E. (1948). Scissor-tailed Flycatcher in the Chicago Area. *Auk*, 65:614.

Baxter, R. C. (1967). Dead Alewives attract migratory Turkey Vultures to southern Lake Michigan beach. *Ind. Aud. Quart.*, 45:117.

Bellrose, F. C. (1976). *Ducks, geese & swans of North America*. Stackpole Books, Harrisburg, Pa, 544pp.

Bennett, H. . (1952). Fall migration of birds of Chicago. *Wilson Bulletin*, 64:197-220.

Blake, E. R. (1936). The season: Chicago region. *Bird-Lore*, 38:389-390.

Bognar, A. J. (1951). Wilson's Phalarope and Yellow-headed Blackbird. *Ind. Aud. Quart.*, 29:11-12.

Bohlen, H. D. (1978). *An annotated check-list of the birds of Illinois*. Illinois State Museum Popular Science Series, Vol. IX.

Brennen, G. A. (1923). *The Wonders of the Dunes*, Bobbs-Merrill, Indianapolis, 326pp.

Bretsch, C. (1927). Birds of Indiana Dunes, extensions of their range, and a few late records. *Ind. Aud. Bulletin*, pp.18-19.

Brock, K. J. (1979). Birdlife of the Michigan City Area, Indiana. *Ind. Aud. Quart.*, 57:95-113.

— (1980). Indiana's first record of the Curlew Sandpiper. *Ind. Aud. Quart.*, 58:120-122.

— (1981). A summer Burrowing Owl in Lake County, Indiana. *Ind. Aud. Quart.*, 59:58-60.

— (1982). Kirtland's Warbler, a rara avis extraordinaire, occurs in Indiana. *Ind. Aud. Quart.*, 60:30-33.

— (1983). Indiana's first White-winged Black Tern: an inland sight record. *American Birds*, 37:109-111.

— (1984). Further details on some rare birds reported in the Field Notes. *Ind. Aud. Quart.*, 62:95-98.

— (1986). A Second Marbled Murrelet Record for Indiana. *Ind. Aud. Quart.*, 64:77.

— (1987). Indiana's First Nesting Record of the Herring Gull. *Ind. Aud. Quart.*, 65:15-17.

— (1989). Frigatebirds Return to Indiana. *Ind. Aud. Quart.*, 67:117-119.

— (1990a). Deletion of the Tufted Duck from the Indiana Avifauna. *Ind. Aud. Quart.*, 68:48-54.

— (1990b). Indiana Dunes Spring Hawk Flights. *Ind. Aud. Quart.*, 68:165-175.

— (1991). Confirmed Ring-billed Gull nesting in Indiana. *Ind. Aud. Quart.*, 69:258.

— (1994a). Slaty-backed Gull Sight Record for Indiana with Comments on Identification. *Meadowlark*, 3:47-50.

— (1994b). Barred Owl taking duckling Wood Ducks. *Ind. Aud. Quart.*, 72:156.

— (1995). Kirtland's Warbler: Indiana's first fall record, *Ind. Aud. Quart.*, 73:1-2.

— and T. T. Cable (1981). A first Band-tailed Pigeon record for Indiana. *Ind. Aud. Quart.*, 59:116-120.

— , P. B. Grube and E. M. Hopkins (1978). The Black-headed Gull: an Indiana record. *Ind. Aud. Quart.*, 56:1-2.

—, and S. F. Jackson (1988). The Mew Gull: an addition to the Indiana Avifauna. *Ind. Aud. Quart.*, 66:107-110.

Brodkorb, P. (1926). The season: Chicago Region. *Bird-Lore*, 28:347-348.

Butler, A. W. (1898). *The birds of Indiana*. Ind. Dept. Nat. Res. 22nd Ann. Rep. 1897, Indianapolis, Ind., pp.515-1187.

— (1906). Some notes on Indiana birds. *Proceedings of the Indiana Academy of Sciences*, 16:145-150.

Cutright, N. (1976). 1975-1976 Annual Report Bailly Nuclear-1 site. Reported by Texas Instruments Inc.

— (1978). Bird kill over Lake Michigan, *Ind. Aud. Quart.*, 56:76-77.

Dancey, H. E. (1983). Winter foraging habits of a Snowy Owl. *Ind. Aud. Quart.*, 61:136-144.

— (1996a). A December vireo in Michigan City, Indiana, *Ind. Aud. Quart.*, 74:83-85.

— (1996b). A Summer Bird Survey of Oak Ridge Prairie County Park, *Ind. Aud. Quart.*, 74:123-134.

Eifrig, C.W.G. (1918). The birds of the sand dunes of northwestern Indiana. *Proceedings of the Indiana Academy of Sciences*, 28:280-303.

— (1922). A mild winter and its effects on the migration of birds at Chicago. *Wilson Bulletin*, 34:90-94.

Fields, Clyde (199)). Late Acadian Flycatcher nesting, *Ind. Aud. Quart.*, 68:199.

Ford, E. R. (1956). *Birds of the Chicago Region*. Chicago Academy of Sciences Special Publication No. 12, 117pp.

—, C. C. Sanborn and C. B. Coursen (1934). *Birds of the Chicago Region*. Chicago Academy of Science, 5:17-80.

Graber, R.R and J. W. Graber (1971). *Illinois birds: Turdidae*. Illinois Natural History Survey No. 75.

— and E. L. Kirk (1973). *Illinois birds: Lanidae*. Illinois Natural History Survey No. 83.

— (1974). *Illinois birds: Tyrannidae*. Illinois Natural History Survey No. 86.

— (1983). *Illinois birds: Wood Warblers*. Illinois Natural History Survey No. 118.

Grow, R. (1952). Rare and semi-rare winter visitants in northern Indiana. *Ind. Aud. Quart.*, 30:31-34.

Hine, A. (1924). Burrowing Owl in northern Indiana. *Auk*, 41:602.

Keller, C. E. (1957) and (1958). The shorebird families: Charadriidae, Scolopacidae, Recurvirostridae, and Phalaropidae of Indiana. Four parts. *Ind. Aud. Quart.*, 36:2-39.

—, S. A. Keller and T. C. Keller (1976). House Finch in central Indiana: An addition to the avifauna of Indiana. *Ind. Aud. Quart.*, 54:108.

— (1979). *Indiana birds and their haunts*. Indiana University Press, Bloomington, Ind., 214pp.

Landing, J. (1962). Exotic bird records for Michigan City, LaPorte County, Indiana: An addition to the avifauna of Indiana. *Ind. Aud. Quart.*, 40:15-16.

— (1966). Jaeger migration in Northwestern Indiana. *Ind. Aud. Quart.*, 44:32-37.

Mlodinow, S. (1984). *Chicago area birds*. Chicago Review Press, Chicago, Ill, 220pp.

Moore, P. A. (1959). *The Calumet Region*. Indiana Historical Bureau, 654pp.

Mumford, R. E. (1954). Brewer's Blackbird nesting in Indiana. *Wilson Bulletin*, 66:61-63.

— (1966). Some 1965 summer bird records for Indiana. *Ind. Aud. Quart.*, 44:98-100.

— (1967). Notes on the Loggerhead Shrike in Indiana. *Ind. Aud. Quart.*, 45:113-114.

—, and C. E. Keller (1984). *The birds of Indiana*. Indiana University Press, Bloomington, Ind. 376pp.

Nelson, E.W. (1876). Birds on northeastern Illinois. *Essex Inst., Bull.*, v. 8, 1876, p.90-155.

Payne, R. B. (1983). A Distributional Checklist of the Birds of Michigan. Museum of Zoology, University of Michigan, Ann Arbor, Michigan, 71pp.

Peattie, D. C. (1930). *Flora of the Indiana Dunes*. Field Museum of Natural History, Chicago, Ill., 432pp.

Perkins, J. P. (1964). 17 flyways over the Great Lakes, Parts I & II. *Audubon Magazine* 66:294-299 and 67:42-45.

Pitcher, E. B. (1974-79). Black oak and sassafras woods. *American Birds*, volumes 28-33.

Pitelka, F. A. (1938). Say's Phoebe in northern Indiana. *Auk*, 55:280-281.

Segal, S. (1960). Bird tragedy at the Dunes. *Ind. Aud. Quart.*, 38:23-25.

Simon, A. C. (1977). The Black Rail returns to Indiana. *Ind. Aud. Quart.*, 55:2.

Smith, H. M. (1936). Unpublished check list of birds of the Calumet and Dune region. 40pp.

— (1950). Notes on the birds of the Chicago region. *Auk*, 67:109-110.

Squires, B. (1991). Hawk Movements at the South End of Lake Michigan. *Ind. Aud. Quart.*, 69:225-241.

Stoddard, H.L. (1917a). The Roseate Tern on Lake Michigan. *Auk*, 34:86.

— (1917b). Rare winter visitants in northern Indiana. *Auk*, 34:487.

— (1921). Rare birds in the Indiana sand dunes. *Auk*, 38:124.

— (1969). *Memoirs of a Naturalist*, University of Oklahoma Press, Norman, 303 pp.

Thomson, T. (1983). *Birding in Ohio*. Indiana University Press, Bloomington, Ind., 256pp.

West, H. C. (1954). A wintering Sanderling in Lake County, Indiana. *Ind. Aud. Quart.*, 32:62.

— (1956). The status of the grebe family in Indiana. *Ind. Aud. Quart.*, 34:42-55.

Woodruff, F. M. (1907). *The birds of the Chicago area*. Natural History Survey, Bulletin No. VI, Chicago Academy of Sciences. 221pp.

INDEX

Boldface numbers refer to primary reference.

Ani, Grove-billed, **126**
  Smooth-billed, 30
Avocet, American, 7, 21, 83, **87**
Baileytown, **23**
Bailly Generator, **23**
Berry Lake, **23**
Beverly Shores, **18**
Bittern, American, 6, **39**
  Least, 12, **40**
Blackbird, Brewer's, **222**
  Red-winged, 6, 7, 21, **219**
  Rusty, 6, **221**
  Yellow-headed, 21, **220**
Bluebird, Eastern, 6, 7, **160**
Bobolink, 7, **218**
Bobwhite, Northern, **76**
Boyd, Donald F., **2**
Brant, 12, **48**
Bufflehead, **61**
Bunting, Indigo, 7, 18, **203**
  Lark, 14, 16, 204, **208**
  Snow, 12, 18, 204, **218**
Burr Street Dump, **22**
Canvasback, **54**
Cardinal, Northern, 6, **201**
Catbird, Gray, **165**
Chat, Yellow-breasted, 18, 176, **198**
Chickadee, Black-capped, 7, **152**
  Boreal, **152**
Chuck-will's-widow, 18, **132**
Coot, American, 21, **81**
  white-shielded, 82
Cormorant, Double-crested, **37**
  Great, 30
Cowbird, Brown-headed, 6, **223**
Cowles Bog, **23**
Crane, Sandhill, **82**
  Whooping, 30
Creeper, Brown, 6, **154**
Crossbill, Red, **226**
  White-winged, **226**
Crow, American, 7, **151**
Cuckoo, Black-billed, **125**
  Yellow-billed, **125**
Curlew, Long-billed, 30
Dickcissel, **203**
Dove, Mourning, 6, **124**
  Rock, **124**
Dowitcher, Long billed, 21, 83, **102**
  Short-billed, 22, 83, **102**
Duck, American Black, **49**
  Harlequin, 10, 12, **58**
  Ring-necked, **55**
  Ruddy, **64**
  Tufted, 30
  Wood, **48**

Dunes State Park, **16**
Dunlin, 7, 83, **99**
Eagle, Bald, 9, 66, **67**
  Golden, 9, 66, **73**
Egret, Cattle, **43**
  Great, **41**
  Snowy, **42**
Eider, Common, 30
  King, 14, **57**
Falcon, Peregrine, 9, 66, **75**
Finch, House, **225**
  Purple, 6, **225**
Flicker, Northern, 6,7, **138**
Flycatcher, Acadian, 16, 18, 20, **142**
  Alder, 2, 18, **142**
  Great-crested, **145**
  Least, **144**
  Olive-sided, **140**
  Scissor-tailed, **146**
  Willow, 18, **143**
  Yellow-bellied, **141**
Frigatebird, Magnificent, 14, **38**
Furnessville, **23**
Gadwall, **52**
Gallinule, Purple, 16, **80**
Gannet, Northern, 7, 12, 14, **36**
Gary Sanitary Landfill, **22**
George Lake, **20**
Gibson Woods Preserve, **22**
Gleason Park, **21**
Gnatcatcher, Blue-gray, **160**
Godwit, Hudsonian, 21, 22, 83, **92**
  Marbled, 21, 22, 83, **92**
Goldeneye, Common, **61**
  Barrow's, **61**
Goldfinch, American, 7, **229**
Goose, Canada, **48**
  Greater White-fronted, **47**
  Snow, **47**
Goshawk, Northern, 9, 66, **70**
Grackle, Common, 7, **222**
Grebe, Eared, **35**
  Horned, **34**
  Pied-billed, **33**
  Red-necked, **34**
  Western, 12, 16, **36**
Grosbeak, Black-headed, 30
  Blue, **202**
  Evening, **229**
  Pine, **224**
  Rose-breasted, 7, **202**
Grouse, Ruffed, **76**
  Sharp-tailed, 30
Grow, Raymond, 2, **4**, 8
Gull, Black-headed, 14, 111, **113**
  Bonaparte's, 111, **113**

California, 14, 111, **114**
Franklin's, 7, 22, 111, **112**
Glaucous, 2, 5, 10, 12, 22, 111, **117**
Great Black-backed, 5, 12, 22, 111, **118**
Herring, 111, **114**
Iceland, 5, 22, 111, **115**
Kelp, 111, **117**
Laughing, 12, 22, **111**
Lesser Black-backed, 14, 22, 111, **116**
Little, 5, 7, 111, **112**
Mew, 14, 111, **116**
Ross', 30
Ring-billed, 111, **114**
Sabine's, 5, 7, 111, **119**
Slaty-backed, 14, 111, **117**
Thayer's, 5, 12, 22, 111, **115**
Gyrfalcon, 66, **75**
Hammond Cinder Flats, **22**
Harrier, Northern, 9, 66, **68**
Hawk flights, 8
Hawks, Broad-winged, 8, 9, 16, 66, **71**
  Cooper's, 9, 66, **69**
  Ferruginous, 66, **72**
  Red-shouldered, 9, 16, 66, **70**
  Red-tailed, 8, 9, 66, **72**
  Rough-legged, 9, 66, **73**
  Sharp-shinned, 8, 9, 66, **68**
  Swainson's, 9, 66, **71**
Heron, Black-crowned Night, **44**
  Great Blue, **40**
  Green, **43**
  Little Blue, **42**
  Yellow-crowned Night, **45**
Heron Rookery Unit, **20**
Hummingbird, Ruby-throated, **134**
  Rufous, 30
Ibis, Plegadis, **45**
Inland Marsh, **23**
Jaeger, annual counts, **109**
  composite records, **108**
  Long-tailed, 7, 109, **110**
  Parasitic, 5, 7, 109, **110**
  Pomarine, 5, 7, 14, 109, **109**
  totals 107
  unidentified 107
Jay, Blue, 6, 7, **150**
Johnson Beach hawk-watch, 16
Junco, Dark-eyed, 6, **216**
Kestrel, American, 9, 66, **74**
Killdeer, 6, 7, 83, **86**
Kingbird, Eastern, 7, **146**
  Western, 14, **145**
Kingfisher, Belted, **135**
Kinglet, Golden-crowned, 6, **158**
  Ruby-crowned, 6, **159**
Kite, American Swallow-tailed, 66, **67**
  Mississippi, 16, 66, **67**

Kittiwake, Black-legged, 2, 5, 7, 10, 12, 111, **118**
Knot, Red, 2, 5, 10, 83, **93**
LaPorte County landfill, **23**
Lark Horned, 12, **146**
Liverpool, **23**
Long Lake, 12
Longspur, Lapland, 6, 12, **217**
  Smith's, 6, **217**
Loon, Common, **32**
  Pacific, 12, **31**
  Red-throated, 7, **31**
Magpie, Black-billed, **151**
Mallard, 21, **50**
Martin, Purple, 6, **147**
Meadowlark, Eastern, 6, 7, **219**
  Western, 6, **220**
Merganser, Common, 12, **63**
  Hooded, **62**
  Red-breasted, **63**
Merlin, 9, 66, **74**
Michigan City Harbor, **12**
Migrant Trap, 9
Migration, 4
Migration, longshore, 7
Miller see Millers
Miller Beach, 2, **10**
Millers, **23**
Mineral Springs, **23**
Mockingbird, Northern, **165**
Moorhen, Common, 21, **81**
Moraine State Nature Preserve, **23**
Mount Baldy, **18**
Murrelet, Ancient, **124**
  Kittzlitz's, 30
  Marbled, 14, **123**
Nighthawk, Common, **132**
Nuthatch, Brown-headed, **154**
  Red-breasted, **153**
  White-breasted, **153**
Oak Ridge Prairie County Park, **24**
Oldsquaw, **58**
Oriole, Baltimore, 7, **224**
  Orchard, **223**
Osprey, 9, **66**
Ovenbird, 16, 176, **192**
Owl, Barred, 16, 18, 129, **129**
  Burrowing 129, **128**
  Common Barn **126**
  Eastern Screech, 6, 129, **127**
  Great Horned 129, **127**
  Long-eared, 6, 12, 129, **129**
  Northern Hawk, 30
  Northern Saw-whet, 6, 10, 14, 129, **131**
  Short-eared, 10, 18, 129, **130**
  Snowy, 10, 12, 129, **128**
Park, Dunes State, **16**
  Gleason, **21**

249

Oak Ridge Prairie County, **24**
Whiting, **9**
Parula, Northern, 176, **179**
Pelican, American White, 12, **37**
Brown, **37**
Pewee, Eastern Wood, **140**
Phalarope, Red, 5, 7, 83, **106**
Red-necked, 21, 22, 83, **105**
Wilson's, 20, 22, 83, **104**
Phoebe, Eastern, 6, **144**
Say's, **145**
Pheasant, Ring-necked, **75**
Pigeon, Band-tailed, **124**
Passenger, **124**
Pintail, Northern, **50**
Pipit, Northern, **167**
Plover, American-golden, 83, **84**
Black-bellied, 2, 83, **84**
Piping, 20, 83, **86**
Semipalmated, 2, 83, **85**
Snowy, 83, **85**
Port of Indiana, **12**
Prairie-Chicken, Greater, **76**
Rail, Black, **77**
King, 6, **78**
Virginia, 6, 10, **79**
Yellow, 6, **77**
Raven, Common, **151**
Redhead, **54**
Redpoll, Common, **227**
Hoary, **228**
Redstart, American, 20, 176, **191**
Reuter-skiold, Virginia, 2, **3**, 8
Robin, American, 6, 7, **164**
Roxana Pond, **21**
Ruff,   83, **101**
Sanderling, 2, 5, 83, **94**
Sandpiper, Baird's, 2, 5, 10, 83, **97**
Buff-breasted, 83, **101**
Curlew, 20, 83, **100**
Least, 83, **96**
Pectoral, 83, **98**
Purple, 2, 5, 10, 12, 83, **99**
Semipalmated, 83, **95**
Solitary, 83, **89**
Spotted, 83, **90**
Stilt, 21, 22, 83, **100**
Upland, 83, **91**
Western, 83, **95**
White-rumped, 83, **97**
Sapsucker, Yellow-bellied, 6, **137**
Scaup, Greater, **56**
Lesser, **56**
Scoter, Black, **59**
Surf, **60**
White-winged, **60**
Shoveler, Northern, **52**
Shrike, Loggerhead, **169**

Northern, **168**
Siskin, Pine, **228**
Skimmer, Black, **123**
Snipe, Common, 6, 83, **103**
Solitaire, Townsend's, 12, **161**
Sora, 6, 10, **80**
Sparrow, American Tree, 6, 204, **205**
Bachman's, 204, **205**
Chipping, 6, 204, **206**
Clay-colored, 10, 16, 204, **206**
Field, 6, 16, 204, **207**
Fox, 6, 204, **212**
Grasshopper, 6, 204, **209**
Harris', 10, 204, **215**
Henslow's, 10, 14, 204, **210**
House, 204, **230**
Lark, 10, 204, **208**
LeConte's, 6, 10, 204, **211**
Lincoln's, 6, 204, **213**
Nelson's Sharp-tailed, 204, **211**
Savannah, 6, 204, **209**
Song, 204, **212**
Swamp, 6, 18, 204, **214**
Vesper, 6, 204, **208**
White-crowned, 204, **215**
White-throated, 204, **214**
Starling, European, 6, 7, 204, **170**
Stilt, Black-necked, 83, **87**
Stoddard, Herbert L. Sr., 2, **3**
Swallow, Bank, 7, **149**
Barn, 7, **150**
Cliff, **149**
Northern Rough-winged, **148**
Tree, 7, **147**
Swan, Mute, **46**
Trumpeter, **46**
Tundra, 12, **46**
Swift, Chimney, **134**
Tanager, Scarlet, 7, **200**
Summer, **200**
Western, **201**
Teal, Blue-winged, 21, **51**
Cinnamon, **51**
Green-winged, **49**
Tern, Arctic, 14, 21, **121**
Black, 20, **123**
Caspian, 2, **120**
Common, **121**
Forster's, **122**
Gull-billed, 7, **119**
Least, **122**
Roseate, **120**
Royal, 14, 21, **120**
White-winged, **122**
Thrasher, Brown, 6, **166**
Thrush, Gray-cheeked, **162**
Hermit, 6, **163**
Swainson's, **162**

Varied, **164**
Wood, **163**
Titmouse, Tufted, **152**
Towhee, Eastern, 6, **204**
Tremont, **24**
Turkey, Wild, **76**
Turnstone, Ruddy, 2, 83, **93**
Veery, 2, 6, 16, **161**
Vireo, Bell's, **171**
  Philadelphia, **173**
  Red-eyed, **174**
  Solitary, **171**
  Warbling, **173**
  White-eyed, 2, 6, 16, 18, **170**
  Yellow-throated, **172**
Vulture, Black, **65**
  Turkey, 9, **65**
Warbler, Bay-breasted, 176, **188**
  Black-and-White, 176, **190**
  Blackburnian, 176, **184**
  Blackpoll, 176, **189**
  Black-throated Blue, 176, **182**
  Black-throated Gray, 16, 176, **183**
  Black-throated Green, 176, **184**
  Blue-winged, 16, **176**
  Canada, 2, 16, 176, **198**
  Cape May, 176, **182**
  Cerulean, 16, 18, 20, 176, **189**
  Chestnut-sided, 2, 16, 176, **180**
  Connecticut, 176, **195**
  Golden-winged, 176, **177**
  Hooded, 2, 16, 176, **196**
  Kentucky, 176, **194**
  Kirtland's, 10, 14, 176, **186**
  MacGillivray's, 30
  Magnolia, 176, **181**
  Mourning, 176, **195**
  Nashville, 176, **179**
  Orange-crowned, 176, **178**
  Palm, 176, **187**
  Pine, 176, **186**
  Prairie, 2, 16, 176, **187**
  Prothonotary, 176, **191**
  Swainson's, 30
  Tennessee, 176, **178**
  Townsend's, 16, 176, **183**
  Wilson's, 176, **197**
  Worm-eating, 10, 176, **192**
  Yellow, 18, 176, **180**
  Yellow-rumped, 6, 176, **183**
  Yellow-throated, 20, 176, **185**
Waterthrush, Louisiana, 2, 16, 18, 20, 176, **194**
  Northern, 176, **193**
Waxwing, Bohemian, 12, **167**
  Cedar, 7, **168**
West Beach, 12
Whihala Beach, **24**

Whimbrel, 7, 83, **91**
Whip-poor-will, 6, 10, **133**
Whiting, 9,
Whiting Park, **9**
Wigeon, American, **53**
  Eurasian, 12, **53**
Willet, 2, 10, 83, **90**
Wilson Shelter, 16
Wolf Lake, **20**
Woodcock, American, 6, 10, 18, 83, **103**
Woodpecker Black-backed, **138**
  Downy, 6, **137**
  Hairy, 6, **138**
  Pileated, **139**
  Red-bellied, **136**
  Red-headed, **136**
Wren, Bewick's, **155**
  Carolina, 6, **155**
  House, 6, **156**
  Marsh, 21, **158**
  Sedge, 6, **157**
  Winter, 6, **156**
Yellowlegs, Greater, 83, **87**
  Lesser, 83, **88**
Yellowthroat, Common, 18, 176, **196**